Our Canadian names come from all over the world and have fascinating meanings.

Check these out!

Shania Twain – *Shania* means 'on my way' in the Ojibwa language.

Keanu Reeves – Keanu is Hawaiian for 'cool breeze.' *Ke-ahe-anu is* literally 'the breeze cool.'

Neve Campbell – *Neve is* Portuguese for snow. Campbell means Crooked Mouth in Scottish Gaelic.

Mike Bullard – His surname means 'slick trickster' from Middle English *boule* 'deceit.'

Fly-fornication and Faint-not – In Puritan England these were legal given names for men.

Alcock – No, it's not every high-school boy's fantasy state. It really means 'Little Alan.'

Chuck Scarborough – Toronto has its Scarborough Bluffs. Scarborough means *Harelip's Fort.*

Wagstaff – This began as the nickname of a pompous beadle like Mr. Bumble in *Oliver Twist.*

Byron – Sooo uppercrust. But originally it's Byrom from Old English *byrum* 'at the cowsheds.'

Gulliver – means 'glutton'

Turnbull – literally, strong enough to turn aside a charging bull

All these and more surprising surnames of Canadians are INSIDE!

What's in a Canadian Name?

THE ORIGINS AND MEANINGS OF CANADIAN NAMES

Bill Casselman

McArthur & Company

TORONTO

First Canadian edition published by McArthur & Company, 2000

Canadian Cataloguing in Publication Data

   Casselman, Bill 1942-
      What's in a Canadian name? : the origins and meanings of
      Canadian surnames

   ISBN 1-55278-141-0

   1. Names, Personal – Canada. I. Title.

   CS2385.C37 2000   929.4'2'0971   C00-930294-8

Composition & Design by *Michael P. Callaghan*
Cover by *Tania Craan*
Typeset at *Moons of Jupiter, Inc.* (Toronto)
Printed in Canada by *Transcontinental Printing Inc.*

McArthur & Company
322 King Street West, Suite 402
Toronto, ON, M5V 1J2

10 9 8 7 6 5 4 3 2 1

The publisher wishes to acknowledge the financial support of the
Government of Canada through the Book Publishing Industry
Development Program (BPIDP) for our publishing activities.

for my dear friend, Keith Thomas

Obscurum explanat per obscurius

Contents

Preface

Names have to be appropriate. Therefore I spend a lot of time reading up on the meanings of names, in books like Name Your Baby.

– Margaret Atwood
discussing how one novelist selects characters' names in an interview from *Margaret Atwood: Conversations, 1990*

Why should you read a book about where names come from? Well, you've got a name or two yourself, right? What does your last name mean? Nothing? Wrong! Every name, first, middle, or last, began with meaningful roots and has a story to tell that will delight and startle you. The next paragraph presents one intriguing example.

Canadian actress and Hollywood movie star Neve Campbell has to my mind typically Canadian names, given and family names with a zesty multiplicity of origins, the kind of personal naming that happens often here in our relatively new world on this side of the Atlantic.

Neve is the Portuguese word for snow, pronounced Nev to rhyme with Bev.

Campbell is a Scottish surname based on the insulting nickname of the founding ancestor. There is proof that such a Campbell laddie was alive at the dawn of the thirteenth century. But we must guess that early in his life he suffered a stroke that left paralyzed some of the muscles of his face, in particular those that control the mouth and lips, muscles with sonorous and daunting anatomical labels like *orbicularis oris, depressor anguli oris, buccinator,* and *musculus zygomaticus major.* Whew! That's enough Latin to start a rogue mass under a gurney. Such a stroke befalling a person in the days when surnames were just forming could alter that person's name. The surname *Campbell is* made up of two Scottish Gaelic roots. *Cam* 'crooked' + b*uel* 'mouth' equal Campbell! Notice the infixing of the spurious letter *p*, popped in by some English speaker attempting to have the name Campbell make sense as an English-based name. Of course, Campbell has nothing whatsoever to do with a bell ringing in camp. The illiterate intrusion of letters like *p* into the legitimate roots of a surname like Campbell was dubbed by one Victorian studier of names, "the infix euphonious." He thought the letter *p* had been dropped into the middle of Campbell to make the name sound more pleasing!

In its original Scottish Gaelic sense, Crooked Mouth is a most unpleasant moniker. Yet both Scots and Vikings among other peoples liked nasty nicknames. Consider a Viking raider whose real name was Snot. He and his marauding Norse pirates invaded Britain and built a fortress called in Old Scandinavian *Snottingsheim* (literally 'the home of Snot's people'). Today it is the English city of Nottingham.

If Crooked Mouth, the ancestral Campbell, didn't suffer a stroke, then he may have received a sword slash to the head that severed one or more facial nerves. In any case, he had a crooked mouth, that first Campbell, quite unlike the pleasing and bilaterally symmetrical smile of Neve Campbell—even when she is fending off homicidal male wackos in slasher movies.

Upon contemplating a book whose subtitle contains the phrase "Canadian Surnames," one quibble may dribble into the mind of the professional fussbudget. In fact, a fussbudget might squawk like a berserk parrot. My own eardrums have rung in the company of that more erratic sort of academic pest. Well, all ye tenured lads and lassies who scamper through the subsidized halls of envy—er—ivy, relax, gulp a Prozac, and apply a Tensor to your throbbing doctorate. How, you may ask, can any surname be called Canadian except perhaps those of aboriginal peoples? Certainly Inuit and Cree and Ojibwa names were the first ones heard across the land that would become Canada, and you will discover the origins of fascinating First Nations names throughout this book. Consider pop singer Shania Twain, whose aboriginal first name is Ojibwa for "on my way." But surnames from all over the earth are Canadian too, brought here by immigrants speaking many languages. If you had tried telling my late Scottish grandmother Gordon that her family, almost two hundred years on this land that would become Ontario, if you had even hinted that Gordon, her married name, and Munro, her maiden name, were not Canadian surnames, albeit Scottish in origin, well!—you would damn well have had an argument, if not a dour look, if not a broom slap across your impudent arse!

The reader will find surnames of many languages explained in this book, including examples from Arabic, Armenian, Blackfoot, Chinese, Cree, Czech, Dutch, English, French, German, Greek, Hebrew, Icelandic, Inuktitut, Iranian, Irish, Italian, Polish, Punjabi, Russian, Scottish Gaelic, Slovakian, Spanish, Stoney, Ukrainian, Welsh, and Wendat.

Up pop in this book startling stories behind famous Canadian names. Movie star and Canadian Keanu Reeves has a given name that is Hawaiian and means 'cool breeze.' *Ke-ahe-anu* is literally 'the breeze cool.' And one of his ancestors was a reeve or *gerefa* in Old English.

Among the Anglo-Saxons a reeve was a high-ranking official appointed under the aegis of the king, often as the chief magistrate of a town. But by 1300 the position had dwindled into what might have been called more fittingly a reevelet, because by that time a reeve was a mere bailiff or landlord's overseer. *Reeve* as a word was slapped on any office-holder of low rank. Years later, long after it had become an English surname, reeve took on its special sense in early Canada. Every township or village of small size would elect a reeve and several deputy-reeves to govern it, as larger centres might elect a mayor and councillors.

Now, many books list the meaning of last names and devote one line to each individual name. Such volumes of reference are fine for their purpose. But they seldom get into the nitty-gritty of onomastics, that is, the **reason** last names mean what they mean, how precisely last names began, how each language has differing rules for the kinds of words that may become part of its stock of naming words. Here I do try to tell you what's in a name. For any reader interested in genealogy and surnames, the introduction gives a colourful and amusing overview of how English surnames arose. Then the main part of the book examines individual surnames of famous Canadians.

The names we inherit at birth are the most personal gifts life offers. Yet how many of us know much at all about their meaning? Even if we don't know the original sense of our family name, it is still precious, personal, and not to be defiled by coarse lips. I recall the sting of a taunt by a Grade 5 classmate who called me "Cat's-ass-elman." The same Torquemada-in-training then tiptoed after me around the recess yard, singsonging "Silly Billy. Silly Billy. Silly Billy." An iced snowball fired at his protuberant mandibular region caused him to reconsider singsong as a career. He remained a bully as an adult. Twenty-seven years later—I'm sad to report— a large transport truck brought his inquisitorial potential to a pulpy end.

Don't mess with my name! And so say all of us. Names have a ritual sanctity that is made plain at baptism. Yes, they are just labels. But they label both the outer, physical us and the inner, proprioceptively-tuned us. Over the years as we acquire an experienced and self-created character, our names come to share our mystical and inviolable aura of selfhood. Therefore in this little study no name is mocked. Oh, there's fun and enlightenment and astonishment galore in the story of Canadian surnames. But I make fun with names, not of names.

Not everyone likes the names glued on at birth. Canadian media guru Marshall McLuhan disliked his own names intensely and said, in his 1964 book *Understanding Media,* "The name of a man is a numbing blow from which he never recovers." And there are people who find the names of others loathsome. Shakespeare has a deft reply for them in *As You Like It:*

> *Jaques: I* do not like her name.
>
> *Orlando:* There was no thought of pleasing you when she was christened.

If you do not like the names I have chosen or indeed find your own name odious—as apparently Marshall McLuhan did—I can only conclude this little preface by quoting Groucho Marx. The great American comedian was once asked if Groucho were his real name. "No," replied Marx, "I'm breaking it in for a friend."

May 1, 2000
Bill Casselman
205 Helena Street
Dunnville, Ontario, Canada NIA 2S6

Introduction:
How Last Names Began in English

Names, once they are in common use, quickly become mere sounds, their etymology being buried, like so many of the earth's marvels, beneath the dust of habit.

—Salman Rushdie
The Satanic Verses, 1988

The First English Names like Wade

To understand English surnames—many of which stem from given names—one must know how the very first single personal names arose among the English people. The Angles, Saxons, and Jutes who invaded and settled the British Isles between AD 449 and 700 spoke a Germanic language and brought it with them to Britain. The Angles called their language *ænglisc*. Today we call it English. After AD 500 certain Germanic or Anglo-Saxon names may be labelled English names. Anglo-Saxon is an earlier term for the language we now prefer to call Old English (OE).

Now these Germanic tribes brought with them single names, some already moss-clad from their birth in prehistoric Indo-European homelands. To begin with, each human being needed only one name. The first personal names in Old English were single-root ones like *Wada*. In modern English, Wade is a given and a family name. It harks back to a figure in German mythology. Wado was a sea-giant who lived along the Baltic Sea and North Sea. His name is related to the Old High German verb *watan* 'to go (through water or thick mud).' It is cognate with our English verb, to wade. Sprung from the same root is the modern German word for the human calf muscle, *die Wade*. If you do enough wading, do you develop remarkably buff calf muscles? Movie fans can await some future Schwarzenegger action flick where Arnold's character foghorns to the ingenue, "*Ja*, you can stroke my gastrocnemius, Baby, but remember, it's the most superficial of my calf muscles."

But why would parents name an innocent newborn child after Wado, a hideous sea-giant? Well, they had had no chance to read Dr. Spock on naming children. And there was the apotropaic reason. In many human cultures, it is believed evil influences can be prevented by acknowledging the evil in some way. *Apotrepein* is a Greek verb that means 'to turn away.' And that's what apotropaic names do. They ward off evil and evil creatures. You name your kid after Godzilla, so the superstition goes, and Godzilla is so charmed, he never attacks and devours the kid. He might even keep Mothra away from the cradle with a pervasive spritz of Moth-Off now and then.

Simple Anglo-Saxon Names

Other single-root personal tags from the Old English name hoard are, for example, totemic bird names for men: *Cocca* 'cock, rooster,' *Fugol* 'fowl,' *Heafoc* 'hawk,' and **Meaw* 'mew, a gull-like seabird.'

By the way, the asterisk (*) after *Meaw* indicates a hypothetical form, adduced from its modern forms, usually in the Indo-European (or IE) family of languages to which English, and most other languages of Europe belong. Consult a large dictionary with a chart of the hundreds of languages which belong to this ancient family. The forms are hypothetical and marked with an asterisk because the Indo-Europeans had no system of writing.

Anglo-Saxon men and women also took adjectives of colour as single personal names. Consider *Brun* 'brown,' *Cola* 'black as coal,' *Grene* 'green,' and *Hwita* 'white, with fair complexion.'

The Patronym

Within the conventions of Anglo-Saxon nomenclature, a father could name his child after himself. Such a single personal name based on the father's name is a patronym. Patronymics were formed in Old English with the suffix *-ing*. A personal name still in use during the twelfth century was *Hwiting* 'son of White.' From Hwiting arose modern surnames like Whiting, Whitting, and Witting.

The Anglo-Saxon Clan Name

One might have a Germanic clan name as one's single personal name, like *Hwitling* 'one who belongs to White's clan or tribal unit.' From Hwitling came the current English surname Whitling. Another male of the same clan might bear the sole personal name *Hwitmann* 'male of a clan led by a chief called White,' which in time would give rise to surnames like Whitman, Whiteman, and Wittman.

Compound Names

Next in Germanic naming history appeared compound warrior names of a standard type, often called dithematic by scholars, indicating that such names have two distinct roots. Such a dithematic name was Cuthbert from *cuth* 'known' + *beorht* 'bright, shining, famous.' One of the earliest Anglo-Saxon names is Herbert. In Old French it was Hébert, and recalls one of Québec's finest writers, the late Anne Hébert. In Old English, Herbert was *Herebeorht*, itself derived from older Germanic roots *harja* 'army' + *berhta* 'bright.'

Note that the two roots that made up Germanic warrior names, male and female, did not have to make literal sense. Instead, pairs of such elements were selected from a small group of word stems thought suitable for naming. For the most part, these roots denoted things and abstractions and qualities held in high regard among prehistoric Germanic tribes. Some name elements had a magic purpose, like *ælf*, the root for elf or supernatural forest spirit. Alfred in Old English was Ælfræd = *ælf* 'elf, sprite' + *ræd* 'advice.' Bellicose components of names in Germanic languages like Old English included roots that meant: daring, battle, bold, war, warrior, spear, powerful, victory, fortress, protection, guard, and ruler.

The Germanic name hoard shared words with Scandinavian languages for familiar totem animals of northern tribes, like wolf, bear, and raven. From them came individual given names like the Germanic Wolfgang 'goes fast like a wolf' and the Old English Beowulf 'bee-wolf,' a synonym for a bear with reference to its love of honey.

Viking Personal Names

Scholars today call the language spoken by the Vikings invaders Old Scandinavian. It used to be termed Old Norse. Vikings who settled in Britain came first from Denmark and then from Norway.

The modern English surname Rankill begins as the Viking personal name Hrafnkell from Old Scandinavian *hrafn* 'raven' + Old Scandinavian *kell* 'cauldron.' Now a guy named Raven-Cauldron might summon to our minds a dude in a cow-horn hat, waiting with an empty skull as his cup for a ladle of bird soup thickened with purée of enemy brain. But to ancient Norsemen, Hrafnkell was a potent sound announcing the bonds of a clan whose totem was the sleek, wise, black raven.

Alas! Poor Ragnar! I Knew Him, Horatio.

By the way—if the reader will permit a brief detour—modern archeology has shown that the Vikings did use skulls as bowls and drinking cups. Think of the modern Scandinavian drinking toast: *skål*! This toast wishing good health is common to Danish, Norwegian, and Swedish. Its root is Old Scandinavian *skál* 'bowl.' The earliest reflex of the *sk*-vowel-*l* root appears in the Old Scandinavian word for seashell, *skel*. The larger Atlantic seashells were used as scrapers and as drinking scoops by all coastal peoples of northern Europe. Was their first bowl a shell found as wrack on a Baltic beach? At the dawn of the Scandinavian languages did the white bone of human skulls seem made of material similar to thick white seashells? Perhaps Old Scandinavian *skoltr* 'skull,' the bowl-like skeletal cranium, has its root in *skel* 'seashell'? Or, was a larger bowl that would hold more mead or water discovered when someone broke off the lower jaw and axed in half a dried human cranium? Not attested in sagas is this Viking tongue twister: I sell sea skulls shilled with scored shells. Skole!

Anglo-Saxon Female Names

Female names, although fewer in number than male names, were made from the same group of root words. Edith <OE *Eadgyth* = *ead* 'riches' + *gyth* 'strife.' Sometimes the modern avatar of one of these old names is a shortened version. Hilda as a female first name is a contraction of Old Germanic compound names like Hildegard, Hildebrand, Hildebald, Hildegund, Hildemut, or Hildrun. Sometimes Hilda stems from the Viking version, for example, the Old Scandinavian Hildibrandr. *Hild* meant 'battle.' *Brandr* meant 'flaming sword.' A woman whose name was Battle-Flaming Sword was, perhaps, not to be trifled with.

Rearranging Elements in Compound Names

While some Old English compound names like Alfred and Emma persisted into the twenty-first century, most declined in use and disappeared. Seldom today do we meet anyone named Wulfstan, from Old English *wulf* 'wolf' + *stan* 'stone.' Wulfgar (OE *gar* 'spear') has not been popular for eight hundred years, although the Anglo-Saxon word for spear still peeks through, often unrecognized, in modern English words like garlic (*gar* 'spear' + *leac* 'leek, onion') and in the garfish with its spear-like snout.

These Old English two-stem names could have the order of their elements shuffled to make different names. We have records of people with single names like Wulfgar and Garwulf (*gar* 'spear' + *wulf* 'wolf'). There existed also Beorhtsige and Sigebeorht from OE *sige* 'victory' and OE *beorht* 'bright, famous.' For the modern, related German form of *sige*, think of the creepy and mindless Nazi mass shout *Sieg Heil!* 'Hail, Victory!' Both Beorhtsige and Sigebeorht survived to modern times. Beorhtsige became the English surname Brixey, and Sigebeorht became Sigbert and Siegbert (German given names) and Seabert, Seabright, Sebert, and Sibert (English surnames).

The Anglo-Saxon personal name *Ælfgar* (elf, sprite + spear) led to the surname of a British composer, best known for his five *Pomp and Circumstance* marches, Sir Edward Elgar. Several personal names with the *gar* 'spear' root survive happily in many of the languages of modern Europe and also in modern English, some having been re-introduced in their Norman-French forms:

- Garbalt   German form: Gerbald, Italian surname form: Garibaldi *gar* 'spear' + *bald* 'bold'
- Garhart   Norman form: Gerard, Frisian form: Gerrit, Hungarian form: Gellért *gar* 'spear' + *hard* 'brave'
- Garthruth   Norman form: Gertrude, Dutch form: Geerta, English pet forms: Gertie, Trudy *gar* 'spear' + *thruth* (some times pronounced *drud)* 'strength'
- Garwald   Norman form: Gerald, Italian form: Giraldo *gar* 'spear' + *wald* 'rule'

Huge numbers of Anglo-Saxon names became obsolete after the Conquest, when a Norman ruling class began to introduce French personal names into Britain. Often Norman-French versions of

Anglo-Saxon and Viking names replaced older forms that had been widely used in Britain. For example, Old English *Hreodbeorht* 'fame-bright' and its Old German form *Hrodebert* disappeared quickly and were replaced by their exact equivalent in Norman French, Robert. The father of William the Conqueror was named Robert. Robert enjoyed instant popularity in England, *Hreodbeorht* vanished, and Robert went on to become one of the most popular personal names in British history, at first with a French pronunciation in which the final *t* was silent and the accent was placed on the final syllable. Eventually the English pronunciation became more common, with the accent on the first syllable and the final *t* sounded.

Compound Names in Older Languages

English and most of the languages of Europe and many of the languages of India derive from one, ancient mother tongue called Indo-European. All these tongues, believe it or not, are related and share common word roots and they also share compound warrior names: French, German, Russian, Spanish, Italian, English, Hindi, Bengali, Greek, Latin, Persian, Pali, and Sanskrit. For a full list of the dozens of languages that evolved from Indo-European, consult a good dictionary or encyclopedia where you will often find a comprehensive chart. Indo-European (IE) is sometimes called Proto-Indo-European (PIE).

Linguists dispute the precise homeland of the first Indo-European speakers. Some scholars posit an area in the eastern Ukraine, whereas others suggest a place south of the Black Sea; still others say the Indo-Europeans were neolithic farmers around 7000 BC in Anatolia, the central plain of Turkey. Various reasons for migration and dispersal of the Indo-Europeans by 2000 BC towards Europe and towards India have been suggested: population increase, domestication of the horse and subsequent invention of the chariot for warfare, enemy attack, and/or weather changes that brought persistent crop disasters.

All these hypotheses of locative origin are partially based on comparative vocabulary studies. The earliest strata of Indo-European texts in languages like Hittite, Vedic Sanskrit, and Linear B Greek share common word roots for fish, but not for sea. That is, the various words for sea were not native IE but were borrowed from neighbouring languages that were not Indo-European. Therefore, the original home of IE speakers probably was not situated on a sea. There is a common IE word root for grain, but none for grape. Thus, grape-growing regions of Europe and Asia are not likely candidates for any Indo-European *Heimat*. Note that the German word for homeland is often used in linguistics. In a similar fashion, there is an IE word for birch tree, but not for maple tree. Scholarly guesses about the IE Heimat are formed after subjecting the entire IE vocabulary to such winnowing.

As well, Indo-Europeans had a patriarchal society, if we are to trust the prominence of male names and the extensive vocabulary of words naming male relatives, in the face of the extreme scarcity of IE words for female relatives. The vocabulary of IE—deduced by examining words in all the languages derived from Indo-European—also suggests that these neolithic farmers had a priestly caste, a warrior class, artisans, and other specialized trades. The IE mother tongue and those who spoke it possessed all these specialized occupations before their migrations, before the subsequent breaking-up of the IE mother tongue into its many daughter languages. How male names were formed in the earliest and oldest daughter languages is strong evidence that compound warrior names were the normative method of naming IE people.

So, Indo-Europeans appear to have used two-root warrior names, similar to Germanic ones with words denoting totemic animals like wolves and bears. For example, Vedic Sanskrit is a very old member of the Indo-European language family, a specialized form of language not spoken in daily life but used to record and recite religious texts composed around 1000 BC Varkakarman. *Varka* is the Sanskrit word for wolf. *Karman* is the Sanskrit word for action or acting. So Varka-karman 'acting like a wolf' could almost be a translation of the Germanic Wolfgang 'going like a wolf'! Classical Greek, another ancient Indo-European language, has Lykophron as a man's name. *Lykos* is the ancient Greek word for wolf. *Phron* here means 'mind, thinking.' Thus, the first Greek man to be named Lycophron was, perhaps, a warrior who thought like a wolf, a crafty hunter who pursued game in a pack with his buddies, just as wolves do. Lykophron is then very close in meaning to old Germanic warrior names like Wolfgund 'wolf-like in battle' and Wolfrad (or Wulfrat) 'giving or taking wolfish advice.'

Compound male names close to Germanic types appear also in the Slavic languages. The oldest Russian names, condemned and banned after the Russian Orthodox Church gained power over baptism, display this form. Consider Vladimir 'rule-great' and the Polish given name Slawomierz 'glory-great.' Polish Bronislaw is 'armour-glory.' Russian Miroslav means 'great glory.' The Czech Ludomir means 'tribe-glory.' In fact, throughout most of the Indo-European languages, the glory names appear early and frequently. The famous Greek Pericles, an Athenian statesman who died around 429 BC, bore a name that meant 'much glory.' *Kleos* in ancient Greek meant 'fame' or 'glory.' Although *peri* is a Greek preposition often meaning 'around,' in onomastic composition it is merely intensive. Thus Periander, the tyrant of Corinth, had a name that meant 'very manly' from Greek *aner*, *andros* 'man, male.' Cleopatra was the *kleos* 'glory' of her *pater* 'father.' Returning to Germanic names, we find Ludwig 'glory-warrior' from Old Germanic *hlud* 'glory' + *wig* 'warrior.'

Transformed as it was borrowed into different languages, Ludwig became Ludovicus in medieval Latin, Lodewijk in Dutch, Lajos in Hungarian, Ludwik in Polish, and Louis in French and then in English.

To sum up, in most Indo-European languages the dithematic or compound warrior names are the earliest. Shorter forms and monosyllabic male names appear actually to have come after the compound names, and in many instances the shorter names are derivatives of the longer ones. With this in mind, we can return to that most persistent feature of a living language, change, and see how English names were altered forever by one of the most important events in English history.

Radical Changes in Naming After the Norman Conquest

1. Anglo-Saxon Names

The preferred style of personal name was different for the Anglo-Saxons, the Vikings, and the Norman French, and these preferences deeply influenced the development of English surnames. The Anglo-Saxons did not like to repeat names. The magic attached to the individual attached also to his or her name. Each son or daughter might be given a name with one element of each parent's name. But Anglo-Saxon fathers did not want their sons to have precisely the same name as themselves. For example, a man with the name Brungar (*brun* 'brown' + *gar* 'spear') might have a child with a woman named Eadgyth (Edith, *ead* 'riches' + *gyth* 'strife'). That child might have been called Eadgar (Edgar, *ead* 'riches' + *gar* 'spear').

2. Viking Names

On the other hand, Scandinavians like the Danish and Norse raiders we call Vikings thought it fitting to honour and recall the names of great fighters and seafaring heroes, so they preferred to pass along the same name in a family. A Viking father and son might both be named Leif. But they would add a patronymic byname, to make clear which individual was being referred to. Leif the father might have had a father himself whose name was Erik. The father then was named Leif Eriksson. Leif the son would be Leif Leifsson. Thus emerges the important point that a true patronym is not hereditary. The second or byname would change with each new generation. Interestingly, this system of naming is still in full force in Iceland where non-hereditary patronyms are used. Thus a girl may be Gudrun Magnusdottir, Gudrun daughter of Magnus. A boy may be Gunnar Eriksson, and later that boy's son may be Thor Gunnarsson. It is customary to alternate such names from one generation to the next. When Icelanders emigrate to other countries they often choose to make a non-hereditary surname legally hereditary, to conform with standard Western naming habits. Russian patronymics are true ones too, being the names of one father only. Therefore, the patro-nyms change with each generation. A father is Ivan Arkadievich 'John, son of Arkady.' His son is Sergei Ivanovich 'Sergei, son of John.' But Russia also uses hereditary family surnames.

3. Norman Names & The Beginning of Hereditary Surnames

By the time of their invasion and conquering of England, the Norm-ans preferred to use a small stock of male and female names and to show differences by adding various kinds of bynames after the indi-vidual name. A man's everyday given name might be Henri, but, when he had land to bequeath to a son in a will, the clerk who wrote the will might make very clear which Henri owned the property by adding Henri's father's name, the name of the estate or village where Henri lived, a nickname Henri had picked up during his life, or even what he did for a living. In such testamentary records from the eleventh century onward are the beginnings of hereditary last names. Here is a sample entry from a collection of documents called the Holme Cartulary written down late in the twelfth century, well after the Battle of Hastings in 1066 had introduced Norman power, influence, and the French language to alter English and English names forever.

Before the sample, take this brief detour for some Latin word lore. A cartulary was an archive, a room or container where charters and records were kept. Compare Late Latin *cartula* 'little charter, document.' The ancient Greek word for papyrus stalk *khartes* goes into Latin as *charta* 'sheet of papyrus paper' which in turn passes through French to give, in modern English, the doublet words *card* and *chart*. Note that the Classical Latin *charta*, reflecting as it does a rough Greek *chi*, was pronounced by Romans with a hard *c*. The Roman poet Catullus was not fond of his rival poet Martial, and thought Martial's work lewd and obscene. Catullus referred to a scroll containing some poems of Martial as *cacata charta* 'a shitty sheet.'

As you read the following entry showing the begining of English surnames, remember that, before the advent of competent dictionaries in the eighteenth century, English spelling was chaotic. In this passage, a man named Warren is listed using four spellings of his first name and using several bynames. This entry was written by a clerk who was a monk.

***Guarinus minister noster, Gwarinus dispensarius noster,
Warinus dispensator, Warinus de Thoftes.***

My translation of each monkish unit of Latin follows in boldface with a few comments on each unit.

Warren is our good helper who waits upon us.

The prime meaning of *minister* in medieval Latin was attendant, one who acts under the authority of another. In classical Latin *minister* meant waiter, servant, accomplice, one who abets in a good or bad way. In each phrase of this entry, some form of the verb to be (here *est* 'he is') is understood but not expressed.

Warren is the stewart of our religious house.

Dispensarius and *dispensator* are medieval Latin synonyms. Later, a *dispensarius* would signify a place in a great home or monastery where drugs and medicines were mixed and also the person by whom such pharmaceuticals were prepared, giving the modern English word *dispensary*. At a very large monastery or grand estate, a spencer was much like a head stewart, responsible for ensuring that proper supplies of food and drink were available either from the work of the brothers at the monastery or through donations and purchases from outside. At a humbler monastery, a spence was the room in which food and drink were stored, a pantry or buttery, and the dispensator was more like a larder, a person whose responsibility was to keep the pantry provisioned. Later dispensator would refer to a butler.

Warren of Toft is also his name.

Note the bit of French, *de*, in the midst of the Latin, showing the Norman influence and method of indicating residence or birthplace. *Thoftes* could refer to Warren's place of birth, a village named Toft or Tofts. There are two in Norfolk, one in Cambridgeshire, and several more in other parts of Britain. But *Thoftes* may be the scribe's attempt at a local farm name, The Toft. A toft was a curtilage, a kind of homestead with attached, covered areas, based on a style of farm home brought to Great Britain by the Vikings (Old Scandinavian *topt* 'covered farmstead').

Why Are *Real* French Names So Germanic?

The Norman French were descended from Scandinavian invaders, the same race of Vikings who had raided Great Britain beginning about AD 400. The Old French designation *Normans* came directly from the Old Scandinavian plural noun *Northmathr* 'north men.' Soon after they settled in northern France during the tenth century, these Northmen gave up their pagan ways and quickly took up Christ-ian-ity, French, and French-style names. But, by an odd quirk of language rebound, most French names were historically of Germanic origin! It's odd because French is a Romance language directly derived from the Latin of Roman soldiers who surged north to conquer Gaul in the days of Julius Caesar. Consider the accountant-like statement of fact that opens Caesar's *De Bello Gallico* 'The War in Gaul.'

In Latin: *Gallia est omnis divisa in tres partes.*

In Modern French: *Toute la Gaule est divisée en trois parties.*

In Modern English: The whole of Gaul is divided into three parts.

French is hard Latin polished smooth through time and shaped to fall with grace upon the listening ear.

Then why are so many French names Germanic? It is due to the vagaries of French history. Names that seem to exude pure French-ness like Louis, Charles, Henri, Richard, Robert, Roger, and thou-sands of the French surnames are in fact Germanic. Henri, for example, is from Old German *Haimirich* (*heim* 'house' + *ric* 'owner, ruler'). It was Heinrich in Frankish and the final *-ch* loses its Germanic rough breathing, becomes a smoother and lighter *ch* sound, and then disappears to give earliest French Heinri, then Henri. The name's popularity increased greatly after Henry of Bavaria (died 973) was made a saint in 1146. Saint Henry in turn made the name a suitable one for princes and potentates and kings-to-be. Named Henri or Heinrich or Henry were four kings of France, seven German kings, eight kings of England, and a great many more ob-scure princelings and kinglets of Europe.

The Rise of the Germanic Franks

French appeared about 700 as a dialect of Latin spoken by the off-spring of soldiers of Rome who had been posted to the outskirts of the empire for centuries. French was preceded as the language of Gaul by several Germanic tongues, the most important being Frankish, the language of the Franks, who gave their name to both France and French. The French word for the French language actually means 'Frankish' and is of course *français*. The *Franci* as the Romans called them were to the Italian masters of the world mere Teutonic barbarians lurking on the northern Rhine frontier of the empire. Frankish kingdoms existed from about 200 to 900. At their greatest extent under Charlemagne in 800, the Franks controlled all of central Europe, including what would become France, Belgium, Holland, Germany, Italy, Austria, and parts of Yugoslavia. This success began around 450 when Roman power in northern France collapsed, as the last soldiers hurried back to Rome to defend it from invading barbarians. After more than 400 years of occupying northern Gaul, generations of Roman soldiers had intermarried with local people and their descendants spoke a lively Latin dialect heard in northern France particularly around Paris. Bits of street Latin had filtered into local Germanic languages like Frankish, just as words from Frankish entered the new Latin dialect that would become the French language. The largest number of Germanic roots were in common given names. Other Frankish borrowings that are still in modern French are *fauteuil* 'armchair' from Frankish *faldistol* 'folding stool,' a chair carried on campaigns by Frankish warriors. The modern French word for marsh or swamp, *marais*, is also Frankish, and is in fact related to the English word *marsh*. The French verb *rôtir* 'to roast meat' is Frankish.

Frankish was the Germanic speech of the court of Charlemagne (742–814) and some given names like Gervais that were to become common in Modern French (as Gervase) first gained wide use because they were prominent in Charlemagne's court.

Like many mighty empires, the kingdom of the Franks began to crumble when it attained its widest breadth, and the problems were faulty communication and inadequate legislative and executive structures. Charlemagne himself had paid rotating visits to each little duchy and principality. Even he could not control the great landowning families who had grown richer than the king from land given by the king for services rendered in war and given also to retain the loyalty of these counts and dukes. Around 950 the economy of western Europe was buoyant. Agriculture improved; crop yields increased; trade brought even more wealth to these Frankish plutocrats and soon the whole map of France was dotted with virtually independent duchies and counties. The Frankish wars of conquest were long completed, and there was no more new land for a king to dole out to greedy dukes. In 987 when the last Frankish king was ousted, the bastion of regal power was the tiny royal domain of the Île de France with its city of Paris growing more important with every decade and with the new French, its Latin-based language, replacing Germanic Frankish in importance. The Vikings had planted colonies along the northern coast of France; one of them under King Rollo had become the Duchy of Normandy. But these Scandi-navian invaders integrated with locals and by 1066 had given up their language and many of their customs to become Northmen, that is, Norman, French. Many of their descendants were powerful lords in Normandy.

Popular Norman-French Names in England

A bastard son of Robert, Duke of Normandy, decided in 1066 that he had claims upon the throne of England. His name was William. After the victory of William the Conqueror, Norman-French names replaced Old English names quickly. The Normans introduced to Great Britain male personal names like Alan, Bernard, Brian, Denis, Geoffrey, Gerald, Gervase (Jarvis), Henry, Hugh, Louis, Maurice, Oliver, Piers (Norman form of Peter), Ralph, Richard, Robert, Roland, Walter, Warren, and William. William came in as French

Guillaume and even as German Wilhelm, all of them from a dithematic Germanic two-parter, *will* 'resolution' or 'strong will' + *helm* 'helmet.' The name of the conquering King William was soon heard at every baptismal font.

Into the English stock of female names the Normans imported such popular damsels as Adela, Alice, Avis, Constance, Emma, Jocelyn, Laura, Maud, Rosamond, and Yvonne.

Biblical Names: A Major Source of Surnames

Names from both the Old Testament and the New Testament entered Great Britain with the first serious Christian missions to the island. Tradition says Saint Augustine and forty monks sent by Pope Gregory the Great began these missions of conversion in AD 597. For the next five hundred years, until the end of the period of Old English, Latin loanwords used by Christian scribes filtered slowly into English along with personal names like Abraham and Mary and John. The Norman French were Christian, too, and brought their forms of Christian names to Britain. Here are early references in written English documents to Biblical names:

• Abel, a male name popular in the thirteenth century
• Abraham, the name of a priest in the Domesday Book of 1086
• Agnes (Norman-French, medieval English, Scottish forms: Anis, Annis, Annice) a female given name recorded in 1160 in the Pipe Rolls of Cambridgeshire
• Augustin (modern English surname forms: Austin, Austen), a very popular medieval name recorded in 1153
• Benedictus (medieval English form: Bennett), a Christian name popular from the twelfth century onward

Adam was a widespread given name for males. Its etymology is fascinating, too. Check the entry for Canadian singer Bryan Adams.

Eve, on the other hand, was never as common a name as Adam. After all, the lady gave in to the snake and brought sin into the Garden of Eden. Just ask the male oinkers who wrote the Book of Genesis.

The popularity of Old versus New Testament names has waxed and waned through the centuries, the fashionability of an individual given name dependent often on whatever religious shenanigans were current. After the Protestant Reformation in the sixteenth century, early Lutherans and other Protestant sects shunned names they considered Catholic, particularly Mary. The names of Catholic saints were also avoided. So out the clerestory window went Augustine and Benedict, Agnes and Barbara. The Protestants liked solid Hebrew personal names from the Old Testament, names untainted by popery, hence the surge in use during the sixteenth and seventeenth centuries of Biblical monikers like Benjamin, Daniel, David, Joshua, Samuel, Saul, Deborah, Leah, Rachel, and Sarah.

The Puritans, true to their extremist Protestant notions, decided that even names from the Bible were taboo. They invented slogan names for their children. Legal given names registered in Puritan England include: Faint-not, Stand-fast-on-high, and Fly-fornication. How'd you like to saunter into a schoolyard with one of those doozies printed on your middy? On the other hand, the Puritan virtue-names for girls, being not so outrageous, became popular outside of the sect, and gave English a new stock of female personal names: Amity, Charity, Faith, Felicity, Grace, Honour, Hope, Joy, Mercy, Patience, and Prudence.

Roman Catholic saints, with their birthdates entered into a long calendar, have provided more personal names and surnames than any other source in European history. Sometimes mandated by law as in France, saints' names include Church fathers like Saints Basil, Gregory, and Jerome; martyrs like Agatha, Laurence, and Sebastian ("Ew! Those quivers tickle so!"); blessed seers like Anthony and Teresa; and other canonized stalwarts like Bernard, Dominic, Christ-opher, Bern-adette, and—Saint George, whacking away manfully at dragons.

As we have seen then, Anglo-Saxon, Scandinavian, Norman-French, and Biblical sources provide the chief but by no means all of the origins of those first names that became English surnames.

Four Kinds of Surnames

We turn now to the classes and types of surnames that have developed in English. There could be a dozen subdivisions of varieties of surnames from the British Isles alone. But it is convenient to present them in four broad categories, as all but the fussiest onomatologists have done. In general, we can say that surnames developed:

1. from an ancestor's first name (e.g., Ben Johnson, Brian Williams)

2. from the ancestral place of birth or the locality of held land (Peter Kent, Sir Sandford Fleming [literally 'man from Flanders']) or from a topographic feature near the ancestor's homestead (Stanley Knowles, from Old English *cnoll* 'top of a hill' and Knowle is the name of villages in four English counties, so Knowles can be a locative genitive meaning 'of [the village of] Knowle.')

3. from the occupation or status of the founder of the family (actress Kate Trotter [messenger], Tommy Hunter, Douglas Fisher)

4. and, producing the smallest number, surnames derived from the nickname of an ancestor (Elizabeth Smart, novelist, author of *By Grand Central Station I Sat Down and Wept;* Otto Lang [lang = long = tall]). Here belong the now rare clausal surnames of jittery warriors like Shakespeare and pompous beadles like Wagstaff. To picture a pompous beadle, think of Mr. Bumble in *Oliver Twist* by Charles Dickens.

The majority of English surnames stem from the first two categories above: from a male ancestor's given name and from the name of his homestead, his native village, or some feature of the land or water near his farm.

Throughout the late Middle Ages, roughly from 1100 to 1500, English and European surnames were forming and being passed down from father to son unchanged. Trade grew; city life throve; population boomed in spite of many wars; Christian churches exerted massive influence. Indeed religion oozed into every cranny and flowed over every facet of medieval life, including how people named their children and their families. By the late sixteenth century most surnames, a huge number drawn from Biblical given names, had achieved their final form, but not their final spelling. Let's glance at the four types of English surname.

1. Surnames from Ancestors' First Names

During the entire history of Britain, the majority of its people never knew what their own names meant. In the high Middle Ages, while surnames were becoming hereditary and regular in form, the average person had no knowledge of Old Germanic or Old English. So the meanings of names like Robert and Alfred and Winnifred were quite lost to those who bore them. On the whole, children were baptized with socially acceptable current names that were precisely similar to their parents' names or to the names of other relatives. As to the many Biblical and saints' names, people might know where in the Bible such names occurred and which saint was the patron of which cause, but ordinary citizens were very unlikely to possess any knowledge of Latin, Greek, or Hebrew, to help them decipher the meaning and provenance of names like Mark, Elizabeth, or Bathsheba.

In the Old Testament, Elisheba was Aaron's wife; in the New Testament, Elizabeth is the mother of John the Baptist, but few English people knew Elizabeth belonged to a class of Hebrew names that made complete sentences or phrases in the ancient tongue. *Elishebath* means 'God is my oath.' Likewise, Michael is a question in Biblical Hebrew and means 'Who is like God?'

Bathsheba, *Batsheva* in modern Hebrew, means 'daughter of the oath,' and not 'daughter number seven' as some opine. Think of the Jewish ceremony of religious initiation for girls, bat mitzvah, which means 'daughter of the commandment.' It is the female version of the bar mitzvah for boys.

How Andrew Became Anderson

In England, few surnames existed until the twelfth century. So, let's say in the early Middle Ages there was an English villager named Andrew. Andrew, or versions of it, is one of the most popular first names in the Christian world. Andrew was the first disciple to be called by Jesus. In the Koine Greek of the New Testament, Luke (6:14) calls him Andreas based on the Greek *andreios* 'manly, bold.' But it is unlikely the first apostle had a Greek name at all. Andreas is probably a translation of a Hebrew name indicating maleness or boldness, like Adam 'first man, earthly one, created one' or Gabriel 'strong man of God.'

Now let's return to Merry Old England where quite soon in our putative little village there were three men named Andrew. No language has an infinite number of first names. In any society of ample population, duplication of first names will occur early, and the need to differentiate two people with the same personal name had grown critical by the early Middle Ages. Because the upper classes had large amounts of property and riches to bequeath to their descendants, they needed names more precise than Long Andrew and Short Andrew to denote specific heirs listed in wills. Surnames thus began first among the landed wealthy. Often the addition to the name was the father's first name: John, son of

Andrew. Or the added tag might appear in the possessive case: John Andrewes. Later, dropping the *e*, the name appears as John Andrews. In documents and in street parlance, John, son of Andrew, was shortened frequently to John Andrews. However, the crucial step was taken when William, the son of John, also adopted his father's last name and was known in legal documents and around his own native village as William Andrews. And in that act of practical testamentary specificity we have the arrival of the hereditary surname, not only in English but also contemporaneously in all the Indo-European languages of Europe (see chart). The use of surnames began in southern Europe among land-owning Italian nobles and quickly spread northward during the later Middle Ages.

ANDREW LEADS TO MANY SURNAMES

English	French	
		Andrez
		Andrian
Anderby	Anderlin	Andricq
Anderson	Andrat	Andrieux
Anderton	Andraux	Andrillet
Andison	André	Andrillon
Andress	Andréa	Andriolet
Andrew	Andreant	Andrion
Andrewes	Andréas	Andrisse
Andrews	Andreault	Andriu
Andrewson	Andrée	Andriveaux
Andrey	Andreix	Andrivet
Andrus	Andrel	Andrueton
Aunderson	Andréol	Andry
Danson	Andres	Andryeux
Enderson	Andreus	Dreiu
Tancock	Andrevon	Dreux
Tandy	Andrey	Drevet

French *(cont'd)*

Drius
Drivet
Landré
Landrieux
Landriu

•

German

Anderer
Anderl
Anders
Andersen
Anderssohn
Andert
Andrasch
Andreesen
Andrich
Andrick
Andriske
Antrag
Drehsel
Dreisel
Dreiss
Dreuss
Ender
Enderl
Enderlein
Endermann
Enders
Endrass
Endress
Endriss

•

Hungarian

András

•

Italian

Andreani
Andrelli
Andreoletti
Andreolli
Andreotti
Andretti
Andrucci

•

Scandinavian

Andersholm
Andersqvist
Anderssen
Andersson

•

Scottish Gaelic

Dand
Dandie
Dandison
Dandy
Gillanders
Kendrew
McAndrew

•

Slavic

Anders
Andrássy

Andratski
Andreachuk
Andreev
Andreiov
Andreivitch
Andrej
Andreychuk
Andrianov
Andric
Andritski
Andropov
Androschek
Andrushky
Andruskevich
Andrzejewski
Handrock
Jander
Jendryschik
Jendrzejski
Jendrzek
Ondra
Ondrej
Ondruchuk
Wandrei

•

Spanish

Andrez
Andrillos

•

Welsh

Bandra
Bandrew
Bandrey

Another example of rendering names as more specific, copied directly from listings in medieval registers is: John, Andrew's son. This became John Andrewson or, in the common Scottish spelling, John Anderson. Dialect pronunciations gave other spellings like Enderson. A pet form of Andrew like Andy gave the surname Andison.

Surnames from Pet Names

Let's say the ancestral founder of the family was named William. His son and descendants might bear the surname Williams, like best-selling Canadian writer Stephen Williams, author of *Invisible Darkness* (1996), the most interesting and most controversial account of murderer Paul Bernardo. If three or more men named William lived near one another in the same English hamlet, they might be differentiated with a hypocoristic—a pet name like Will, Willie, or Wilkin. Such affectionate diminutives of first names are called hypocoristic in linguistics and are associated with playful terms of endearment that parents give to children, hence the English noun and adjective from the Greek verb *hupokorizesthai* 'to play the child, to behave or speak like a child.' *Koros* and *kore* are the classical Greek words for boy and girl. Many English surnames arose from such pet names. Consider the singer and star of the musical *Phantom of the Opera*, Colm Wilkinson. His surname means 'descendant of Wilkin,' that is, Little Will. Wilken in certain parts of England was shortened to Wilk and gives surnames like Wilkes and Wilke, as in the eighteenth-century political gadfly and reformer John Wilkes and his later, less reputable American namesake John Wilkes Booth. A popular Scottish form, also giving a surname, is Wilkie, as in London-born William Wilkie Collins, author of the early detective novel, *The Moonstone* (1868).

Pet names using the affectionate suffix *-kin* are quite productive of last names. A boy called Little Simon in a medieval English family could also be addressed as Simkin, which produces surnames like Simpkins. If Tommy grew bored being called Little Tom, his siblings could try Tomkin, giving last names like Tompkins and Tompkinson.

Yet another hypocoristic suffix in Middle English was *-cock*. Thus, another way to say Little Will was Willcock. From that sprang surnames like Willcocks, Wilcox, and the many variants.

Perhaps a Norman-French family added a French diminutive to a son named William and produced the fairly common pet name of Willet? Surnames like Willett, Willetts, and Willet result.

Another Norman-French pet suffix was *-ot* added to a boy's name. So the mother of a William or Guillaume might call him Wilmot or Guillemot. Wilmot gives surnames like Willmet, Willmitt, Willmott, Willmetts, and Willmuts. *Guillemot* 'Billybird' is the name, in modern English and in French, of a seabird of the Atlantic coast, an auk with a narrow bill.

If the pet form of William was simple Will, then resulting surnames include Wills, Willis, Willing, and Willison. Canadian novelist Ethel Wilson (1888–1980) comes to mind immediately, one of our first fiction writers to present with power the wilds of British Columbia and their influence on an independent woman, all this in her first and best novel, *Swamp Angel* (1954).

2. Surnames from Place Names

Surnames based on places and geographical features near the home of the founder of a family are often easy to interpret: Blackwell, Holbrook (brook in a hollow or ravine), Mayfield, Norwood, Westbrook. Equally clear are last names like Banks, Bridges, Downs, Fields, Hill, Lake, Meadows, Townsend, and Woods.

A few dozen topographical words from Early and Middle English, though obsolete in everyday modern speech, are still here in surnames, words like *wic*. Canadian cartoonist and philanthropist Ben Wicks possesses a surname that harks back to an ancestor's homestead. *Wic* in Old English had this series of meanings: dwelling place, abode, homestead, several homesteads (that is, hamlet), village, and town. Then in the twelfth and thirteenth centuries it meant a specific kind of farmstead, a dairy farm, and gave rise to village names like Gatwick (literally 'goat farm,' now a British airport location), Chiswick (cheese farm), and Butterwick. There are dozens of little villages in England named Wix, Wick, Wyke, and Week. Ben Wicks's ancestors may spring from such a place. As a suffix in hundreds of British village names, *-wic* can indicate a small settlement, specialized farm like a dairy operation, trading place, or a harbour. Surnames like Eastwick come from villages where ancestors lived. There are six towns in various English counties called Southwick, one or all of which may have given rise at different times to the surname Southwick. Old English nouns, like modern German ones, had declensions, and sometimes a modern spelling hides an ancient declined form, as in the town of High Wycombe, wherein lurks an Old English dative plural *wicum* 'at the settlements or dairy farms.'

Some snooty families—surely not in Britain?—embarrassed by the humble nature of their surnames have tried to disguise low origins by alterations in spelling. The most famous of this class of red-faced surnames is Byron. It was originally Byrom or Byram from Old English *byrum* 'at the cowsheds,' a dative plural of location, and not perhaps the noblest placement of an ancestor's abode. Certainly, Byrom had an etymology not sufficiently seemly to suit so exalted a personage as the poet, George Gordon, Lord Byron. What would people say? Have you seen Lord Cowshed's latest ode? Quite, quite bovinely inspired! He must have been courting the Moos. The family changed Byrom to Byron very early in the thirteenth century. The word *byre* meaning cowshed lingers still in English, particularly in some English dialects.

Another common place-name suffix that appears in English surnames is-*ham* 'homestead, village, manor, estate.' Canada's pert political journalist Allan Fotheringham's last name may spring from an ancestor who once dwelt in the wee Scottish town of *ffodryngay* (so it was entered in a document of 1261). This settlement in turn had been named after Fotheringhay, a locality in Northamptonshire founded years earlier. Fotheringhay means 'island where cattle can be grazed,' that is, supplied with fodder. -*Hay* is probably a dialect pronunciation of the Old English word *eg* or *ieg*. It could mean island, but also, less stringently, it could mean a parcel of land only partly surrounded by water. *Eg* could refer as well to a dry hummock of land rising above marshy ground.

As the population of Anglo-Saxon Britain expanded, so did the meanings of certain Old English words. *Tun*, for example, in its prime meaning was a simple, enclosed farmstead. Later it was something grander like an estate or a mansion. Tun acquired an additional meaning of two or three farmsteads together, perhaps at some particular geographic feature. This use of tun produced place names like Eaton (island farm), Eton (river farm), Houston (Hugh's tun or farm), and Norton. Tun is still with us in its modern form of *town*. Many such place names were the sources of well-known surnames, like Stratton that began as *stræt tun* 'farm beside a Roman road' from Latin *strata via* 'paved road.' Old English *stræt* is Modern English *street*.

The first name and surname Winston began as *Wynnes tun*, Wine's town, that is, the farmstead of an Anglo-Saxon man with the common male name of Wynn 'friend.' Its Middle English spelling was Wine and it is still seen as Wynne, a given name for boys or girls. The etymon or root of Wynn and Wine is not related to fermented grapes. That wine is from Latin *vinum* 'wine.' Winston became a frequent given name passed down through many generations of the Churchill family. A trifle more exotic is the name of a farmstead near a Celtic burial mound owned by another Anglo-Saxon family named Wynn. This place in Buckinghamshire was first called *Wynnes hlaw* 'Wynn's mound' and is now the the place and the surname Winslow.

Viking Places Yield Surnames

The Old Scandinavian word for village or settlement was *by*. In areas of Britain conquered by Vikings, it appears as a suffix at the end of many town names like Ashby and Kirby that produced surnames. The Viking form of Ashby was *Askr by* 'village where ash-trees grow.' There are dozens of places named Ashby in northern England and in the Midlands. Kirby is a shortened form of Kirkby, both common place names in the Danelaw. The Old Scandinavian form was *Kirkju by* 'church village.' Think of the Middle English and still Scottish *kirk*, a word for church borrowed from the Viking language.

Quite early in the Norse and Danish invasions of Great Britain arose the place name that is the origin of the surname of Canadian politician the Hon. John Crosbie of Newfoundland. The Vikings were not Christian, but soon after they stopped merely plundering Britain and actually settled and built farmsteads and small communities, these marauders began to accept Christianity. Oh, there would be holdouts, villages where the message of Christ was rejected. But a traveller coming over a hill and spying in the distance a small settlement could often tell if the place was Christian or not. Its very name gave away its religious status. In the north of Britain were many places called in Old Scandinavian *Krossa by* 'village with crosses.' By 1190 one of them was being recorded as Crossby, and variants like Crosby and Crosbie soon appeared.

New York City has a newscaster and novelist named Chuck Scarborough. And Toronto has its Scarborough Bluffs. Scarborough means '*Harelip's Fort*,' a fact no doubt unknown to Elizabeth Simcoe when she named the village because the local bluffs reminded her of cliffs near the town of Scarborough in Yorkshire. The wife of Upper Canada's first governor general, John Graves Simcoe, needed only to add a knowledge of Old Scandinavian to her many accomplishments and she might have thought twice about that place name. Scarborough in England was a Viking settlement originally. We know because it was recorded in a Viking saga that one Thorgils Skarthi founded the North Yorkshire settlement around AD 965. Now Viking warriors liked frightening and sometimes repellent nicknames. *Skarthi* meant harelip in Old Scandinavian, as we today call the language spoken by the Vikings. In Old English the settlement was *Skaresborg*, Harelip's Fort. One further example of Viking naming habits is found in the origin of Nottingham. Its first name was *Snottingsheim*, or in Old Scandinavian 'farmstead of a Viking named Snot.' Yes, his name indicated that this Viking needed Kleenex. And, yes, Nottingham became a person's last name. In printed registers as early as AD 1169 is a record of land held by one Thomas de Notingeham.

Our federal minister of foreign affairs is the Hon. Lloyd Axworthy. His surname has two possible sources. *Akes worthig* in Old English is oak homestead, a dwelling or farm home enclosed by oak trees. *Worth*, *worthig*, and *worthign* were variants in OE and all referred to an enclosed farmstead. The other possibility is Axworthy from Hakesworthy with a lost initial *h*. A common Viking male name was Haki, a nickname that meant bent or crooked in Old Scandinavian. So Old English *Hakis worthig* is Haki's enclosed homestead. As its population grew, it may easily have become a little village. When a man moved from that village to another part of Britain, he might be known and entered in a medieval register as Tom of Akesworthie. .

Actor Neil Vipond's ancestors may have originated in Vieuxpont 'Old Bridge,' a place in Calvados in northern France. Or, the family founder may have built a homestead *au vieux pont* 'beside the old bridge' somewhere in Norman Britain or France.

Surnames of Nationality

Although these national last names deserve their own category, they fit snugly here under local surnames. A medieval arrival in London might have been a lively lad named *Jean le breton*. This John from Brittany might found a family with any of the following surnames: Breton, Brett, Britt, Britten, and Britton. Consider one of the great ornaments of the British stage, Dame Judy Dench. Dame Dench is Danish, her surname based on one of the following: Old English *denisc*; Middle English *denshe, dench*; Scottish *Dence, Dens*—all meaning Danish. The late Canadian hockey broadcaster Ward Cornell had ancestors from Cornwall. Other surnames from the same place are Cornish and Cornwallis. Immigration from various departments of France produced some English family names. Surnames that positively drip British disdain and haughtiness turn out—delightfully—to be of peasant origin. The snobbish-sounding Gascoynes were mere upstarts from Gascony. The Lorings came by cart and then by boat from Lorraine. The Jarmans and Jermyns were just Germans. A little more deviously, the Pettengales and the Pettingells and the Puttergills were Portuguese, while the Wallaces, the Wallises, the Welches, the Wellsmans, and the Walches were Welsh.

3. Surnames from Ancestors' Occupations

Renowned Canadian contralto Maureen Forrester had an ancestor who was a medieval gamekeeper. Last names took their final hereditary forms, as we have learned, between 1300 and 1600, therefore the occupation surnames reflect a late medieval world of manual labour and craft skills. The large number of different occupation names in Late Middle English is astonishing. More than two hundred different occupations have their own agent nouns. Sir Martin Frobisher (1539–1594), who gave his name to Canada's Frobisher Bay, had an ancestor who was a furbisher, that is, he burnished armour. He put the final polish on swords and lances so they would sparkle on the day of the joust.

Canadian publisher James Lorimer sports a surname derived from the agent noun for a medieval craftsman who forged the metal bits and studs used to adorn and strength the harnesses put on horses. It's from Old French *loremier* 'bit-maker' from OF *lorain* 'straps of a harness' from Late Latin *loranum* 'harness strap' from Latin *lorum* 'leather thong, strap.' A variant of lorimer, loriner, was far more common in everyday speech and in documents. Lorimer as an agent noun is completely obsolete. But loriner survives in the title of one of the hundred or so London livery companies, those splendid remnants of the medieval guilds that once regulated trade apprenticeship and marketing, forerunners of labour unions. The Noble Company of Loriners and Spurriers (makers of spurs) still marches proudly through London streets in the Lord Mayor's annual parade.

CBC Radio sportscaster Dave Naylor boasts a founding ancestor who cast nails and spikes at a forge. That nailer also sold nails. Star of TV's *The Urban Peasant* cooking show, James Barber, had a forebear who, of course, cut hair. But medieval barbers also pulled out teeth, hence the spiralling red line representing blood on barber poles. Barbers also performed minor surgeries without benefit of anesthetic. The philanthropic Chalmers family of Ontario may boast an ancestor who was a chalmer, that is, a chamberlain, a personal servant in a great mansion, or, if the family name originated a little later in English history, a chalmer was a kind of jack-of-all-trades at a country inn or city tavern. The late Canadian firebrand and broadcaster extraordinaire, Jack Webster, bore a name that means weaver. Canadian playwright George F. Walker did not inherit a family name from Elizabethan sprinters. Walker is an occupation name from medieval cloth manufacture. After the cloth had been dyed and set, it was washed, and then walkers trod upon the cloth in order to clean it. Fuller is yet another surname from the cloth trade. Fuller's earth was used to stiffen the cloth, clean it, and make it easier to tease up the nap on woven goods. A fuller actually used the prickly heads of the dried teasel plant. To Canadians teasel is an unpleasant weed. Vast fields of teasel grew beside cloth-making buildings in medieval England. Anyone named Ledbetter had an ancestor who worked with the metal lead as a lead-beater. A hayward was a hedge-guard, a village official in charge of the maintenance of fences and enclosures. In Middle English a travers collected tolls. Tolls were exacted not only at toll bridges, but on certain roads through estates and towns. The surname Travers was as widespread throughout Great Britain as medieval tolls. A few occupation names are much older than the medieval ones. Mather, for example, is pure Anglo-Saxon. In Old English, *mæðere* was a reaper or a mower.

4. Surnames from Ancestors' Nicknames

Bassett is a double diminutive of a nickname. *Bas* meant of short stature or low in Old French and the diminutive form *basset*, with the suffix *-et* or *-ett*, often referred to an actual dwarf. Of course, a few marriages over a few generations with taller women would soon render the possibly offensive nickname meaningless, as indeed would the temporal and linguistic change that saw *bass* disappear completely from the adjective stock of modern English, although its noun cousin *base* is still here.

Under the rubric of nicknames reside surnames of skin and hair colour like Black and Blake, Brown and Burnett, Dunn and Gray, Hoare (greyhaired) and Read or Reed (redhaired), Snow (whitehaired), and even Sorrell (reddish-brownhaired). Nicknames can be insulting too, and we have surnames that are, like Bossey (hunchbacked), Cruickshank (crooked legs), Crump (stooped), Doggett (dog head), Gulliver (glutton), and Smollett (small head). But nicknames may be complimentary as well, like Bellamy (French *bel ami* 'handsome friend'), Fairfax (beautiful hair), Goodfellow, Hardy (courageous), Prowse (Old French *proos*, *prooz* 'brave'), Sharp (quick thinking), and Turnbull (literally, strong enough to turn aside a charging bull).

Canadian comedian and TV host Mike Bullard has a very interesting surname based on a nickname. In Late Middle English bulling was fraudulent scheming. A bulle or boule or bole was a deceitful act, a trick. The noun suffix *-ard* very often had a pejorative meaning. Think of nouns like bastard, coward, drunkard, laggard, and sluggard. But remember one who is too wise, a wizard. A bullard then was a cheater or deceiver. Although the prime force of the root is definitely depreciatory, we must not forget human nature. Folks often admire a slick trickster. Insulting surnames don't last very long. Who wants to have a name that's an insult? So, for the surname Bullard to appear and to persist, the original nicknaming term must have had something of praise in it as well. When the gullible are duped, sympathy often goes to the duper, not to the duped. Whew! I wiggled out of that one nicely. So, please, Mike, if I'm ever in the audience for your TV show, be gentle!

The Power of Babel

Well, that concludes my sketch of English surname history. As a poet once sighed, "Had we but world enough and time . . ." Then I could write a thousand-page guide to surnames in all major languages of the world. Not in a mass-market paperback, Billy. The reader will find surnames of many, many languages explained in this book, including examples of surnames from Arabic, Armenian, Blackfoot, Chinese, Cree, Czech, Dutch, French, German, Greek, Hebrew, Icelandic, Inuktitut, Iranian, Irish, Italian, Polish, Punjabi, Russian, Scottish Gaelic, Slovakian, Spanish, Stoney, Ukrainian, Welsh, and Wendat.

The Meaning & Spelling Traps

Although original meanings of surnames surprise and fascinate, let's bong one gong of caution. Names don't mean in the same way most words mean. A word can represent an actual thing or feeling or sense perception like colour. A name may have started life as a signifier, but as it became specialized—some might say fossilized—as a name, and joined the select word-hoard of surnames (perhaps 100,000 in English) the word as surname loses part of its referential, signifying quality. We do not expect a lady whose last name is Hunter to charge about the forest athwart a mountain lion, clad in deerskin skimpies, picking off dangerous killer raccoons with a .357 magnum. In short, her name is Hunter. She is not one. It is likewise in other languages. Even if we know Arabic, no one nowadays expects a person named Haddad to be a blacksmith. Yet *haddad* is one Arabic term for such a craftsman. The complete name of an individual signified that person alone, so that we may say the meanings of the words that comprise that individual's name have altered completely. The semantic focus of the name words has narrowed. Their meanings have shifted from the general to the specific. As a surname, Hunter is no longer a general agent noun. It has become the specific identifier of an individual.

In a short piece, *A Toast to Ava Gardner*, the poet and anthologist Robert Graves wrote:

In Spain, a married woman keeps her maiden name, but tacks on her husband's after a de. *Thus, on marrying Wifredo Las Rocas, our Majorcan friend Rosa, born an Espinosa, became Señora Rosa Espinosa de Las Rocas—a very happy combination. It means 'Lady Thorny Rose from the Rocks.' Rosa was luckier than her maternal cousin Dolores Fuertes, who thoughtlessly married a lawyer named Tomás Barriga, and is now Dolores Fuertes de Barriga, or 'Violent Pains of the Stomach.'*

Sound a second warning gong for those setting out to discover the "meaning" of a surname. English spelling was illiterate chaos until well into the eighteenth century when dictionaries appeared in cheap editions that humble registry clerks could afford to buy. Especially chaotic are the spellings of surnames from families none of whose members were literate. If you are tracing family names, keep written track of every spelling variation and try to find documents containing the family name from medieval times when surnames of most Western countries were forming. Or, if your quest is informal, you can relax and smile as Fielding did. British novelist Henry Fielding (1707–1754), whose masterpiece was *Tom Jones*, was once visiting the Earl of Denbigh. The earl's family name was Feilding, and naturally, one rook-streaked twilight, over goblets of finest malmsey, the two men discussed Fielding's belonging to the same family line. The earl wondered why the names were spelled differently. Fielding replied that he could give no reason, "except perhaps that my branch of the family was the first to know how to spell."

Shakespeare supplied the title of this book. What's in a name indeed? In *Romeo and Juliet*, Juliet is fibbing when she says, "that which we call a rose by any other name would smell as sweet." In fact, given the synesthetic muddle of memory stimulated by sight, sound, and smell, if we called a rose a gezoxtehoogen, it would not smell exactly the same as something called a rose would smell. After you have discovered their meaning, last names will never again be dull labels. So spur your curiosity to the charging point and set forth with these Shakespearean words, with which King Henry V exhorts his troops on the eve of the Battle of Agincourt:

Then shall our names,
Familiar in his mouth as household words, . . .
Be in their flowing cups, freshly remembered.

Abbreviations, Symbols, & Linguistic Terms

I have tried to keep abbreviations and symbols to a minimum. Nevertheless, I use a few in tracing the origins of surnames.

1. What do < and > mean in linguistic descriptions?
When one states the origin of words or roots in earlier languages or when one shows how a root developed in a later form of the same language or was borrowed into a different later language, linguistics borrows two arithmetical operator signs from mathematical notation. As a mathematical symbol > means 'greater than' and < means 'less than.' But in language study > means 'develops into, is the root of.' And < means 'stems from, derives from, is related to a previous form like.'

2. In discussions of the parts that make up a whole surname, the equal sign (=) means 'is made up of the following roots or elements.'

3. The only frequent abbreviation is OE for Old English.

4. The asterisk *
The asterisk (*) indicates a hypothetical form, usually in the Indo-European (or IE) family of languages to which English, and most other languages of Europe belong. Consult a large dictionary with a chart of the hundreds of languages that belong to this ancient family. The forms are hypothetical and marked with an asterisk because the Indo-Europeans had no system of writing, so the prehistoric roots are adduced from their modern forms. This ancient mother tongue is sometimes called PIE for Proto-Indo-European. It

accounts for the similarity in many common terms across now widely separated languages, for example, explaining why father, *pater*, *pitar*, and *Vader* are all related and all mean 'father.'

5. Why are there so many forms of some Latin and Greek words?
The simple or nominative case of a Latin or Greek noun is not always the form that entered a later language like French or English and so influenced the making of a last name in those languages. For example, many Latin and Greek nouns do not contain the full root form in the nominative case, but do show the full root form in the genitive. Thus, it is traditional in learning Latin and Greek nouns to quote a noun in its nominative and genitive case. You have seen it frequently in dictionaries. You will see it in this book occasionally. For example, one might list a root like *chrom-* and say it derives from *chroma, chromatos* Greek, colour of the skin, then any colour; used as a combining form signifying 'colour.' The Greek is given as *chroma, chromatos* because English has borrowed both the nominative and the following genitive of the Greek word for colour to make new scientific words. For example, in science, the word *chromosome* uses only the nominative stem. And the English scientific word *chroma* uses the Greek nominative in its original form. But the adjective referring to colour, *chromatic*, uses the genitive stem.

Like all languages whose nouns have declensions of different case endings, and whose verbs have many conjugational endings, Latin and Greek words had many forms. Different parts of Latin and Greek nouns and verbs have been used over the centuries to make or to influence the making of new surnames, especially of course in the Romance languages derived from Latin. That is why a classical word may appear in several forms.

The Origins & Meanings of Some Canadian Surnames

Presented in Alphabetical Order

A

ABBOTT

Sir John Joseph Caldwell Abbott 1821–1893

The lawyer and politician became the third prime minister of Canada (1891–1892) and was the first Canadian-born prime minister.

Abbott is of course from abbot, the head of a monastery or convent. Abbots were priests and were celibate, so they could not found families. And even if they did enjoy a quick tryst under the table in a moonlit refectory with a scullery wench, it would have been unwise to make known the fact by labelling one's bastard spawn in public registries. Therefore Abbot as a surname usually meant the founding ancestor of the family was the lay servant of an abbot or was someone who worked on the estate or in the household of an abbot. Surprisingly then, the Scottish Gaelic surname MacNab does mean '**son of** the abbot.' Two questions arise and are answered if you see the entry for Archibald McNab.

The word *abbot* entered English from ecclesiastical Latin *abbas*, itself from Koine Greek *abbas*, borrowed directly from Biblical Hebrew *abba* 'father, abbot.' And compare Aramaic *abbá* 'father.' In modern Hebrew *abba* with the first syllable stressed means 'father, daddy, papa, and abbot.' The ancient Hebrew root *ab* could refer to God the Father and begins many Hebrew personal names:

• Abigail   'father of exaltation'
• Abner   'father of light'
• Abraham   'father of many'

In Genesis 17:5 the derivation of Abraham is given as the Hebrew words *av hamon* (*goyim*) 'father of a multitude of nations.' But, like very many derivations in the Old Testament, it is not supported by the facts of linguistic change and is therefore probably a folk etymology. The true origin of the name *Abraham* is uncertain.

• Absalom   'father of peace'

Compare *shalom* in Hebrew and *salaam* in Arabic, the beautiful greeting of peace common to both these members of the Semitic language family.

Some Hebrew and Arabic Names

Salaam and *shalom* bring us to a little digression about Semitic languages, and about Hebrew and Arabic first and last names. The verbal roots in Hebrew and Arabic are said to be triliteral. Most of them are based on three consonants. And *salaam* is an example worth discussing because it gives us two words widely used in English. The Arabic triliteral root *s-l-m*, expressed usually as the verbal form *salima* or *salama* has a basic meaning of 'be safe and sound' and developed meanings like 'be at peace' and 'be in the peace of Allah' and hence 'give in or submit to the will of Allah.' If we take the *s-l-m* root, prefix an *i* and perform a few other abstract-noun-forming shenanigans, we get the noun *islam* 'submission or surrender,' which becomes the name of a great religion, Islam 'submission to the will of Allah.' One who has submitted to the will of Allah is a *muslim*, where the passive, preterite prefix *mu-* is added to the *s-l-m* root. Muslim thus has a literal meaning of 'one who has submitted to the will of Allah.'

Next, consider the beautiful given name borne by many male muslims the world over, Salim. This means 'safe and sound' or 'healthy' when stressed on the last syllable. When Salim is stressed on the first syllable it means 'free, secure.' An even older, pre-Islamic Arabic female name is Salma, based on the same *s-l-m* root. Salma is Salima, a female version of Salim, with the stress on the first syllable so strongly pronounced that the second syllable, a short *i* to begin with, gradually drops out. Try saying the name Salima and punching the first syllable very strongly, and you will hear the weak *i*-sound begin to disappear. This is precisely what happened in spoken Arabic over the course of many years.

Salma follows a strange path indeed into English. An eighteenth-century Scottish poet and translator named James Macpherson (1736–96) published what he claimed were the works of a long-lost Gaelic poet named Ossian. The book of translations was phenomenally popular all over England and Europe. Macpherson was later revealed to have perpetrated a vast hoax on the reading public. He had made up the poems from bits and pieces of Gaelic folklore. But that did nothing to stem the sweeping tide of Ossian mania. People began naming their children after characters in the poems. Macpherson had named Ossian's castle: Selma. It seems Macpherson must have come across some book featuring Arabic names like Salma. In Germany and Scandinavia there was a sudden vogue to name female babies Selma. Although never thereafter widely popular, the name is still found in the West, for example, in the name of American comedy writer, Selma Diamond.

The Hebrew reflex of the triliteral root *s-l-m* changes the s to *sh* sometimes, so that the root is *sh-l-m*, to give nouns like *shalom* 'peace.' Peacefulness is *shulamit* in Hebrew. The terminal *t* is a common marker of grammatical and sexual femininity in Semitic languages. Shulamit is a familiar female name today in modern Israel. It is also seen as Shelomit, Shulamite, and Shulamith or contracted to Shula.

Perhaps the most infamous name derived from the *shalom* root is Salome, a late Greek version of the Aramaic *Shalamzu*, itself an abbreviation of Aramaic *Shalomziyon* 'peace of Zion.' The sinuous and lissome Salome danced for King Herod and so jolted the royal undercarriage that he offered Salome anything she desired. She wanted the severed head of John the Baptist brought to her on a plate. This scene so imprinted itself on the medieval Christian imagination that Salome became a taboo name for girls until almost the twentieth century, and even today it wins no popularity contests.

From the *sh-l-m* root as well is Shlomo, a modern Hebrew form of Solomon (Hebrew *Shelomoh* 'peaceful'). The Arabic form of Solomon is Sulayman, best known to Western history in the name of that mighty sultan of the Ottoman empire, Suleiman the Magnificent (1496–1566). The Yiddish form of Solomon is Zalman, whose pet form Zal is common. Fans of 1960s mellow pop music will remember Canadian Zal Yanovsky, lead guitarist for the Lovin' Spoonful whose hits included "Do You Believe in Magic?" and "Day Dream."

So we see how one Semitic root, *s-l-m*, can weave its way through the centuries into a multitude of Hebrew and Arabic names, and from those languages of the Middle East, principally by means of holy books such as the Bible and the Koran, the *s-l-m* names have spread over the entire planet.

ABERHART
William "Bible Bill" Aberhart 1878–1943
He was a radio evangelist, then premier of Alberta from 1935 to 1943, and, as such, head of the world's first Social Credit government.

The surname Aberhard is German, a variant of the personal name, Eberhard. In Old German Eburhard was *ebur* 'wild boar' + *hardu* 'tough, enduring.' The two elements in such warrior names did not have to combine to make literal sense, rather they were composed of a stock of word roots that came to be set aside as suitable for name-making, giving compound Germanic names like *Reich-hardt* 'powerful-brave' that led to the English Richard.

Consider also Old German *Gairhard* 'spear-hard,' which evolved into the modern German given name *Gerhardt*, French *Gérard*, English Gerard, and Irish Garret.

ACORN

Milton Acorn 1923–1986

Born in Charlottetown, Prince Edward Island, this populist was a carpenter by trade and a poet by calling. A most prickly man in his dealings with friends and loved ones, Milton Acorn championed the validity of the daily experience of working people, both their joy and their pain, in collections like I've Tasted My Blood *(1969) and, referring to the original Mi'kmaq name for Prince Edward Island, the collection* This Island Means Minago *(1975). The best all-round sampling of his feisty verse is in* Dig Up My Heart: Selected Poems 1952–1983.

Acorn, if an English surname and not a translation from a foreign language or a surname made up by the bearer, could arise as the nickname of an ancestor who was short, swarthy, and nut-shaped, much as we might call someone "Stubby" today. Or it may be an occupational name by metonymy for one who collected mast, the nuts of forest trees, chiefly beech and oak, used as food for domestic swine.

Metonymy is a technical term for a common figure in speech, in poetry, and in prose. It is a label for one of the ways language departs from the everyday mode in order to achieve some special effect or heightening. Because we'll meet it now and then in discussing the origin of surnames, let's define it. Metonymy is a kind of metaphor in which an associated part stands for the whole. A Canadian news story might say, "Parliament Hill turned down their request." The reference however is to the government of the day, not the actual buildings. "No comment from Rideau Hall." The governor-general's official residence is Rideau Hall, but metonymy allows the residence to stand in the sentence for the governor-general herself or himself. A British newspaper might report that "the Crown has made it clear." They mean that the Queen has made it clear. "I like the stage" could mean "I enjoy theatre." Something associated with a thing is named instead of the thing and stands in for it. This metaphorical substitution or change of name freshens language, and is the source of the word itself in Greek rhetoric where *metonumía* means literally 'cross-naming' or 'change of name,' being composed of the Greek prefix *meta* across + *onuma* name (*onoma* is the Attic form of the word; *onuma* is the form in the Aeolian dialect of ancient Greek) + *ia* Greek noun suffix borrowed through Latin.

The Attic form of the Greek word for name, *onoma*, gives the scientific name for the study of personal and place names, onomastics, from the Greek adjective *onomastikós* 'related to names.' This book is but a quick toe dip into the ocean of onomastics.

Milton Acorn himself would have been delighted to know—if he did not indeed well know—that the modern form of the Old English *aecern* has been corrupted by folk etymology. At one time it was thought to contain *ac*, Old English for oak, then Elizabethans had the notion it derived from the same root as corn, hence the modern spelling acorn. In fact, *aecern* is related to acre and the Latin *ager* 'field,' and to its closer cousins in Old Scandinavian *akarn* 'fruit of the forest,' Danish *agern,* and Dutch *aker.*

ADAMS

Bryan Adams 1959–

The Canadian superstar rock singer and composer was born in Kingston, Ontario. Probably his most popular song is "Everything

I Do, I Do It for You." The music video of his 1998 hit "A Day Like Today" is considered one of the best rock videos ever made in Canada. In 1999, adding another quiver to his bow, Adams published a very popular book of his own startling and evocative photographs of women, famous and not, titled* Made in Canada.

The majority of English surnames are based on the first name of the founding male ancestor of the family. Yes, it was oinky and chauvinistic of those frowsy Saxons to deprecate female names, but, shall we revise history? No, *herstory* won't work as one peruses the rise of surnames.

As we might expect, Adams was in medieval English a genitive form, *Adames* 'of Adam.' This could be appended in a parish registry to a first name like John, so that John Adames would mean John, son of a man named Adam. But note that it could also commonly refer to anyone of the household of a man named Adam. If that Adam had servants, his underlings' newborn children could be baptized with their master's name. So Adams can also mean 'servant of Adam.' If a family wished to make clear that the child being baptized was a legitimate heir of the founding ancestor, the relationship was stated plainly by putting "Adam's son" after the first name, so that John, Adam's son would become in time John Adamson.

In Scotland, MacAdam was the form, and one of that name, a surveyor, John Loudon McAdam (1756–1836) helped pave the way for better roads by suggesting many layers of broken stone as a roadbed. He also gave us a verb "to macadamize." Another illustrious bearer of the name was John Macadam, an Australian chemist, after whom is named the Australian tree whose fruit we eat as macadamia nuts.

Spelling did not become standardized in England until the spread of dictionaries and general literacy. So variant forms of the surname appear as Addams, Adems, and Adhams.

Sometimes the founding ancestor's pet name, often a diminutive form, was the origin of the surname. Pet names for Adam in medieval English included Addy, Ade, Adcock, Adekin, and Adnett. These pet names produced a profusion of Adam-based surnames that include Adcocks, Addey, Addis, Haddy, Addison, Addyman, Ades, Adey, Adkins, Atkins, Adnitt, and so forth. There is an Irish-Gaelic diminutive form, too, that appears in the name of the eighth-century Irish St. Adamnan, 'Little Adam.'

The majority of first names in all countries of Christendom were taken from the names of Christian saints, often by legal enforcement. For example, in 1563 the Council of Trent decreed that children baptized in the Roman Catholic Church must be given names that appear in the Catholic calendar of saints' names. This stricture was made to combat the then-growing Protestant habit of using Old Testament names. What the anti-Semitic Council of Trent was actually in a racist tizzy about, of course, was the fact that most Old Testament names were Hebrew, and Rome did not want the entire population of Europe tagged with Jewish names. Well, this may be a *goyishe welt*, but that ploy didn't work. A very large percentage of all first and *last* names in every language of Europe can be traced back to Hebrew originals in the Old and New Testament. Thus failed one bit of papal anti-Semitism.

And so it behooves any bearer of the name Adam or Adams to know just what the name of the first man means in Hebrew. One striking feature of the Adam and Eve creation myth in Genesis is the pottery metaphor: a god formed humans from clay. This is a worldwide element in creation stories. Compare the Hebrew and Christian version in Genesis 2:6, 7 as translated in the King James version of 1611: "There went up a mist from the earth, and watered the whole face of the ground. And the Lord God formed man of the dust of the ground. . ." So, even today, in brickyards of the Middle

East, does the brickmaker sprinkle water on the clay before he kneads it into shape. The Bible's name for the first man reflects this too. Adam means 'human being, person.' With only a slightly different voicing, *adom* means 'red.' Both may be related to Hebrew *adamah* 'clay' or 'red earth of Israel.' In Old Testament Hebrew it is usually *ha adam* and the definite article makes some scholars suspect that the name, like some others in Hebrew, was very early borrowed from neighbouring Assyrians. If so, it might stem from Assyrian *adamu* 'to make or produce.' Thus Adam would mean 'the made one, the created one.'

The ultimately Latin word 'human' also reflects this pottery myth in creation stories. The prime meaning of Latin *humanus* is 'clayey' or made of *humus* 'earth, soil, clay.' The Roman word for human being or man, *homo*, as in our species *Homo sapiens*, also stems from the same root. In Old Latin it was *hemo* 'the earthen one' or 'the person of clay.' The idea must have occurred early in human history, when primitive humans first dug up an interred body to discover bones and dust. Dust thou art; to dust shalt thou return.

ADARIO
Adario
The early seventeenth-century Huron chief was the prototype of the "noble savage."

Adario was chief of a tribe of the people whom the French called Huron. A French explorer's report about Adario's life inspired the French writer Jean-Jacques Rousseau to write about the 'noble savage,' the shining example of natural goodness, dignity, and nobility untainted by the evil of civilization. Rousseau propounded this Romantic stereotype particularly in *Émile,* his 1762 novel about the education of children. Adario's name in his native Wendat language means 'muskrat.'

AFFLECK
Raymond Tait Affleck 1922–1989
The renowned architect's projects included Market Square in Saint John, as well as Place Bonaventure, Place Ville Marie, and Maison Alcan in Montréal.

Affleck is a Scottish Gaelic field name, from which village names and then surnames arose. It began as a local pronunciation of Auchinleck whose Gaelic meaning is 'stone field.' Affleck or Auchinleck is a place name in the former Scottish counties of Angus, Lanark, Ayr, and Wigtown. The one in Ayrshire lays claim to a connection with English literature, being the lairdship of James Boswell's father, the Lord of Auchinleck. Boswell was the companion, toady, sidekick, and biographer of Samuel Johnson, composer of the first great dictionary of English. The first mention of the name in written records is Patrick de Achenlek in 1296.

AIRD
John Black Aird 1923–1995
He was a lawyer, senator, lieutenant-governor of Ontario, and chancellor at Wilfrid Laurier University and at the University of Toronto.

Aird is a place name in the former Scottish county of Ayrshire and also in the former Wigtownshire. In Scottish Gaelic *aird* means 'peak, direction, or point of the compass,' and so would be used to name an elevation of land that helped indicate direction to early settlers or travellers along a path or trail. It is not, as several amateur books about Scottish surnames suggest, derived from the name of the River Aire. Aire is a very old river name and probably means 'river.' Aire might stem from Old Scandinavian *eyjar* 'islands' or possibly Aire is Celtic or pre-Celtic for 'flowing strongly.' There is no instance of a terminal *d* suddenly and mysteriously being tacked on to the end of a river name to make a Gaelic surname.

AITKEN

Kate Aitken 1891–1971

She was a well-known radio broadcaster during the 1930s, 1940s, and 1950s; she was also a cook, a writer, and the guiding spirit of the Canadian National Exhibition's Women's Division.

Max Aitken 1879–1964

William Maxwell Aitken, first Baron Beaverbrook, the financier who created Stelco and Canada Cement, became a British politician, author, and publisher. He took the title of his peerage "Beaverbrook" from a little stream near his birthplace in Maple, Ontario. Aitken had become a millionaire by 1910 when he moved to England to begin his newspaper empire.

Aitken or Aitkins are Scottish forms of Atkins, 'son of Little Adam,' based on early diminutive forms of Adam like Adekins. See the *Adams* entry. Aitken is among the one hundred most common surnames in Scotland.

The diminutive suffix -*kin* formed a few English nouns and survives in some surnames. It ends words like catkin, lambkin, and nursery names like Peterkins, but not apparently bumpkin, pipkin, or pumpkin. Surnames using it include Aitkens, Jenkins, Simpkins, Tompkins, Watkins, Wilkinson, and most famously, Dickens (Dick + kins = a double diminutive of Richard).

The suffix is not related to the kin in kinship, but is related to similar diminutive endings in other Germanic languages. Compare *Häuschen*, German for 'little house' and *Kindchen* 'little child.' The French word *mannequin* 'little man' is borrowed from *manneken* in Dutch, which also uses the suffix. The English word *manikin* is a borrowing from Dutch. Ramekin, the little dish for baking individual portions of food, entered English from French *ramequin* borrowed from a Middle Dutch **rameken* ' little dish for cream.'

ALAN ALLAN ALLEN

Andrew Edward Fairbairn Allan 1907–1974

He was the leading director of CBC Radio drama during its golden age in the 1940s and 1950s, producing more than four hundred plays for the "Stage" series from 1944 to 1956. Critic Robert Fulford wrote that Andrew Allan gave many young CBC Radio listeners "our first hint that there were Canadian writers who had something interesting to say."

Sir Hugh Allan 1810–1882

During the 1830s, this Montrealer was one of the world pioneers in transatlantic steamship service.

Ralph Allen 1913–1966

One of Canada's great journalists, he was the best-loved editor of Maclean's *magazine (1946– 1960), the author of a popular history of Canada,* Ordeal by Fire, *and of a 1954 satirical novel about the CBC,* The Chartered Libertine.

Ted Allen 1916–1995

This was the pseudonym of Alan Herman, professional Communist, actor, writer of radio and TV scripts, and biographer, some would say hagiographer, of Norman Bethune. His wonderful, warm screenplay, Lies My Father Told Me, *all about growing up Jewish in Montréal, was nominated for an Academy Award.*

Allan became a popular name for men right after the Norman Conquest of Britain in 1066 for this very good reason: two of William the Conqueror's French generals were Alain, Count of Brittany, and Alain, 1st Earl of Richmond. To be in favour with the French who controlled Britain, parents rushed to give their children French names. Earlier, Alain was also the name of the Bishop of

Quimper who became a popular Breton saint. And many Bretons came to England after the Norman Conquest, settling particularly in Lincolnshire where Alain was among the ten most popular names in the twelfth century.

There is much dispute about what Alan means, but three contending theories have emerged. One posits a direct borrowing from the name of an ancient Scythian nomadic tribe named The Alan who dwelt near the Caspian Sea two millennia ago and spoke an Iranian language. Although no direct record of the Scythian tongue exists, related roots suggest that *alan* meant 'the people' in their language. The second theory suggests that Alan derives from what the earliest speakers of French would have called Germans, namely, *Alemanni*. This meant 'all the men' or 'the people' in Proto-Germanic, and gives rise to the present French word for Germany which is *Allemagne*. A third theory suggests that *Alan,* the saint's name in the Old Breton language, may be related to Gaelic *ail* 'rock.' Some of the Scottish surnames spelled Allan in English certainly derive from the Gaelic names *Ailene* and *Ailin.*

ALBANI
Dame Emma Albani 1847–1930
Albani was the stage name of a Canadian-born opera singer who became world-famous during the last thirty years of the nineteenth century. She had been born Marie-Louise-Cécile-Emma Lajeunesse at Chambly, Québec, and later made up a stage name that would sound Italian, since this was common practice among non-Italian opera hopefuls of the day.

Her inspiration for the stage surname Albani was a place, Albany, now the state capital of New York on the Hudson River, where she had studied opera happily. Albany had been named in 1664 at the time of the English occupation to honour the Duke of

York's Scottish title, Duke of Albany. King Charles II had entrusted the colony to him. Alba was an early Gaelic name for Scotland. So were Alban and Albany. Saint Alban was the first Christian martyred in the island of Britain. His name is either from Late Latin *albanus* 'white, of fair complexion' or from the locative adjective *Albanus* 'pertaining to the ancient Rome town of Alba,' centre of the Latin League. Or he may have been born in the *Monti Albani,* the limestone Alban Hills near Rome. And, serendipitously, Albani does happen to be a legitimate Italian surname, much like White in English.

ALCOCK

Norman Z. Alcock

He was a Canadian peace researcher and author of books such as The Bridge of Reason *(1961),* The War Disease *(1972), and* The Logic of Love *(1976).*

No, this name does not have its origin in the common fantasy of adolescent males. Alcock was an affectionate nickname for someone named Alan. First the founding ancestor may have been known by the shortened form, Al; then, as Basil Cottle puts it succinctly in *The Penguin Dictionary of Surnames*, cock, "the strutting barnyard fowl, became a generic term for pert lads, and was attached as a suffix to diminutive forms."

In Elizabethan English a mother could call her son "my little cock robin." Cock as a noun was applied to servant boys and apprentices. It gives rise to several common English surnames: Adcock, Simcock, Wilcock, Wilcox, Wilcoxson, and the matronymic Babcock 'son of Bab.' Bab and Babs were/are pet forms of Barbara. Simcock is from Sim, pet name for a Simon.

Although the cockerel was a domestic fowl, the phallic meaning of cock distressed certain English gentry, especially it seems after any Simcock family acquired wealth, and so, to remove even a hint of low, anatomical taint such as might bring a blush to a dowager's dewlap, Simcock was altered by some families to Simcoe, including the one that produced Lord Simcoe, the first lieutenant-governor of Upper Canada, whom Ontario celebrates by calling its August civic holiday, Simcoe Day.

Note also Silcox for Silcocks, Sil being a pet form of Sylvester or the Norman *Sylvein*. Pocock, on the other hand, is an attempt to disguise Peacock, a surname from a nickname, probably not based on fine dress, but on the strutting arrogance of the ancestor.

ALMIGHTY VOICE
Kakeesay-manitou-wayo 1874–1897
A Cree man turned outlaw by white policies toward First Peoples, he was arrested in 1895 for killing and butchering a farmer's cow. He escaped and evaded capture for almost two years, murdering four men including a North West Mounted Police officer. He and two companions were run to ground and blown up by NWMP cannons in 1897.

Kakeesaymanitouwayo means 'voice of the Great Manitou' in Cree. Manitou is a spirit, and the Great Manitou may be translated as 'God.' It's essentially an Algonquian verbal construct that signifies 'he has surpassed all.'

ALMOND
Paul Almond 1931–
The Montréal-born director of CBC television dramas went on to helm an important trilogy of Canadian feature films starring his then wife, actress Geneviève Bujold: Isabel *(1968),* Act of the Heart *(1970), and* Journey *(1972). He directed* Captive Hearts *in 1987 and* The Dance Goes On *in 1991, again with Bujold.*

Almond only looks like a nut. It has nothing to do with almond which is *amande* in French. The French surname derives from an ancestor's first name, *Alamond*, which was a French version of the compound Germanic warrior name *Adalmund*, whose elements are *adal* 'noble' and *mund* 'protection.'

ANDRÉ

Frère André (né Alfred Bessette) 1845–1937

The Roman Catholic healer, a brother of the Congregation of the Holy Cross, founded St. Joseph's Oratory on Mount Royal in Montréal, which became the most visited Catholic shrine in Canada. Brother André was the most revered religious figure of twentieth-century Québec. As usual, the leaders of the Roman Catholic Church in Québec were at first appalled by the tawdry miracles attributed to the intervention of Frère André's patron Saint Joseph, but soon they were persuaded by the immense popularity of the illiterate brother to spend the years 1924 to 1955 erecting a vast basilica and oratory beside the humble little chapel he began.

André (Andrew) is one of the most popular first names in the Christian world. Andrew was the first disciple. In the Koine Greek of the New Testament, Luke (6:14) calls him 'Andreas' based on the adjective *andreios* 'manly, bold.' But it is unlikely the first apostle had a Greek name at all. Andreas is probably a translation of a Hebrew name indicating maleness or boldness, like Adam 'first man, earthly one, created one' or Gabriel 'strong man of God.' Saint Andrew is the patron saint of Scotland, Russia, and fishermen. For the meaning of his birth surname, see the entry for Gérard Bessette.

The root *andro* is common in English words. For example, Polyandry is the practice of one woman having many concurrent husbands. Gynandromorph is a term in biology to denote an individual who has male and female characteristics.

ANGLIN

Ann Anglin 1942–
Toronto stage, radio, and TV actress

Margaret Anglin 1876–1958
The Ottawa-born stage actress had her own classical company, plus success as Roxanne in Cyrano de Bergerac, *in classical title roles like* Antigone, Medea, *and* Electra, *and in contemporary plays such as her last Broadway drama,* Watch on the Rhine *(1943).*

Timothy Warren Anglin 1822–1896
Born in County Cork, he came to Canada at the age of twenty-seven, fleeing the Great Famine, to become a journalist, politician, and Speaker of the House of Commons. His daughter Margaret became a famous actress, his son Frank a chief justice of the Canadian Supreme Court.

Anglin is an Irish Gaelic surname that originated in county Cork from the nickname of the founding ancestor. *Anglond* in Irish means 'heroic deed, exploit' and then came to denote the hero or champion who performed the deed. Various spellings, all found in Cork, include Angland, Anglim, Anglind, and Angylond.

ANHALT

István Anhalt 1919–
This Hungarian-born Canadian composer of avant-garde music that combines traditional and electronic instruments with the human voice has taught, composed, and performed at McGill and Queen's universities. Among his works are La Tourangelle *(1975), a musical about Marie de l'Incarnation, the mystic and nun who founded the Ursuline order in Canada after landing at Québec in 1639. In 1994 Anhalt completed* Traces, *a new opera.*

Anhalt is a German name. The founding ancestor came from Anhalt, a former duchy in central Germany north of Saxony. In 1848 Anhalt comprised some 898 square miles of territory. As a noun in medieval German, *Anhalt* suggested a place at which a rider or a coach might make a temporary stop, and this sense is likely to be the origin of the duchy's name and the surname, the founding ancestor living at or operating an important inn or imperial stopping place on a major route. It occurred frequently as a local place name throughout German-speaking Europe with spelling variations. Compare Anholt in Westphalia and compound place names like Wasserburg Aneholt.

István is the Hungarian form of Stephen from the common Greek personal name *Stephanas* 'wearer of a laurel crown for some achievement' from *stephanos* 'crown.' Its widespread use in Christian Europe is due to the popularity of Saint Stephen, the first Christian martyr. English surnames derived from Stephen include Stevens, Stevenson, Stinson, Stimpson, Stenson, and Steenson.

ANKA

Paul Albert Anka 1941–

The Ottawa-born pop singer and composer of fifties hits like "Diana," "Puppy Love," "You Are My Destiny," and "Lonely Boy," wrote Sinatra's signature tune "My Way," moved to the U.S. and became a star of Las Vegas nightclubs.

Anka is a Lebanese surname, based on a nickname of the ancestor. The root in Standard Arabic *naqiy* has a form *aniq* 'neat, elegant, chic' and *anka* is a Lebanese Arabic dialect form. Another possibility is a derivation from the Standard Arabic form *ankha*, plural of the noun *nakhw* 'direction, part, method, manner, mode, fashion.' It must be remembered that almost any lexical item can become a surname in Arabic, although names related to Islam have been most popular through the centuries. Especially popular as male names are the so-called 99 names of Allah, including such common first names as Akbar.

APPLEBAUM

Louis Applebaum 1918–2000

He composed music in a broad range of musical styles including Hollywood film scores, and had been associated with the Stratford Festival, CBC, the National Film Board, CAPAC, and played many gigs as musical administrator.

Applebaum is a partial Englishing of the Jewish surname Apfelbaum 'apple tree.' Variant spellings may indicate the origin of the founder. Among Polish, Hungarian, and Russian Jews, those speaking Western Yiddish, it can be Apelboim or Appelboym. Eastern Yiddish speakers, like some Lithuanian Jewish families, may spell it as Apelbeym.

In certain German-Jewish families, the surname is traceable directly to the medieval Frankfurt ghetto called the *Judengasse* 'The Street of Jews.' House numbers and street names were not common until the end of the eighteenth century, simply because most ordinary Europeans were illiterate. Houses and shops bore signs to identify their owners. More than two hundred Jewish surnames arose based on signs and have come down to us from the Frankfurt ghetto alone. Animal signs could represent many German-Jewish first names like Baer 'bear,' Loeb 'lion,' Wolf, Fisch 'fish,' Lachs 'salmon,' Hecht 'pike.' This happened in Poland and Russia too, for example, Polish Karash 'carp,' and Slavic Karassick 'little fish.' Among the tree signs identifying houses and owners were Apfelbaum 'apple tree,' Birnbaum 'pear tree,' Buxbaum 'box tree,' Grünbaum 'green tree,' and Nussbaum 'nut tree.' These house signs sometimes also served to identify a shop or place of business.

But Apfelbaum might also have been pleasing to the pious because of its mention in the Torah and other ancient Hebrew religious texts. Now this is not the fruit in Genesis, nor the apple of temptation in the garden of Eden, a piece of which, folklore says, lodged in Adam's throat to give us the English phrase *Adam's apple*, referring to the little swelling in the front of the neck caused by the projection of the thyroid cartilage of the larynx. No, the pious took note of the apple and apple tree in Proverbs and, for example, in the Song of Solomon 2:3–5: "As the apple tree among the trees of the world, so is my beloved among the sons. I sat down under his shadow with great delight, and his fruit was sweet to my taste. . . . Stay me with flagons, comfort me with apples, for I am sick with love."

Red-faced generations of skittish Talmudic revisionists have rushed to convince readers that the Song of Solomon is not what it plainly is: a luscious passage of ancient Hebrew erotic poetry, composed to be chanted at a wedding feast as a celebration of sexual desire and love. In feats of allegorical exegesis that would cross a rabbi's eyes, commentators have insisted that the apple tree here symbolizes the love between God and his people, Israel. Well, read the Song of Solomon for yourself. The apple tree is a symbol alright, a symbol of a big, healthy, potent bridegroom, full of seed and ready for his wedding night. Later Christian writers also blushed to find such piquant sensuality enshrined in Holy Writ, so Roman Catholic dogma states it's all about the love between Christ and the Church. Not to be outpurged by mere papists, Protestant divines swoon in the moist deeps of the Song of Solomon as well, assuring all sex-hating sects that the poem concerns the love between God and man's soul. Not in the apple of my eye.

Biblical apples harbour a few other worms of contention. The Biblical Hebrew word pronounced 'tapPU'ach' in modern Hebrew and now meaning 'apple,' could never have referred to the fruit of the genus *Malus* that we know today, made big and juicy by hybridizers only in the last two hundred years. The species of the *Malus* genus that throve in the hot places of the ancient Middle East were miserable treelets, stingy with fruit that was tiny, hard, acidic, unpalatable and virtually inedible, that resembled crabapples the size of marbles! Now listen to how the Bible describes its 'apple': Joel 1:12 says it was a tree of the field like the vine, fig, and pomegranate. The Song of Solomon 2:3 and 7:8 says the apple had a sweet perfume and taste. Other passages say it hung in a tree that offered much shade.

I don't want to upset your apple cart but Biblical scholars believe the fruit referred to by the word *tappuach* was an orange, a quince, or, most likely, an apricot. Ancient Palestinian folk wisdom said the apricot possessed aphrodisiac qualities, so its use as a sexual metaphor in the Song of Solomon is most apt. And apricot trees grew throughout ancient Palestine.

So ends our traipse around the orchard. None of this takes away a whit of the delight its bearers may take in the surname Applebaum.

APPLEYARD

Peter Appleyard 1928–

The British-born musician has been in Canada from 1951 as a jazz vibraphonist with much concert, nightclub, and studio work, as well as gigs abroad with musicians like Benny Goodman and Mel Tormé. In 1992 Mr. Appleyard was made an Officer of the Order of Canada.

Appleyard was a place in the West Riding of Yorkshire and a country synonym for orchard. Old English *geard* 'enclosure' (pronounced *yard*) is related to garden, and an Old Scandinavian cognate *garthr* gives English *garth*, an open space within a cloister or a yard, garden, or paddock. Apple trees were a method of identifying fields and houses of founding ancestors, and thus contributed to several English surnames:

- Apperley   'clearing with apple trees'
- Applin   '(among) the apples' from the Old English dative plural *aepplum*
- Appleby   'apple farm' with Old English *by* 'a farmhouse' then 'a village,' with cognates in Swedish and Danish *by*, all akin to Viking word *byr* 'a farm'
- Appleford   from one of several place names describing the shallows of a river where livestock could cross easily and where apple trees grew beside the ford
- Applegarth   'apple enclosure'
- Applegate   ultimately from Old Scandinavian *apaldrsgarðr* 'apple-orchard'
- Appleton   'apple farm' with Old English *tun*, a common suffix on English place names. The meaning of *tun* expanded through history. Its initial sense was a hedge, a fence, an enclosure, a homestead, then a farm, a manor, a settlement, a hamlet, and finally a village. Our modern form of the word is *town*.
- Applewhite   from Applethwaite 'a clearing with apple trees' where thwaite is Old Scandinavian for 'meadow, enclosed land'

Apps

Charles Joseph Sylvanus "Syl" Apps 1915–1998

The athletic all-rounder (British Empire Games, 1936 Berlin Olympics) was famous as centre for the Toronto Maple Leafs from 1936

to 1948, where he was one of professional hockey's best team play-
ers, and an especial favourite of fans.

Apps locates the ancestor as living at or near aspen trees. Another
form of the same surname is Asp. The *p* and the *s* have been trans-
posed in a natural linguistic process called metathesis. A good modern example is the non-standard English for ask, as in "Don't **aks**
me no questions."

Some consonant clusters give speakers trouble, so the brain makes
our speaking apparatus interchange the offending consonants. Some
young English-speaking children say *pesghetti* instead of spaghetti
because children cannot always immediately utter all the consonant
sequences in a language. Some clusters remain tricky even for
adults who may say *perscribe* for prescribe. Historical examples of
this reordering in English are wasp from Old English *waeps*, bird
for Old English *bridd*, Manx for Middle English *Manisk*, and third
for Old English *thridda* (compare the modern German *dritte*).

AQUIN

Hubert Aquin 1929–1977

The important avant-garde Québec novelist and influential politi-
cal activist has an œuvre that includes Prochain épisode, Trou de
mémoire, L'Antiphonaire, *and* Neige noire.

Aquin also appears in the forms Achin, Achain, and Acquin, a
French surname from an ancestor who bore the Germanic warrior
name *Acwin*, a compound of *ac* 'blade of a sword' and *win* 'friend.'

ARCAND

Denys Arcand 1941–

He is a leading Québec film director, screenwriter, sometime actor,
and movie producer whose films include Réjeanne Padovani
(1973), Le déclin de l'empire americain *(1986),* Jésus de Montréal

(1989), and Love and Human Remains *(1994). For television he directed a searing story about homeless people on the streets of Montréal,* Joyeux Calvaire *(1997).*

Arcand is probably from an Old Germanic adjective used as a first name, *Ercan* 'genuine, sincere, excellent.' It may even be a shortened form of the common Old German name *Ercanbald* 'sincere-bold' that gives Archibald in English, and French surnames like Archambaud. A much remoter possibility would be an origin from Latin *arca* 'box, chest,' as a nickname or signifying one who made and sold wooden chests.

Archambault

Gilles Archambault 1933–
A Montréal-born novelist, his works include La Fleur aux dents *(1971),* À Voix basse *(1983), and* Le Regard oblique *(1984).*

Joseph-Papin Archambault 1880–1966
The Montréal-born Jesuit priest, an early militant French-Canadian antisocialist and nationalist, worked with Abbé Groulx at the periodical l'Action française.

Louis Archambault 1915–
The Montréal-born sculptor has been called the "greatest Canadian sculptor of his generation."

Archambault is one of the earliest French surnames to become established in Québec. In France, the founding ancestor of the family bore the Old Germanic warrior name *Arcanbald*, a French variant of *Ercanbald*, a compound first name containing the Germanic elements *ercan* 'genuine, sincere' and *bald* which is cognate with English 'bold.' There are several variants: Archambault, Archaimbaud, Arcambal, and Arquimbau.

ARGUE

Hazen Robert Argue 1921–1991

The Moose Jaw–born CCF, NDP, and Liberal politician was the Saskatchewan MP for Assiniboia (Wood Mountain) from 1945 to 1963. Appointed to the Senate in 1966, he ended his political career as minister of state for the Canadian Wheat Board.

Argue is an Irish surname. The family emigrated from Ireland to Ottawa in 1821 and counts many distinguished Canadians in its ranks. The surname is widespread in County Cavan, and may derive from Irish Gaelic *arg* 'noble' as an adjective, 'hero' as a noun.

However, another school of thought maintains that Argue belongs to the wave of Norman-French surnames that swept over Ireland at various times after the Conquest. That school posits an origin for Argue in one of the French place names that begin with an element like *Aigre-* or *Aigue-* which both mean 'sharp, pointed' and appear in town names like *Aigremont* 'pointed hill.' *Aigre* was also a French nickname for a man who was difficult to deal with, of a "sharp" personality. The *aigre-* school would require metathesis to have taken place in which the *g* and the *r* changed places, implying that the Irish could not pronounce the consonant cluster in *aigre-* words easily. That is nonsense. But other French surnames could have evolved into the Irish Argue. Argout is a prime candidate, itself from the dithematic Germanic warrior name Argwald (Old High German *arg* 'bad, wicked' + *wald* 'ruler'). But Argout is not a Norman name. It originates in southwestern France.

ARSENAULT

Aubin-Edmond Arsenault 1870–1968

In 1917 he became the first Acadian premier of a Canadian province, namely Prince Edward Island and later sat as a judge of P.E.I Supreme Court.

Arsenault is a common Acadian surname. A spurious etymology is attached to this last name in several popular books about French surnames. It has nothing whatsoever to do with the ancient Ionic or Attic Greek adjective *arsen* 'male, virile.' Arsenault belongs to the class of French surnames that arise from the occupation of an ancestor, in this case, medieval textile-making, where *Arsenault, Arsonneau,* and *Arsonneaud* are regional spelling variants and local diminutives of *arçonneur*, a person who made looms for the wool trade—specifically the *arçon*, the felter's bow, an instrument for carding wool or for teasing up the nap on other forms of woven cloth. The *arçon* was shaped like a wooden bow with an arch-shaped curve, and this is the origin of the French word. *Arçon* derives directly from *arcionem,* the accusative singular of the Late Latin *arcio* 'little bow.'

ASSMAN

Dick Assman 1934–

A service station attendant who pumps gas at a Petro-Canada station in Regina, Saskatchewan, he became famous after his name was ridiculed on The David Letterman Show *in the 1990s. Good-naturedly he agreed to appear on the show, obtained the services of an agent, and made a few bucks from his unusual surname.*

Assman is an Englishing of the not uncommon German surname *Assmann* whose variants include Asmann, Assmus and Asmus. We don't wish any Assman to be the butt of a joke, and thus we happily point out that all variants have a most noble origin. They derive from Saint Erasmus, a fourth-century Christian martyr who, pious legend states, was dispatched by having his intestines wound out of his body on a windlass. Now a windlass resembles a ship's capstan, and so Erasmus became the patron saint of sailors—so says another coincidence-crammed legend that stretches resemblance and credulity the snapping point. One nickname of Erasmus is Elmo. St. Elmo's fire of nautical note refers to Erasmus. St. Elmo's fire is a luminous electrical discharge sometimes seen by seafarers sparking off the masthead of a ship during a storm. To further ennoble the surname Assman, let us report that the saint's name derives from the Greek adjective *erasmios* 'lovable, pleasant, desired, beloved.' Note, however, that the German names *Assmann, Asmann, Assmus,* and *Asmus* do not derive from the Erasmus who lived from 1469 to 1536. That Dutch humanist and most famous scholar of his day was born after the German names first appeared in print during the thirteenth and fourteenth centuries. The humanist Erasmus was named after the saint, too. I hope, David Letterman, this will teach you not to make ignorant fun of Canadian names of such noble lineage, you hoser! Perhaps, Dave, you might better reflect on the origin of Letterman, which is an americanization of Ledermann 'leather-man,' a medieval German surname from an ancestor who was an itinerant huckster of cheap leather goods on the dusty roads of fourteenth-century Europe. Touché, eh?

ATTFIELD

Roger Attfield

He is a Canadian trainer of thoroughbred racing horses whose steeds have won the Queen's Plate seven times.

Attfield is a locative denoting the ancestor's place of residence, namely 'at the open field.' The first one of that name in printed records is Stephen Attefeld, listed in the records of the British county of Essex in the year 1262.

ATWOOD

Margaret Eleanor Atwood 1939–

The poet and critic is one of Canada's most popular novelists whose works include Bluebeard's Egg, Cat's Eye, The Edible Woman, The

Handmaid's Tale, Lady Oracle, Life Before Man, The Robber Bride, *and in 1996,* Alias Grace.

Atwood is a reduced spelling of Attwood 'at the wood.' The earliest person of the name in English records is one Thomas Attewode listed in the Assize Rolls of Somerset for 1243.

A number of English surnames kept the preposition in little phrases added after an ancestor's first name to specify where he dwelt and to differentiate him from others with the same first name. This class of surnames includes:

- Atberry   for Atbury 'at the manor-house,' in Old English *burh*
- Atbridge
- Atbrook
- Atcliff   or Attercliff
- Atcot   'at the cottage'
- Atford
- Atherfold   'at the fold' (perhaps a shepherd?)
- Athoke   'at the bend in the road or river' from Old English *hoc* 'hook'
- Atholl   for *atte Hole* 'at the hollow'
- Atkey   'at the quay' hence a dock worker
- Atlow   'at the hill' Old English *hlaw*
- Attenborough 'at the hill, grove, or fort'
- Attlee   'at the lea' that is, at the wood or clearing
- Attwater
- Attwell
- Attwick   'at the dairy farm'
- Atty   'at the enclosure or common pasture' Old English *teag*
- Atyeo   'at the river'

AUGUSTYN

Frank Augustyn 1953–

The Hamilton-born ballet dancer was a frequent partner of Karen Kain in the National Ballet of Canada and is now a choreographer and teacher.

Augustyn is a Ukrainian surname based on the name of Saint Augustine, whom the Russian Orthodox Church, like the Roman Catholic one, holds in pious regard as one of the fathers of the Christian religion. Aurelius Augustinus (354–430), author of *The Confessions* and *The City of God*, had a second name based on the Latin adjective *augustus* 'venerable, consecrated' but literally 'increased in human regard,' which was of course made popular by the very first emperor of the Romans who himself chose the name Caesar Augustus.

AVISON

John Henry Patrick Avison 1915–1983

The pianist and founding conductor of the CBC Vancouver Chamber Orchestra led this important musical group for forty-two years.

Margaret Avison 1918–

The poet won the Governor-General's Award for Winter Sun *(1960); other collections of her poetry include* The Dumbfounding *(1966),* Sunblue *(1978), and* No Time *(1990).*

Avison shows up in early documents as Thomas Avyce in 1220, Ricardus *filius* Avice in 1332 and Ralph Avyson in 1674. The name was likely to have been brought over by the Norman French. In the records of Roman Gaul are the female and male names *Avitia* and *Avitius*, both derivatives of a recorded Roman cognomen mentioned by Cicero in the record of one of his legal cases, the *Oratio pro Cluentio*, as Aulus Cluentius Avitus. The cognomen is either

from a lost place name or the Latin adjective *avitus* 'of a grandfather, ancestral, ancient,' itself from Latin *avus* 'grandfather, ancestor.' A diminutive form of *avus* is *avunculus* 'maternal uncle' which
gives the learned English adjective *avuncular* 'pertaining to an
uncle' and also gives modern English *uncle* through Medieval
French *oncle*, from *aunclus*, a Late Latin contraction of *avunculus.*

AYKROYD
Daniel Edward (Dan) Aykroyd 1952–
The Ottawa-born TV and film comedian became famous on NBC's
Saturday Night Live, *and then left to pursue a successful career in
comic films, including in the 1980s* The Blues Brothers, Ghostbusters
(co-screenwriter), Twilight Zone: The Movie, Indiana Jones and the
Temple of Doom, Dragnet, *and in the 1990s* My Girl, Grosse Point
Blank, *and* Susan's Plan. *In 1997 Dan came back to Canada to
shoot the CBC-TV drama miniseries* The Arrow *about the creation
and government-involved scuttling of the Avro Arrow plane.*

Aykroyd is a common variant of Ackroyd. Ackroyd was a small
village in the county of West Yorkshire in northern England, and
the surname is common throughout the region. It means 'oak-clear-
ing,' *ac-rod* in Old English. In Yorkshire dialect, 'royd' was the
pronunciation of *rod.* A very large percentage of English surnames
derive from localities where the founding ancestor of the family
worked, lived, operated a farm, or had a place of business.

Individuals had one name to begin with. As population density
increased, with the rise of towns and villages, a method was needed
to differentiate clearly between two or more persons both with the
same single name. For example, a village might have two persons
named John. In the parish register of births and deaths, one might
be a John whose father's name was Robert. He would be entered as
John, son of Robert, and eventually his patronymic surname would

be John Robertson. Another John might have a small farm in a clearing *royd* among oak trees *ac*. He might be John of the *ac-royd*, and eventually be known as John Ackroyd.

Rod, the Anglo-Saxon stem, gave rod and rood in English, rod being originally a stick or a pole, then a measure of length, then a measure of area, specifically of land about a quarter of an acre in extent, and so easily transferred to mean a small area of cleared land.

Rood came to denote a very particular wooden rod, the cross upon which Christ was crucified. That sense gave expressions like Holy Rood, Rood Day, and the roodscreen that separates the nave from the choir in some churches and is so called because the wooden or stone screen was surmounted by a cross. To make the rood-token formerly meant to make the sign of the cross.

The *royd* or *rod* ending appears in other surnames like Murgatroyd which was *Margat's royd* in Yorkshire dialect, Margat being a pet name of Margaret. Thus Murgatroyd refers to Margaret's clearing, an example of an English last name stemming from a woman's property, which is perhaps not rare, but certainly infrequent in British surnames. Another related last name originating in Yorkshire is Royds, and from Lancashire came Ormerod. Ormrod or Ormerod is 'the clearing of a Viking named Orm,' a warrior name that means 'dragon' or 'snake' in Old Scandinavian.

ℬ

BACHMAN
Randy Bachman

The rock guitarist studied with the late jazz great Lenny Breau and became a pivotal member of the seminal Canadian band, The Guess Who, until 1970. Then, with Robin Bachman, Blair Thornton, and Fred Turner, Randy, a convert to Mormonism and father of eight children, formed the megahitter band BTO. Bachman Turner Overdrive sold 20 million records during the mid-seventies, including the million-seller "You Ain't Seen Nuthin' Yet" which was Number One on the Billboard charts on November 9, 1974. Earlier BTO landed on the Top 100 with 1974's "Let It Ride" and, that same year, "Takin' Care of Business." Randy took the band's name from the trade magazine of the trucking industry, Overdrive. *BTO reunited for a successful tour in 1984 and, three years later, Randy Bachman and Burton Cummings did a Canadian tour and worked on a new album. BTO's success was due to the band's musical talents and to the superb management skills of Vancouver's Bruce Allen.*

Bachman is a German surname of locality that means *einer der am Bach wohnt,* 'one who lives on the bank of a stream.' The earliest appearances of the proto-surname show up in medieval German documents in phrases locating the site of an ancestor's house, phrases like *bi dem bach, an der bach, im bach, uf der bach. Bach* as a German noun means 'brook' or 'stream.'

BAILLAIRGÉ

Charles Baillairgé 1826–1906
Architect, civil engineer, surveyor, inventor, writer

François Baillairgé 1759–1830
Sculptor, architect, painter

Jean Baillairgé 1726–1805
Carpenter, joiner, architect in Québec from 1741, he founded a dynasty of architects, painters, and sculptors in the province.

Thomas Baillairgé 1791–1859
Architect, sculptor, painter

William-Duval Baillairgé
Son of Charles, twentieth-century city engineer of Québec City

Baillairgé is a variant of the occupational surname Baillarger, common in history along the Atlantic coast of France. The family has been prominent in Québec professions for six generations. *Un baillarger* was a farmer who grew *baillarge*, a kind of barley with double columns of seeds. This genetic sport of the common cereal was well known in antiquity. The French word stems from the Latin term for this barley *balearicus*, which seems to have originated in the Balearic Islands off the coast of Spain. However, some French etymologists dismiss that as mere folk etymology and prefer the source as a French borrowing from Old English *bærlic* or Middle English *barleche*, both of which seem related to Old Germanic * *baroz* 'barley.'

BAIN

George Bain 1920–
The witty, Toronto-born, former Ottawa columnist and oenophile for the Globe and Mail *taught journalism and was director of journalism until 1985 at King's College in Halifax. He has published the humorous* Letters From Lilac *and several other books.*

Several languages supply possible origins for this surname:
- If the family was of Norman-French origin, *bain* 'public bath' identified an ancestor who owned, operated, or worked at an ancient spa such as Bath.
- The Scottish Bain is Gaelic *bàn* to describe a person 'of fair complexion.'
- The Bain deriving from Old Scandinavian *beinn* singled out a Viking settler who was 'straightforward' or 'ready to oblige.'
- The form Baines sometimes stands for the Northern English and Scottish pronunciation of the nickname-based surname *Bones*,

given to someone unusually thin, gaunt, or gangly. Retired pirates also favoured the moniker and enjoyed stumping into a gin-damp tavern to be hailed by a phlegmy chorus as "Bones!"

BALDWIN

Robert Baldwin 1804–1858
The lawyer and politician fought for responsible government in Upper Canada, influenced Lord Durham's Report, was an early proponent of a bicultural Canada, and a co-premier and attorney-general of Upper Canada who helped establish the University of Toronto.

In the beginning, Baldwin was a first name, an Old German dithematic compound *balda wini* 'bold friend,' a warrior name. Still an English first name for girls and boys is Wynn or Wynne from the same Anglo-Saxon word for friend. Brought to England before the Norman Conquest, the name was reintroduced by Flemish weavers who emigrated to England in the twelfth and thirteenth centuries. As Baudouin it has remained a popular first name in Flanders. Consider Baudouin I, king of Belgium. From Baldwin and its Norman form, Baudouin, arose surnames like Bawden, Boaden, Boden, Bowden, Baudechon, and Bawcock (a double diminutive of Baldwin signifying 'little Bau').

BANTING

Sir Frederick Grant Banting 1891–1941
The surgeon and researcher was a co-discoverer of insulin.

Banting is a type of the common patronymic surname, that is, a last name arising from the name of the father. In Anglo-Saxon, now called Old English, patronymics were often formed by adding *-ing* to the stem of the father's name. Thus English has surnames like Carling 'son of an Anglo-Saxon named Carl' and Keeping 'son of

The Keep,' that is, of a person who looked after the keep of a castle, and was probably the jailor who by metonymy would have a nickname like Keep or The Keep or later John the Keep (for John the Jailer).

Metonymy labels a figure of speech in which the name of an attribute or adjunct of a thing is substituted for the name of the thing itself; for example, referring to the turf for horse racing, to the crown for king, to the stage or the boards for theatrical profession, to the bench for judiciary. Metonymy adds variety and colour to speech and writing, and is a frequently used ploy in the metaphorical bag-of-tricks of most languages. In the making of English last names, metonymy was a frequent source of nicknames and then later of surnames.

Banting is a patronymic that means 'son of an Anglo-Saxon named Bando or Banto.' The Germanic first name Bando is related to our modern English word *band* 'strip of material' and *Bant* in Old High German which meant 'tie, bond, connection.' *Banto* was a common and widespread Germanic first name. Variants of it show up in Italy, Corsica, Spain, France, the Netherlands, Scandinavia, and Russia.

One remote possibility is the origin of Banting as an Englishing of a Norman-French surname, *Bantegny,* itself taken from the French place name Bantigny, a district in the city of Cambrai in northern France. The district took its name from a Gallo-Roman first name, *Bantinius,* which is merely a Latinizing of the Germanic name *Banto*. The swirling mutability of European political boundaries throughout history is mirrored in the transborder ebb and flow of the words used for names. They hop back and forth over customs barriers like Olympic crickets. For example, Germanic *Wido* appears a few hundred years after its start in Germany as *Guido* in northern Italy.

BARBEAU

Charles Marius Barbeau 1883–1969

The father of Canadian folklore studies, collector of French-Canadian and aboriginal songs and texts at the National Museum of Canada, he was also the founder of the Archives de folklore *at Laval University.*

Jean Barbeau 1945–

The Québec playwright made clever, playful use of joual in popular dramas like Manon Lastcall *(1972) and* Joualez-moi d'amour *(1972). Then he broadened his scope to attack modern greed in plays like* L'Abominable Homme des sables *(1989). Although he supports many separatist agendas, Barbeau is a true satirist, not loath to mock his natal fealties, and never above pointing out that the king has only one leg.*

Marcel Barbeau 1925–

Painter, sculptor, filmmaker, performance artist

Barbeau was the nickname of the founding ancestor who probably had a sparse beard. Barbeau is in Old French as early as 1175 as the name of a large European freshwater fish of *Cyprinidae*, the carp and minnow family. It has a few fleshy, antennae-like filaments hanging from its mouth, hence the French name derived from Latin *barbellus* 'little beard' diminutive of *barba* 'beard.' In English the fish is a barbel, and the fleshy protuberances around the mouth of most members of the carp family are barbels. Five hundred years later the common blue cornflower of France was named *barbeau* as well, describing the little 'beard' of ray-like petals that encircle the ovary of cornflowers. But the French surname predates the flower name, so we can be reasonably sure the last name is of whiskery provenance.

BARR

Dave Barr 1952–

Kelowna-born Canadian golf champion had his best year in 1994, winning $300,000 in tournaments and the Dunhill Cup.

Murray Llewellyn Barr 1908–1995

The anatomist and geneticist at the University of Western Ontario was the discoverer of the Barr body, a sex chromatin that is a marker of genetic femaleness and that permitted deeper study and understanding of chromosomal errors and resultant congenital defects. Barr's research helped modern genomics.

Barr as a British or Irish surname stems from the place where an ancestor lived. British places named Barr go back to Celtic *barr* 'hill-top' that has a Welsh reflex *bar* 'summit, top' that appears in the Staffordshire toponym Great Barr, and a place like Barr Beacon as well. The Scottish Barrs take their name from hilly places named Barr in Ayrshire and Renfrewshire.

But there are other locative sources. In Old French and Middle English, a *barre* was a barrier or gateway. An ancestor might have lived beside such a gateway, and taken a last name from it. Bar was used as a synonym for weir, something that barred a stream. A Norman-French group of *Barre* surnames spring from French villages like Barre-en-Ouche and Barre-de-Semilly, and perhaps Barr, a district of Sélestat in the *Bas-Rhin*.

Old French *bare* cannot be discounted as a source of the French surname Barre. *Bare* meant a thin pole, and in later slang, a lanky person, a beanpole. It also denoted a barrier fence around a building and could be used as an occupation name for the person who built such a barrier. There is also the possibility of Old French *barre* 'a long piece of cloth or material' being used as a nickname for a tall, thin ancestor.

Therefore, to determine the precise meaning of a surname like Barre—if indeed that is possible—one must hope that extant documents will indicate the precise place of the founding ancestor's origin and the earliest printed spelling of the name.

BARRETT

David Barrett 1930–

The former social worker was the feisty NDP premier of British Columbia from1972 to 1975.

Barrett, when it is a Jewish surname, may indicate a name change, an Englishing of a European Jewish surname like Barr or Bar. If the family came from Russia or the Ukraine, Barr or Bar may be locative, taken from the town of Bar. This Ukrainian community was founded and named by a sixteenth-century queen of Poland, Bona Sforza, who was born in Bari, Italy! Barrett may also be a change from German-Jewish names like Bär, Baer, Bähr, Behr, Beer, and Bahr, all of which signify the European bear, either as a big, burly, hairy ancestor's nickname or as a house or sign name that indicated he lived *zum Bären* 'at the sign of The Bear.'

Sometimes Barrett is an anglicized form of a French surname like Barrette or Barotte 'little gateway.' Another French source may be Barrat or Barrate from Medieval French *barré* 'wearing striped clothing.' See also the earlier entry on the surname *Barr*.

In all its many spellings (Barrat, Barratt, Barrett, Barritt, Barrott), the English surname begins as a scurrilous nickname in Middle English where *barrat* had a range of meanings that encompassed 'trouble, distress, fraud, deception, or strife.' The vexatious noun did not survive into modern English, but two related and mildly obscure legal terms did. A barrator is a person who causes public discord. In marine law, barratry is gross negligence aboard a ship by the captain or crew, or it is fraud at sea committed against owners of a vessel.

BASSETT

John White Hughes Bassett 1930–1998

The one-time owner of the defunct Toronto Telegram *and of CFTO-TV was a founder of CTV and a flamboyant entrepreneur. His son Douglas became CEO and president of Baton Broadcasting Inc., which owned CFTO-TV in Toronto. His granddaughter Carling Bassett was a championship tennis player.*

The family is not named after the stubby-legged basset hound first bred to run badgers and foxes to ground. The earliest printed reference to the dog is in 1616, while a Ralph Basset is listed in the Domesday Book of Hertfordshire in 1086. In Old French *basset* meant 'of low stature,' a diminutive of *bas* 'low,' perhaps even referring to a dwarf. One ancient commentator said Ralph Basset was elevated by King Henry II *de ignobili stirpe ac de pulvere* 'from low-born stock and from the dust of the ground.' However, this might have been a little pun on the part of a scribe who knew French, or merely the snottiness of some envious, low-born clerk.

BASSO

Guido Basso 1937–

This native Montrealer and long-time ornament of the Toronto jazz scene is one of the world's great jazz trumpet players, combining technique with warmth. The mellow brass of his fluegel-horn adorns jazz cuts on many albums by the Boss Brass, of which Guido is a charter member.

Basso means 'low' in Italian. As an Italian adjectival surname it can refer to a low and melodious voice, to the low land where the ancestor lived, or to his physical shortness. The very ancient surname can also derive from a cognomen of Republican Rome, *Bassus*, itself borrowed from one of Latin's Italian sister-languages, Oscan, where *bassus* meant 'stout, fat.'

Guido as a given name is a Romanized form of the Germanic warrior name *Wido* from the Old High German root *witu* 'wood, forest.' Guido is not related to the English word *guide*. Guide stems ultimately from the Old Provençal verb *guidar*, itself from Frankish **witan* 'to direct, to show the way to' and thus guide is a distant kin to the modern German *weisen* 'to point out, to show' and to all those German adverbs in *-weise*.

BECK

Sir Adam Beck 1857–1925
He was the motive mogul behind the founding of Ontario Hydro.

Some Becks took their family name from the French place of origin of their ancestor. Northern France has many localities named Bec, most of them settled by Viking invaders who camped near a stream, *bekkr* in Old Scandinavian.

Beck as a Scottish or northern English surname is often *bekke*, a Middle English word for stream, also borrowed from Norsemen. There was also a Beck used to denote the occupation of a family founder, a blacksmith who made axes and mattocks, *becca* in Old English. One who sold, made, or used in the field such a mattock was a becker.

Bec was also a Norman nickname for someone with a big or pointed nose, from Old French *bec* 'beak, bird's bill.' Beckard is another related surname with the Old French suffix *-ard* suggesting a person with a prominent or unusual nose. A little nose or small mouth gave the nickname, then the surname of Beckett.

BEECROFT

Norma Beecroft 1934–
A Canadian composer of serious avant-garde music herself, and a tireless promoter of Canadian composers, she worked often for

CBC Radio as a producer and host. Her own works were heard frequently on the national radio service for many years. In 1994, after sixty years of musical life, three new works were premiered: Images for woodwind quintet, String Quartet, *and* CJRT 1994.

Beecroft, like Beeman, is a surname based on the ancestor's occupation. In Old English a croft was a fenced field next to a house in which crops were grown, and where, sometimes as here, beehives were set.

BÉLIVEAU

Jean Béliveau 1931–

He joined the Montreal Canadiens in 1953 and led the most powerful team in hockey history through eighteen smash seasons. He retired in 1993 as vice-president of Les Canadiens.

Beliveau is from a medieval nickname, *beli, beslif*, an adjective in Old French that meant 'on a slant' or 'the wrong way' or of a body part 'crooked.' It would be equivalent to *de travers* in the modern French sentence *Il a la jambe de travers* 'he has a crooked leg.' For example, it might have been the nickname of an ancestor who limped, or one who tottered because he tippled too much of the fermented grape.

Bell

Dr. Leslie Richard Bell 1906–1962

He founded the Leslie Bell Singers, a popular Canadian choral group of the 1940s and 1950s.

Marilyn Bell 1937–

The swimmer crossed Lake Ontario in twenty-one hours in 1954 to become a Canadian sports heroine. All Canada had rapture of the lake for the plucky mermaid.

Bell is among the one hundred most widespread English surnames because of its manifold sources. As a matronymic, where the family name derives from the mother's first name, Bel was a frequent affectionate diminutive for Isabel.

It was also one of the rare sign names in English; compare John atte Belle listed in a document of 1332. This may have been a merchant who did business at the sign of the Bell, or one who lived near a church or town belltower or bellhouse. As an occupational surname, it denoted a bellman or bellringer, while Beller was one who cast bells in a foundry.

BENGOUGH

John Wilson Bengough 1851–1923

He was the most renowned Canadian political cartoonist of the nineteenth century. His work appeared frequently in George Brown's Globe, *in* The Canadian Illustrated News, *and in* Grip *(1873–1994), the comic weekly founded by Bengough.*

Bengough is a surname based on an ancestor's nickname from a Welsh adjective, *pencoch* or *bengoch* 'redhaired.'

BENNETT

Richard Bedford Bennett 1870–1947

He was the prime minister of Canada from 1930 to 1935. Born in New Brunswick, the stuffy, unsympathetic lawyer led Canada through the worst years of the Depression. Massively defeated in 1935, Bennett retired in bitterness to England in 1937.

W.A.C. Bennett 1900–1979
William Richards Bennett 1932–

Both father and son were popular and controversial premiers of British Columbia.

Bennett is among the most common surnames in the English-speaking world. It was the customary pet form of Benedict in Middle English, and was far more frequent a first name in England than Benedict ever was. *Benedictus* meant 'blessed' in Latin (literally and originally 'spoken well of'), and was made especially popular by Saint Benedict, founder of the Benedictine Order and writer of the Holy Rule, still used by some Christian monks. He was born in Umbria around 480 and died in 547 at Monte Cassino, the majestically perched Italian monastery that he founded in the Apennine foothills midway between Rome and Naples.

BENOÎT

Jehane Benoît, née Patenaude 1904–1987

Madame Benoît was a Cordon Bleu authority on Canadian and Québecois food, made famous through radio and television appearances and her many cookbooks.

Benoît is the early French form of the Latin name *Benedictus* 'blessed' made popular by Saint Benoît de Nurcie (480–547), founder of the Benedictine Order, patriarch of Western monks, and known in English as Saint Benedict.

BERTON

Pierre Berton 1920–

He is Canada's most popular and best-selling historian, as well as a journalist and television and radio personality.

The surname Berton stems from a French ancestor who bore the Germanic pet name of *Berhto* or *Berhta*, both from *berht*, Old High German adjective meaning 'shining, famous.' The English word *bright* has the same root. *Berhto* was a nickname for bearers of compound Germanic names beginning with this root, for example, *Berhthraben* 'bright raven,' *Berthold*, and *Bertlinde*.

BETHUNE

Dr. Henry Norman Bethune 1890–1939

Norman Bethune was a surgeon, designer of surgical implements, and a hero to the Chinese people whom he assisted in 1938–1939, dying in the service of the Communists and prompting Mao Zedong's essay "In Memory of Norman Bethune," *which made the surgeon then and now the most famous Canadian in China.*

Bethune means the founding ancestor came from the little French town of Béthune in the Pas de Calais. The town in turn was named after a man with the Germanic pet name of Betto. Betto was short for any compound German name that began with OHG *berht* 'shining, bright, famous.' So that makes it the semantic equivalent of the surname Berton.

BICKERT

Edward Isaac Bickert 1932–

Toronto-based Ed Bickert is one of Canada's most agile jazz guitarists, in solo and combo work, and performing with Canada's greatest big band jazz ensemble, the Boss Brass. Bickert's lean pickings in the guitar permit a tight, well-balanced style, that fans await with eagerness.

Bickert is a French or German surname common in Alsace-Lorraine derived from the Germanic first name *Bichardt*. A compound name, like so many of Germanic origin, its first element, *bick* or *bek* or *bic,* was borrowed into early German from street Latin *beccus* originally '*bill, beak of a bird*,' then in Latin a playful metaphor for the human mouth. Modern French retains this sense, in phrases like *ferme ton bec*! 'shut up' and *avoir bon bec* 'to have the gift of the gab.' The second element in Bickert is the Germanic -*hard* 'tough, severe, hard.' So Grim Mouth might be an English equivalent.

BLAKENEY

Allan Emrys Blakeney 1925–

The Rhodes scholar, lawyer, civil servant, and politician was NDP premier of Saskatchewan from 1971 to 1982.

Blakeney is a surname based on where the founding ancestor of the family lived. Two places in England are named Blakeney, one in Norfolk, one in Gloucestershire. In Old English the place name was *blacan-eg* 'black island,' which referred to the dark soil of a small island or to dry ground in a marshy area.

BOBAK

Bronislaw Josephus Bobak 1923–
Molly Joan Bobak, née Lamb 1922–

Bruno Bobak is an artist and administrator long associated with the University of New Brunswick until his retirement in 1988. He and his artist wife Molly have taught and painted in New Brunswick for decades. In 1992 Molly published Double Duty: Sketches and Diaries of Molly Lamb Bobak, Canadian War Artist, *recalling her days in the Canadian Women's Army Corps.*

Bobak is a Polish occupational or sign surname. *Bób* 'bean' suggests a farmer who grows beans or one who sells them. The other possibility is a surname based on an ancestor's shop sign depicting a bay-tree or laurel from Polish *bobek* 'laurel.'

BOGGS

Jean Sutherland Boggs 1922–

One of Canada's greatest curators and art historians, she was director of the National Gallery of Canada from 1966 to 1976, and was a popularizer of quiet acumen.

Boggs is either Irish or English. If Irish, it refers to an ancestral dweller beside a bog from Irish Gaelic *bog* 'damp, miry.'

Let us stray briefly from the ordained etymological path to consider also the local word in our Canadian Maritimes, 'bogan,' a small creek or branch of a stream, perhaps from Gaelic *bogainn* 'little marsh' but influenced by 'pokelogan,' a marshy place or stagnant pool connected with a river, a backwater. This word is aboriginal, and related to a word in a local language of New Brunswick and Nova Scotia, Malecite, in which *pekelaygan* means 'stopping place' (for a canoe). Of course, bogan and pokelogan have no connection with the surname Boggs.

When Boggs is of English origin, the surname stems from an ancestor nicknamed with the Middle English adjective *bogeys* 'bragging, saucy, stuck-up.'

BONDAR

Roberta Lynn Bondar 1945–

The Sault-Ste.-Marie-born scientist and astronaut was the first Canadian woman in space on January 22, 1992, for which she has received many honorary citations and life memberships in national and local organizations. Indeed, she may have a greater number of awards of merit and recognition than any other woman in Canadian history. For a time she did research under the auspices of the faculty of kinesiology at the University of Western Ontario.

Bondar is the general Slavic word for a cooper, that is, a maker of barrels, casks, and wooden tubs. The English word *cooper* began in Middle English where coop and cupe were baskets used to catch fish and then cages for poultry. Although in Ukrainian and Russian the name appears as Bondar, in another Slavic language, Polish, there occurs a metathetic interchange of the *n* and the *d*, so the Polish word for a barrel-maker is *bednarz*, giving rise to surnames like Bednarski 'son of the cooper.' One patronymic form of the name is that of the great Russian actor and film director Sergei

Bondarchuk, best known for his 1964 version of *War and Peace*. Bondarchuk means 'descendant of the cooper.'

BOROVOY

Alan Borovoy
The lawyer has been long associated with the Canadian Civil Liberties Association.

Borovoy is a Russian surname stemming from an ancestor's nickname, possibly from the neuter adjective *borovoi* 'like a wild boar,' hence persistent.

BORSOS

Phillip Borsos 1953–1995
The gifted Canadian film director was born in Tasmania of Greek stock. His work included an Academy Award nomination for an early short, Nails, *and feature films like* The Grey Fox *(1983) and* One Magic Christmas *(1985), and his one disaster,* Bethune: The Making of a Hero *(1988).*

Borsos is a word in the ancient Greek dialect of the city state of Elis which was located in the western part of the Peloponnesus. Borsos is an Elean word for crucifix, specifically the cross of Christ. But it also refers to the familiar Byzantine cross with two cross-bars, the top bar being slightly shorter than the middle bar. A pious ancestor would take it as a surname. It is equivalent to the standard Greek word for cross or crucifix, *stavros*, which gives a male first name in Modern Greek and also a Greek surname, *Stavros*. The holiness of the word is saved from profanation, so Greeks believe, by shifting the accent from the final syllable to the first. Modern Greek does the same accent-shifting with the word for Christ. The Saviour is *Christós*, whereas the first name for male children is *Chrístos*.

BOURASSA

Henri Bourassa 1868–1952

From a long prominent Québec family, he founded Le Devoir, *one of Canada's most influential newspapers in 1910, and, as an important Québec politician, advanced French-Canadian nationalism in what Laurier and others thought was an extreme manner. He was the grandson of Papineau.*

Robert Bourassa 1933–1996

Twice premier of Québec, from 1970 to 1976, and again from 1985 to 1994, he helped draft the Meech Lake Accord and supported the North American Free Trade Agreement.

Bourassa is a regional variant of the French occupational surname *Bourrassier*, one who makes and sells *bourre de laine* 'homespun cloth of brown wool.' *Bourre* also came to mean the flocking or wadding with which furniture was stuffed. In the spelling *bure*, it was the material from which poor monks' robes were made. The word came into Old French from the popular street Latin of the Romans who conquered ancient Gaul where *burra* meant 'rough wool' or 'a shaggy garment.' *Burrus* was an old Latin adjective for brownish-red, the colour of such clothing. Incidentally, it was also the colour of a small donkey used as pack animal, and Roman soldiers posted to the Iberian peninsula called the animal *burrus*, thus planting the verbal seed for one of the earliest words in the Spanish language, *burro*. In Mexico, a tortilla wrapped around a filling of spiced beef and other yummies looked to eaters like a little donkey loaded down with a colorful pack, and so the diminutive form *burrito* meaning 'little donkey' came to be applied to the food as well. *Burrus* was borrowed from or was akin to the Greek colour adjective *pyrros* 'fiery red, dark red' whose root is *pyr*, which is cognate with English 'fire.' Compare these English words: pyre, Pyrex, and pyromaniac.

BRAITHWAITE

Max Braithwaite 1911–1995

Born in the little Saskatchewan village of Nokomis, he became a novelist, humorist, and author of children's books. Max Braithwaite's best-known book was Why Shoot the Teacher? *(1965), a funny and touching autobiographical story based on his years teaching in a one-room schoolhouse on the Prairies during the Great Depression in the 1930s. It was filmed in 1977.*

Braithwaite is a surname taken from the place of residence of the founding ancestor. Several places in England bear the name, derived from a Viking field name, *Breithrthveiti* in Old Scandinavian, composed of *breithr* 'broad' and *thveit* 'clearing, meadow, paddock.' A subclass of British surnames like Bassingthwaite and Linthwaite 'clearing where flax is grown' bear similar endings. The prime verbal meaning of *thveita* in Old Scandinavian was 'to hew, to cut.' Akin to this root was Old English *thwitan* with a dialect form *thwittle*, and our modern English verb for cutting or paring with a knife, whittle.

A thwaite was any piece of land cut or cleared for a special purpose, like woodland with trees and stumps removed to make it arable. This sense gives English place names and surnames like Applethwaite, Crossthwaite, Ormthwaite, and Seathwaite. Ormthwaite means 'field of a Viking named Orm.' In Old Scandinavian *orm* meant 'snake' or 'dragon' and was a common male personal name.

BRAULT

Jacques Brault 1933–

One of Québec's most accomplished contemporary poets, Brault is also a novelist and essayist whose works Quand nous serons heureux *(1971) and* Agonie *(1984) have won Governor-General's Awards.*

Michel Brault 1928–

Brault is a leading cinematographer of films by Jutra, Poirier, and Mankiewicz, and a director whose own films include Pour la suite du monde *(1963),* Entre la mer et l'eau douce *(1967), and* Les Ordres *(1974). In the 1980s and 1990s he made features, documentaries, and miniseries for Québec television.*

Brault is a contracted variant of Berault, a French surname derived from an ancestor who bore the typically compound Germanic first name *Berwald* whose elements are *bär* 'bear, the animal' and *wald* which means 'power' or 'might.'

BRILL

Debbie Brill 1953–

Born in Mission, British Columbia, this track and field athlete and first woman to clear six feet in the high jump won many medals at the Commonwealth Games, Pan-American Games, and the World Cup during the 1970s. Inventor of the "Brill bend," she published her autobiography, Jump, *in 1986.*

As an English surname, Brill was taken by the founder of the family from the place he lived, a hill in Buckinghamshire that had been named by Celtic-speaking inhabitants of the island long before English was even a gleam in a grammarian's eye. *Bre is the unattested Celtic word for 'hill' and this particular hill was named so long before the arrival of the Anglo-Saxons that, when they arrived and asked local Celts the name of the place, the Anglo-Saxons felt the need to tack onto *Bre an explanatory translation of the term. In Anglo-Saxon or Old English that word was *hyll*. Thus *bre+ hyll = Brill.

Of course, names of similar form are often native to different countries. Brill may also be a Jewish name, and then it often originated as a surname created from a Hebrew acronym—as happened throughout the diaspora wherever Jews were forbidden to have Hebrew elements in their names. For example, Brach could look acceptably German, but it stood for the Hebrew acronym *ben Reb Chaim* 'son of Mr. Chaim.' Brill often stood as an acronym for *ben Reb Yehuda Layb* 'son of Mr. Judah Layb.' But it looked on its surface to be vaguely German, and that satisfied the anti-Semitic authorities.

Brill can be a surname of French origin, and then it is a contraction for the Old French *beril* or *berille* 'a snare to trap birds,' and so the ancestor would have taken his surname from his occupation, that of bird-catcher. We more fastidious bird-lovers of today must remember that in days of yore even tiny songbirds were netted, snared, and trapped with birdlime, then roasted whole on little spits and chomped down, bones and all. The horror, the horror!

Brill can also be of German provenance; some Brills took their name from the medieval town of Bruel in western Germany.

BRONFMAN

Samuel Bronfman 1889–1971

He built a family liquor business into the largest distilling company in the world. Relatives and descendants now control huge real estate, entertainment, and financial institutions.

Bronfman is a particularly apt occupational surname in Yiddish where *bronfn* 'spirits, whisky' gives the original form *Bronfenman* for one who made and sold whisky. *Bronfn* is a dialectic condensing of the German *Branntwein* where the letter *t* drops out, the German *w* becomes a Yiddish *f,* and the final vowel is shortened. By the way, *Branntwein* is literally 'burned' wine, wine that has been distilled over a fire. A similar form in early Dutch *brantwijn* led to *brandewijn* which was borrowed into English as brandywine, and by the middle of the seventeenth century Englishmen were shortening it to brandy, a liquor distilled from wine or fruit juices then reduced over a fire.

BRUHN

Erik Belton Evers Bruhn 1928–1986

The ballet dancer and choreographer was long associated with the National Ballet of Canada.

Bruhn is a Danish surname based on an ancestor's nickname. Brown in Danish is *brun*, and as a nickname indicated hair colour. The old vowel-lengthening *h* is an orthographical sign that disappeared from some modern Scandinavian languages, thus making its retention in surnames a good way to separate such surnames from homophones in the everyday wordstock of a language.

BUCKLEY

Frank Buckley

He's an Ontario businessman whose father invented a patent cough medicine beloved by several generations of Canadians. Buckley's Mixture is the most famous brand made by W.K. Buckley Limited.

Buckley is an Irish surname with an English form, and that's not unusual due to the many times that Irish names and the Roman Catholic religion have been suppressed by English overlords. The infamous Statutes of Kilkenny decreed by King Edward II in 1367 required all colonists to bear English names, use the English language, and keep English customs and styles of dress. It also outlawed marriage between the Irish and the English. Henry VIII did all he could to destroy the Irish, too.

The original Irish form of Buckley is *O Buhilly* or *O Buachalla* 'descendant of a founding ancestor nicknamed Boy. To earn such a moniker, he was perhaps a pert leader whose prowess showed at a memorably early age. Boy or male youth in modern Irish is *buachaill*.

It would be during one of the many periods of repression that some British twit would have decided that *O Buachalla* sounded pretty much like Buckley. It did not, of course. But the surname Buckley already existed in English with two possible sources. Buckley may be from Old English *bucc* 'male deer' + *lea* 'meadow.' This would be a founder who dwelt beside wet ground frequented by deer. Or Buckley can consist of Old English *bucca* 'male goat' + *lea* 'meadow.' Meadows where goats were tethered or deer were spotted (okay, it's a cheap pun) were numerous throughout medieval Britain and so Buckley is a fairly common English town name, for example, Buckley Heath in Sussex, Buckley Green in Warwickshire, and Buckleigh in Devonshire. None bears any ancient connection with the Irish Buckley family.

BULAU

Horst Bulau 1962–

The Ottawa-born champion ski jumper won more than a dozen World Cups.

Bulau is a German surname derived from a place name—Bülau in the northeastern state of Mecklenberg-West Pomerania on the Baltic coast of Germany. The town dates back before AD 1000 and may have been founded by Slavic-speaking people. Some topographic feature near the place may have resembled a breadroll, which is *bula* in early Slavic (compare a Russian diminutive form like *boolachka* 'small French breadroll').

German *Horst* is a shortened form of several compound Germanic names like *Horstmar* 'famous in the little wood' or *Horstwin* 'friend of the copse,' both of which suggest Germanic first names that might have been medieval occupational nicknames for a forester, a guardian of certain woods. In Middle Low German *horst* meant 'coppice.' In modern German *Horst* means 'eyrie,' something high in a wood or on a hill, namely the nest of a bird of prey who builds high up. The German word is akin to the Old English West Saxon noun *hyrst* 'wooded hill,' which appears in numerous British and Canadian place names like Crowhurst, Gravenhurst, Longhirst, Pinehurst, and Whitehurst, not to mention plain Hurst, which is the source of the English surname in all its spellings: Herst, Hirst, Hurst.

C

CABOT

John Cabot (Giovanni Caboto) 1450–1499

In this entry alone, I propose to mix the biographical with the etymological facts. Put it down to Cabot fever! The sea fog of history, with a damp guffaw at human fact-mongering, has shrouded the birth and death of explorer John Cabot. But he was probably born at Genoa in 1450 as Giovanni Caboto. The Genoese navigator later received financial backing for his voyages of discovery from British merchants at Bristol, became a naturalized British subject, and Englished his Italian name. He probably perished at sea off the coast of Newfoundland in 1499.

But his name festoons Canadian mappery. Cabot Head, Ontario, a place name bestowed by John Graves Simcoe to honour the explorer, bears Cabot Head lighthouse built in 1896 to warn ships entering and leaving Lake Huron. Cabot Head is a promontory of Ontario's Bruce Peninsula thrusting forth into the now scubable waters of Georgian Bay. Cabot Strait separates southwest Newfoundland from Cape Breton Island. Cabot Lake in Labrador is drained by the Kogaluk River. Just west of Winnipeg is the little hamlet of Cabot. The capital of Newfoundland, St. John's, was so named to celebrate the traditional discovery of its harbour by John Cabot on the feast of St. John the Baptist, June 24, 1497.

The explorer is obliquely responsible for the early racist term "redskins." The racist notion that all North American native peoples had red skin began in published reports concerning explorer John Cabot's encounters in 1497 with the Beothuk tribes on the island that was later called Newfoundland. The Beothuks, victims of systematic genocide by whites and other native peoples, were extinct by the late eighteenth century. Beothuks ornamented their skin with red ochre for ceremonial and spiritual purposes, hence appearing red-skinned to Cabot and his men.

Not named after early explorer John Cabot is *caboteur*, a French, then an English term for a boat or its captain. A caboteur is a wooden coastal vessel that plies the coast, does not often venture into open sea, but sails from port to port as a cargo vessel. Their individual chronologies prevent derivation of the boat term from the surname. *Caboteur* appears in a French written record as early as 1277. The surname Caboto first appears one hundred years later.

The precise origin of the surname Caboto is disputed, but it certainly begins with Latin *caput, capitis* 'head,' and probably arises from the name of a kind of boat. The following derivative forms are related, but even in classical Latin *caput* had expanded meanings like 'headland of a peninsula.' *Cabo* (from Latin *caput*) is a Spanish word for something jutting out, like a headland, a point, or a cape of land thrusting into the sea. There was a form *cabotz* in Old Provençal (also from Latin *caput*) that meant 'big-headed fish' or 'tadpole,' always a possibility as a sailor's jesting term for any small boat. *Caboto* also may be an early Northern Italian dialect version of the surname *Caputo* 'Big-head.' Early Northern French has *cabot*, *chabot* 'a small vessel that slowly sails along a coast from headland to headland, from port to port. Modern English, French, and Italian now have cabotage, *cabotage*, and *cabotaggio* for 'sailing along a coast in a trading vessel' and 'coastal trade,' to which senses a twentieth-century meaning has been added. Cabotage is allowing a country to regulate airplane traffic in its own skies and over its own territory.

Latin *caput* is the source of our English word *cape* as in Cape Breton Island and our little head covering, a cap, that entered English from French through the language of Provençal. Up it pops in Spanish place names like Cabo de Buena Esperanza, the Cape of Good Hope. As a cape with a hood for the head, it gives French *capote* and thus the surname of American novelist Truman Capote. Mafia movies and American newspapers ring with an Italian derivative, *capo di tutti capi* 'boss of all the bosses.'

Sometimes in etymology what appears a simple borrowing of one word disguises a complex route indeed. Latin *caput* is the origin of the German slang adjective for broken, *kaputt*. We use this in English too but spell it with one *t*, kaput. But caput's path into German was long and twisting. We must go back to a French card game of the seventeenth century called *piquet*, a game for two players. In piquet, when a player was busted and had no tricks left, he or she was said in French *être capot*, to be capotted. Piquet and card games like it were popular throughout Europe. Capot entered German as *kaputt* and Italian as *cappotto*. In Italian hunting jargon, *fare cappotto* is to return empty-handed. Could Caboto be a dialectical variant of *cappotto*? Yes, a jesting name recalling an incident of loss that befell an ancestor long ago.

Canada could have been called Cabotia! Now there's a thought to shrivel your maple leaf. Frighteningly, Canada was not the only name our forebears considered when in 1865 they began thinking about a name for the dominion they wanted to make from the provinces of Upper and Lower Canada, Nova Scotia, and New Brunswick. Let us rejoice that they chose Canada, and not Ursalia (land of bears), Borealia (northern place), Cabotia (after explorer

John Cabot), Tuponia (acronym for The United Provinces of North America), or the hideous tongue-twister Albionora. Get it? Albion (England) of the Nor—th.

Our cartographical Cabotiana conclude by remembering that this Italian sailor's discoveries led to the opening of the North Atlantic fishery and to establishing England's now mercifully defunct claim to North America.

CADILLAC
Antoine Laumet de Lamothe Cadillac 1658–1730
In Québec by 1691 he was a commandant and fur trader. A few years later he founded a fur-trading fort at Detroit, hence the name of General Motors' luxury car. Charges of empire building sent him down to Louisiana as governor from 1710 to 1717. Further charges of sharp dealing sent him with great wealth home to France in 1718.

Cadillac is the name of a place near Bordeaux and of a little town in the Dordogne that springs from the name of a Gallo-Roman territory of ancient Gaul, Catiliacum, itself composed from a Latin cognomen mentioned by Cicero and Pliny *Catilius* and the Latin locative suffix *-acum. Catus,* an adjective in street Latin, meant 'smart, intelligent' and the noun *catus* was a tomcat. The diminutive of that noun *catulus* meant the young of any animal, especially puppy or kitten, and was the nickname of an ancestor of the greatest lyric poet of ancient Rome, Catullus.

CALLAGHAN
Barry Callaghan 1937–
Barry is a poet, founder of a literary press (Exile Editions) *and a literary magazine* Exile, *short story writer, novelist, television producer, host, critic, translator, and professor of English at York University in Toronto since 1966. His published works include* The

Hogg Poems and Drawings *(1978),* The Black Queen Stories *(1982),* The Way the Angel Spreads Her Wings *(1989),* When Things Get Worse *(1993), and* A Kiss Is Still a Kiss *(1995). One of Callaghan's most engaging works is* Barrelhouse Kings: A Memoir *(1998), about growing up in Toronto as Morley Callaghan's son. The memoir bubbles with Barry's frolic and passion, the self-portrait of a man of big talent who takes the space life has given him and occupies it to the fullest.* Barrelhouse Kings *is a masterpiece waiting to be discovered by any reader who likes Canadian autobiography served rare and sizzling.*

Morley Callaghan 1903–1990

How can men and women find spiritual anchorage during the time storm of human life? How do we juggle love and faith with greed and selfishness? How ought a person to live faced with the certainty of eventual death? These questions, central to the fiction of Canada's most intelligent novelist to date, were not ones most Canadians cared to ask themselves in the twentieth century, and that is one reason Morley Callaghan was not as appreciated in Canada as he was in the rest of the English-reading world. His moral genius is however a compelling reason to revisit the work, for the quiz of life did rivet Morley Callaghan, a Roman Catholic from Irish Toronto and a deft wielder of clean prose in novels like Strange Fugitive *(1928),* They Shall Inherit the Earth *(1935),* More Joy in Heaven *(1937),* The Loved and the Lost *(1951),* The Many Coloured Coat *(1960),* A Passion in Rome *(1961),* A Fine and Private Place *(1975), and* A Time for Judas *(1983). Some of his best short fiction is collected in the 1959* Morley Callaghan's Stories. *A strong memoir of Parisian literary life appeared as* That Summer in Paris *(1963), containing Callaghan's famous account of his 1929 boxing matches with Ernest Hemingway and F. Scott Fitzgerald.*

Callaghan describes superbly that heady summer, a high point of his career when he was selling short stories to Ezra Pound's Exile *magazine, to* The New Yorker, Harper's Bazaar, *and* Atlantic Monthly.

For more than forty years beginning in the 1940s Morley Callaghan was also a provocative presence on CBC radio broadcasts as panelist and radio essayist. When I was senior producer in the early 1970s at This Country in the Morning, *it was my pleasure to book Morley Callaghan for conversations with Peter Gzowski. The novelist was a most charming talker—bright as brass with an Irish sparkle and the gab gift of a Jesuit wizard. Callaghan was also a sly debater who easily led interviewers like Gzowski down whatever garden path Morley had decided he would meander. Especially enjoyable were spring mornings when Morley would walk over to the CBC Radio studios on Jarvis Street from his house across the ravine on Dale Avenue, settle into a chair in Studio E, and just chat about things and people he had seen on his jaunt and what those sights might mean.*

Every true Irish surname in its full form, here for example O'Callaghan, is a patronymic, that is, it expresses descent from a father or famous ancestor by means of various prefixes added to the founder's name. The earliest hereditary surnames in Ireland used the prefix *O* or its earlier form *Ua* meaning literally 'grandson.' For example, the first true surname in Irish history was recorded in 916 in County Galway at the death of a great lord named Tigherneach Ua Cléirigh. Nowadays he'd be an O'Clery. Although some think of the Gaelic *Mac* as a Scottish prefix, in Irish, too, *mac* has the literal meaning of son.

O'Callaghan, in Irish O'Ceallacháin, means 'grandson or descendant of a man named Ceallachán.' Now the common diminutive suffix in Irish often appears as -*an*. Ceallach is an ancient Irish single personal name meaning 'bright-head,' or 'shining pate.' What precisely did it betoken to ancient speakers of Irish? Clever, famous, or bald: take your pick. The diminutive suffix could signify actual physical shortness, but more usually diminutives in personal and surnames imply affection. They are little tails of verbal endearment tacked on to the names of loved ones or added to the name of a fondly regarded clan chief. Older etymologies suggested Callaghan means 'strife' or 'frequenter of churches.' These are false.

Ceallachán 'Little Clever One' was a historical personage. He was a king in what is now County Cork in the Irish province of Munster. He died in 954, and we know that the first Callaghan to pass on the hereditary surname was Murchadh Ua Ceallacháin who lived in the eleventh century. Ancestral Callaghan territory comprised land bisected by the River Blackwater near present-day Mallow, land the O'Callaghans ruled for four hundred years from castles at Clonmeen and Dromaneen—homes and fields that by the seventeenth century spread over more than 20,000 acres. In 1996, O'Callaghan was the forty-seventh most populous family in Ireland.

CAMERON

William Cameron 1943–

Vancouver-born Bill is a writer, journalist, television reporter, and CBC-TV host, interviewer, and newsreader.

Cameron, one of the thirty most common surnames in Scotland, stems from an ancestor's nickname, many of which were typically dour. In Scottish Gaelic *cameron* means 'crooked nose, hook-nose' from Gaelic *cam* 'crooked' + *sron* 'nose.' There are several places in Scotland from the same roots, where 'crooked nose' refers to some local feature of topography, for example, a peculiar bend in a river or a rocky outcropping of nasal shape. The earliest spelling of Cameron, and a spelling that persisted, was Cambron. That strongly hints at a derivation from Camberone, now Cameron parish in Fife.

Bearers of this fine Scottish name who have qualms about its etymology can be glad they are not named Cam, a legitimate surname that means crooked-eyed, that is, cross-eyed. The River Cam once had built over it a prominent bridge, and the place became Cambridge. Was the Cam a windy, crooked stream? The Gaelic and Celtic *cam* appears disguised in several English words. A game leg was first a *cam* leg, a crooked or twisted leg. Gammy still means 'disabled by injury' in some English dialects. That part of Greater London known as Camden Town, where Scrooge's clerk Bob Cratchit lived, was named for Earl Camden who took his family name from Campton in Bedfordshire. The prime meaning of Campton is 'farmstead on the River Camel or Cammel' and this river name has Celtic *cam* 'crooked' in its name.

CAMP

Dalton Kingsley Camp 1920–

Mr. Camp is a Progressive Conservative politician and adviser, but, chiefly and resplendently he is a witty writer who in peak form wields one of the most elegant expository prose styles in the history of Canadian political writing, a history composed for the most part of dry academic blather and clumsy partisan bleating. Camp's deft and charming political memoirs include Gentlemen, Players and Politicians *(1970),* Points of Departure *(1979), and* Eclectic Eel *(1981). He is a newspaper columnist and has been a CBC Radio commentator.*

Camp began as an occupational nickname in Old English *cempa* 'warrior.' In Middle English, spelled Kempe, it could mean 'athlete' or 'wrestler.' Old English also had *camp* 'battle' and *campian* 'to fight' both akin to the German *Kampf* 'battle' as in the deranged blatherings of Hitler's *Mein Kampf* 'my struggle.'

Early Germanic mercenaries working for the Romans on the edges of their empire may have borrowed the word *Kampf* into

Proto-Germanic from the Latin *campus* 'level field' on which one could train soldiers, do battle, or pursue studies. In Italian it became *campo* and one who won on the field of battle was a *campione* which French, then English, borrowed as champion and champ. Little mushrooms growing in a French field were *champignons*. A conflict restricted to one field of battle, even a political contest, was a *campagne* 'campaign.' If one were a cowardly rogue, one might run away from a battle and be branded a scamp in its original Italian sense of 'an escape' (Italian *scampare* from Latin *ex* 'away from' + *campare* 'to be in a field'). Now let's scamper away from camp.

CAMPAGNOLO
Iona Campagnolo, née Hardy 1932–
Born on Galiano Island in B.C., she worked as a broadcaster and local politician in Prince Rupert, rising through posts such as Liberal MP for Skeena to become the first female president of the Liberal Party of Canada (1982–1986).

Campagnolo is an Italian surname indicating where an ancestor lived, or in this case, perhaps what he owned, a little group of flat fields. *Campagna* is 'a plain' and *-olo* a diminutive suffix. The surname can also indicate an ancestor who came from the fertile plains of ancient Campania south of and inland from Naples, and in that case the *-olo* is sometimes called an affectionate diminutive, equivalent to some English phrase like "that great guy from Campania."

CAMPBELL
Rt. Hon. Avril Kim Campbell 1947–
After obtaining a degree in political science at the University of British Columbia and pursuing doctoral studies at the London School of Economics, Ms. Campbell became a lawyer and Vancouver politician, being elected in 1986 to the B.C. legislature of Bill Vander

Zalm's Social Credit government. Two years later she ran success-fully as a federal Conservative, rising to become minister of justice and attorney-general for Canada from 1990 to 1992. After the pop-ularity of Prime Minister Brian Mulroney dwindled and he resigned, Ms. Campbell joined the Tory leadership race and beat Jean Charest. In June of 1993, she became the nineteenth and first female prime minister of Canada. In the elections the following November, her attachment to Mulroney and her poor performance on the campaign trail spelled doom for her and almost total wipe-out for the Tories. Kim Campbell went on to a professorship at the Harvard University Kennedy School of Government at Irvine, California. And it was while teaching there in 1996 that Prime Minister Jean Chrétien appointed her to be Canadian consul gen-eral in Los Angeles.

Neve Campbell 1973–

The young Canadian actress was born in Guelph, Ontario, and quit high school in Mississauga at fifteen to work in a Phantom of the Opera *production in Toronto. She went on to headline in the long-running television series* Party of Five*, and to Hollywood movie stardom in films like* Scream 3 *and* Drowning Mona*, both released in 2000. Her first job on TV was acting in a commercial for the Eaton Centre.*

Neve is the Portuguese word for snow, pronounced Nev to rhyme with Bev. Neve Campbell's given name is based on her mother's maiden name. Neves is a female given name in Portuguese and also a surname, derived from Latin *nix, nivis* 'snow.' Both given name and surname spring from one of the religious titles of the Virgin Mary, specifically in Portuguese *Nossa Senhora de las Neves*, or in Spanish *Nuestra Señora de las Nieves* 'Our Lady of the Snows.' Our Lady's title recalls a supposed miracle that occurred during a torrid Roman summer in the middle of the fourth century AD when the Blessed Virgin Mary sent relief to the sweating citizens of the Eternal City by making it snow in August.

Campbell is a Scottish surname based on the insulting nickname of the founding ancestor. There is proof that such a Campbell was alive at the dawn of the thirteenth century. But we must guess that early in his life he suffered a stroke that left paralyzed some of the muscles of his face, in particular those that control the mouth and lips, muscles with sonorous and daunting anatomical labels like *orbicularis oris*, *depressor anguli oris*, *buccinator*, and *musculus zygomaticus major*. Whew! That's enough Latin to start a rogue mass under a gurney. Such a stroke befalling a person in the days when surnames were just forming could alter that person's name. The surname *Campbell* is made up of two Scottish Gaelic roots: *cam* 'crooked' + *buel* 'mouth.' Notice the infixing of the spurious letter *p*, popped into the name Campbell by some English speaker to have it make sense as an English-based name. Of course, Campbell has nothing whatsoever to do with a camp and its mess bell. This ignorant intrusion into the legitimate roots of a surname was dubbed by one Victorian onomastician, "the infix euphonious." He thought the letter *p* had been dropped into the middle of Campbell to make the name sound more pleasing!

Campbell is a common name in Ireland as well. In its prime Scottish Gaelic sense, Crooked Mouth is a most unpleasant moniker. Yet both Scots and Vikings among other peoples liked nasty nicknames. Consider a Viking raider whose real name was Snot. He and his marauding Norse pirates invaded Britain and built a fortress called in Old Scandinavian *Snottingsheim* (literally 'the home of Snot's people'). Today it is the English city of Nottingham.

If Crooked Mouth, the ancestral Campbell, didn't suffer a stroke, then he may have received a sword slash to the head that severed one or more facial nerves. Crooked Mouth could apply also to a harelip, wry-mouth, any disfiguring facial tic, or, topographically, to some local feature of the landscape beside which the founder of the family lived. Campbell is a common name in Ireland as well. It is the family name of the dukes of Argyll and of six other members of the Scottish peerage. In 1958 Campbell was the seventh most frequent name in Scotland.

CARDINAL

Douglas Joseph Cardinal 1934–
He is a Métis architect born in Red Deer, Alberta, whose great works include St. Mary's Church in Red Deer and the Canadian Museum of Civilization in Ottawa completed in 1989. In 1993 he began as principal designer to plan the National Museum of the American Indian, an addition to the Smithsonian Institution in Washington, D.C. His mother was a nurse, his father a provincial wildlife officer of half-Siksika (Blackfoot) heritage. Cardinal has stayed involved in Métis and aboriginal issues, all the while growing as an architect.

Harold Cardinal 1945–
Assembly of First Nations vice-chief, he is a political activist, for a time chief of his natal band at the Sucker Creek Reserve in Alberta, and author of two important books critical of Canada's policies toward First Peoples: The Unjust Society *(1969) and* The Rebirth of Canada's Indians *(1977).*

Tantoo Cardinal 1950–
Born at Anzac near Fort McMurray, Alberta, this Genie Award–winning actress has starred in TV films like Loyalties *(1986) and been featured in important feature films like* Dances with Wolves *(1990),*

Black Robe *(1991), and* Legends of the Fall *(1994). Ms. Cardinal was the star of Sam Shepherd's* Silent Tongue *(1994) and* Where the Rivers Flow North *(1994). She acted in* Smoke Signals *(1998) and in the CBC television drama* The Temptations of Big Bear *(1999) based on Rudy Wiebe's historical novel. She has contributed as well to many educational films in Alberta and other parts of Canada.*

The startlingly coloured cardinal is often a totemic bird of our founding peoples, important in native ritual, myth, and consequently part of the clan-naming vocabulary of First Peoples. Thus the surname Cardinal is usually a translation of aboriginal words for the cardinal, some of which are: *Mihko-piwayesis* (Cree 'small red bird'), *Misko-binesheen* (Ojibwa 'red bird') and *Patliyatjij* (Mi'kmaq 'priest bird').

CARR

Emily Carr 1871–1945

She was a Canadian painter of Pacific forests and beaches, of vanished villages and totem poles, and later in life, when a heart attack made painting difficult, a writer of books like Klee Wyck, *which won the Governor-General's Award in 1941. After her death, four volumes of her journals were published.*

Shirley Carr

She is a union activist who rose to become president of the Canadian Labour Congress (1986–1992) and as such the first Canadian woman to lead a national labour organization.

Carr is a common root in British place names in the Danelaw and then a surname in northern Britain indicating where an ancestor lived. Its root is Old Scandinavian *kjarr* 'marsh, boggy thicket.' Other spellings are Kerr and Ker.

CARREY

James "Jim" Carrey 1962–

Born in Jackson's Point, Ontario, the rubber-faced Canadian actor and comedian of mad excess began in Canadian comedy clubs, moved on to Los Angeles and the Fox Network satire In Living Color, *then to colossal success in violent slapstick films like* The Mask *(1994),* Ace Ventura: Pet Detective *(1994, sequel 1995),* Dumb and Dumber *(1995),* Batman Forever *(1995) where he played The Riddler,* The Cable Guy *(1996),* Liar, Liar *(1997),* The Truman Show *(1998), and* Man on the Moon *(1999), a clever recreation of the juvenile shticks of 1980s comedian Andy Kaufman that failed because the screenplay refused to explain Kaufman's anti-social modes and sociopathic self. Carrey has shown that personality crises that arise from bipolar disorders can sometimes be projected outward to become brilliant comedy "takes" on the manic-depressive nature of modern urban life. The performer's self-love and self-hatred fly out to the audience, interspersed at a mind-boggling rate, and we laugh, sometimes in fear for the performer's sanity, sometimes in fear for our own.*

Carrey is an orthographical variant of Carey and Cary, the latter a British surname taken from the River Cary in Somerset. If Celtic, it is possibly from the Indo-European root **kar* 'hard' or 'stony' in reference to the bed of the stream. If pre-Celtic, you could mug a druid and still be in the etymological dark, for the names of many rivers are of such immemorial antiquity that their true meanings are forever lost. However, of the old river names whose roots we can trace, the great majority mean 'river,' 'wet,' or 'flowing.' Take your pick.

CARVER

Brent Carver 1952–

The Canadian actor and singer won plaudits for his roles in Broadway megamusicals like Kiss of the Spider Woman *(1992).*

Born in Cranbrook, B.C., Carver played Robert Ross in the film version of Timothy Findley's The Wars, *and at Ontario's Stratford Shakespearean Festival he starred in* Hamlet, The Pirates of Penzance, *and* Cabaret.

If of Norman provenance, Carver is Old French *charvier* 'ploughman'; if of English stock, the occupational surname suggests woodcarver or stone mason.

CASSELMAN

Barbie Casselman 1956–

The nutritionist and television cooking expert is also the author of Barbie Casselman's Good-For-You Cooking: A Healthy Eating Guide *(1993).*

Leah Casselman

She is a union leader, president of OPSEU, the Ontario Public Servants' Employment Union, who led a strike in 1996 against the union-bashing tactics of Ontario Premier Mike Harris.

Karen Leigh Casselman 1942–

A writer, broadcaster, lecturer, and fabric artist living in Cheverie, Nova Scotia, she is author of the internationally published Craft of the Dyer *(1980).*

William Gordon Casselman 1942–

It befits a writer, within his own pages, to blush modestly at the words biographical sketch of author *and retire behind the nearest potted palm like some Victorian maiden aswoon with the vapours and fluttering a Japanese fan. Although I did nibble hesitantly on a fern frond while trying to conjure how best to dismiss my life in one sentence, I have come down against specious humility. Abject toady, cringing lickspittle, and base sycophant that I usually am, nevertheless I will make bold to tell a little of my story. The interested reader will find this modest biographical excursus at the end of this book, following the little* envoi.

My Lutheran Kasselmanns fled religious persecution in eighteenth-century Hesse. Many walked from Germany through the Netherlands, and then by boat reached London at the dawn of the eighteenth century. There, to afford passage to the New World, they signed indentures to work with the British Navy. By 1712 my ancestors lived in the small towns of Schoharie and Stone Arabia in the Mohawk Valley, west of the Hudson River in present-day New York State. Earlier, they had worked caulking ships in a navy yard on the Hudson.

During the War of American Independence, most Casselmans remained loyal to King George III, their loyalty buoyed up by the offer of free land along the St. Lawrence River, to which haven they removed themselves with due alacrity as the New York air grew thick with musket shot. But some Casselmans remained in America, enough to make a character named Suffrenus Casselman one of the villains in Walter Edmond's 1936 novel *Drums along the Mohawk*. And Sophrenus was a real given name in the Casselman family's early American history.

Kasselmann is a locative surname that means simply *einer aus Kassel* 'a person from the city of Kassel' in Hesse. Kassel was the site of a Roman fortification on the outer marches of the empire and takes its name from *castellum* 'little camp' and then 'fortified camp;' the same word gives rise to later words like castle, château, chatelaine, and a suffix in British locations named from encampments of Roman legions, places like Chester, Doncaster, Manchester, and home of the pungent sauce: Worcestershire.

When Casselman is a Jewish surname, it is likely to be an anglicizing of Kesselman in which the surname derives from the Hebrew male first name Yekutiel (sometimes Yekusiel), which had a pet form *Kessel* or *Kesseluh*. The Elizabethan transliteration of Yekutiel that appears in the King James version of First Chronicles is Jekuthiel, a son of the scribe Ezra. In Hebrew Yekutiel means 'fear of God.'

Casselman can also be an Englishing of the German occupational surname *Kesselmann* ultimately from German *Kessel* 'kettle, pot, boiler' and so pointing to one who made pots and pans, a boilermaker, or a coppersmith. The more common form was Kessler.

CASSON
Alfred Joseph Casson 1898–1992
Painter, member of the Group of Seven

Here is a rare matronymic in British surnames, where the last name derives from the name of a female ancestor. Casson is a contraction of Cass's son, and Cass is a pet form of Cassandra, the prophetic Trojan princess, a female first name that was widespread in thirteenth-century England when surnames were being created. In Greek, Cassandra means 'she who ensnares men' in her prophesies. Apollo gave her the gift of foretelling approaching evil, but then, as the old Greek gods were wont to do, Apollo fell into a nitpicking snit and put a curse on Cassandra. Yes, she would always foretell the true future, but no one would ever believe her.

Casson may also be a contraction of the medieval surname Cattessone/Catesone, which is 'son of Catt' where Catt is indeed the common feline as a nickname of both males and females.

CHALMERS
Floyd Sherman Chalmers 1898–1993
Editor of the Financial Post, *he was president and chairman of the board of Maclean-Hunter. Mr. Chalmers, his wife Jean, and their daughter M. Joan Chalmers were generous patrons of many*

Canadian arts through the Floyd S. Chalmers Foundation, the Jean A. Chalmers Chair in Canadian Music, and other philanthropies.

Chalmers is a Scottish variant of Chambers 'son of the chamber' which was originally an occupation. The chamber was an official of a great house exactly like a chamberlain, whom today we might call an estate or household manager. Middle English *chaumbre* < Old French *chambre* < Latin *camera* 'room' but originally 'room with a vaulted roof' hence 'large room, public or private' < Greek *kamara* 'anything with an arched covering' < Indo-European root **kam* 'curved, bent.' In linguistics, the symbol < means 'derived from' and the symbol > means 'is the root of, gives rise to.'

An interesting residuum of the IE root **kam* is a Celtic river name in England, the Cam 'crooked' or 'winding.' Near a span over this river grew up a great English university at Cambridge.

CHARBONNEAU

Art Charbonneau
From 1994 to 1996 he was the British Columbia minister of education in the NDP cabinet of Premier Michael Harcourt.

Monsignor Joseph Charbonneau
He was a pro-union archbishop of Montréal, noted for his clashes with Duplessis during the bitter 1949 Asbestos strike in Québec.

Robert Charbonneau 1911–1967
Journalist, editor, poet, novelist, and literary critic, he helped modernize Québec literature during the 1940s.

Yvon Charbonneau 1940–
He is a longtime motive force in and president of the CEQ, an important Québec teachers' union.

Charbonneau 'little charcoal' is a diminutive form of *charbon*, and was applied as an occupational surname, like *charbonnier*, to one who manufactured and sold charcoal, an important fuel in Europe for centuries.

CHAREST

Jean Charest 1958–

Interim leader of the Progressive Conservative Party following the federal election of 1993, the personable MP for Sherbrooke was federal minister of the environment (1991–1993). Charest became the first Québécois to lead the PCs in 1995, and that same year was an important provincial voice in the defeat of the referendum for separation. By the summer of 1997, Charest was more popular than Premier Lucien Bouchard. When the Québec Liberal Party was leaderless in 1998, Charest resigned the federal Tory leadership and a month later became leader of the provincial Liberals. By the middle of 2000, after almost two years of effort, Charest seems to have failed to interest Quebeckers deeply in any Liberal agenda.

Charest is a variant of Charêt, an early French occupational nickname for a carter, one who owned and operated *un char*, in other words a barrowman who transported goods in a handcart, a dogcart, or a tumbrel.

CHIN

Ben Chin

A reporter and affable newsreader who began in Toronto television at CITY-TV after being discovered waiting tables by one of the CITY producers, Ben has moved up to the prestigious desk at CBC's Newsworld and is also seen now on the regular network of the CBC.

The Chinese people were the first to use hereditary surnames. As early as 400 BC, written records show last names passed down from father to son consistently. This may be the benign influence of Confucius (Latin name of K'ung Fu-tse, philosopher, 551–479 who had emphasized and refined the already strong Chinese veneration of ancestors. Relative to other world languages, Chinese permits only a small number of words to be used as family names. Chin is used in China and Korea. Chin is the voicing of several different signs in Chinese, so it can mean 'true,' or be related to verbal roots signifying 'increase' or 'grasp.'

The following are familar Chinese surnames with some of their meanings:

- Chang   'mountain, constantly, draw a bow'
- Chen   'attend, arrange'
- Cheng   'journey, to complete'
- Cho   'to draw a bow, to establish'
- Choi   'turtle'
- Chong   'hanging bell' (echoic word)
- Chow   'everywhere'
- Chu   'bamboo, to bless, deep red'
- Li   'plum, black'
- Lin, Ling   'forest'
- Liu   'willow tree, battle-ax'
- Moy   'plum flower'
- Ng   'crow'
- Wang   'yellow, prince'
- Wong   'wide seas'
- Yee   'I' (first person singular)

COCKBURN

Bruce Cockburn 1945–

The folksinger, songwriter, and political activist is the recipient of many Juno Awards. His 1984 album Stealing Fire *went platinum on the U.S. Billboard charts in 1985. Popular songs he wrote and re-corded include "Goin' to the Country," "Musical Friends," "Wondering Where the Lions Are," "The Trouble with Normal," and "Lovers in a Dangerous Time." His 1997 CD,* The Charity of Night, *included "The Mines of Mozambique," a protest song about anti-personnel land mines, the banning of which was an important cause for Cockburn during the 1990s.*

James Cockburn 1819–1883
The politician was a Father of Confederation and Speaker of the House of Commons from 1867 to 1873.

Cockburn was early altered to euphemistic variants like Cobourne, and so pronounced to avoid what seventeenth-century minds thought was the vulgar meaning of cock. Of course, it began innocently enough. A cock was a rooster or the male of any wild game bird. *-Burn* is often from Old English *burna* or Old Scandinavian *brunnr* 'stream.' Thus Cockburn could mean 'a stream frequented by wild birds,' the name itself a useful hunter's mnemonic. Cock also came to mean 'pert lad,' that is, one who strutted like a cock. It was a term of affection, even used as late as Charles Dickens, who has Mr. Cratchit call Tiny Tim "my little cock-sparrow." And there were Old English personal names like *Cohha and *Cocc(a) so that Cockburn may have been 'Cocca's stream.'

COHEN
Dian Cohen 1937–
The economist, financial commentator, and journalist in print, radio, and television, has won national business-writing awards. In 1993 she was created a member of the Order of Canada. She is the author of Money *(1987). Dian Cohen's opinions have been called "negotiocentric.'*

Leonard Cohen 1934–

The Montréal poet, songwriter, and novelist wrote Beautiful Losers *(1966), one of my personal literary amulets in the late sixties. I now find it much less amulet-like. Another novel was* The Favourite Game *(1963). His work includes books of poetry like* Let Us Compare Mythologies *(1956),* The Spice-Box of Earth *(1961),* Flowers for Hitler *(1964),* Parasites of Heaven *(1966),* Book of Mercy *(1984), and in 1993 a major anthology of his collected work,* Stranger Music: Selected Poems and Songs. *Among albums of his own songs are* Songs from a Room *(1969),* Death of a Ladies Man *(1977),* I'm Your Man *(1987),* The Future *(1992), and* Cohen Live *(1994).*

Matt Cohen 1942–1999

The Kingston-born novelist dealt with small-town Ontario life in his Salem Quartet: The Disinherited *(1974),* The Colours of War *(1977),* The Sweet Second Summer of Kitty Malone *(1979), and* Flowers of Darkness *(1981). Other works that delve into his Jewish heritage include* The Spanish Doctor *(1984) and* Nadine *(1986). Among his last novels were* Emotional Arithmetic *(1990),* Freud: The Paris Notebooks *(1991),* The Bookseller *(1993), and* Last Seen *(1996). In 1999,* Elizabeth and After *won the Governor-General's Award for fiction. Matt Cohen also wrote wonderful books for children under the pseudonym Teddy Jam, beginning in 1988 with* Night Cars *and including* Doctor Kiss Says Yes, The Stoneboat, *and* The Fishing Summer.

Samuel Nathan Cohen 1923–1971

Born in Sydney, Nova Scotia, Mr. Cohen became Canada's most influential theatre critic in the 1950s and 1960s in the pages of the Toronto Star, *as well as a popular panelist on CBC radio and television.*

Cohen, Cohn, Cahn, Kahn, Kagan, Kogan, Kaplan, Kohani, Ca-hana, and variants all stem from a Hebrew word for priest, *kohen*. The brother of Moses, Aaron was the first of the *kohanim*, priests who performed sacrifices and religious services in the simple sanc-tuaries during the desert wanderings and later in glory in the great Temple at Jerusalem. Post-exilic Jews passed the title of *kohen* down as a surname even after the specific priestly office no longer existed.

COLICOS

John Colicos 1928–2000

The superb Toronto-born character actor performed at our Stratford Festival in title roles as King Lear *and* Cyrano de Bergerac, *at the Old Vic, at the American Shakespeare Festival, and memorably as Winston Churchill in Hochhuth's* Soldiers. *He was a veteran of many CBC and American television dramas and international films, such as* Anne of the Thousand Days *(1971) where he acted a spooky, ice-veined Cromwell and an excellent remake of* The Postman Always Rings Twice *(1981) where he played Nick, the victimized husband. His films included work in* Shadow Dancing *(1988),* The Last Don *(1997), and for Canadian television the CBC's* The National Dream *(1974) and* Love and Hate: A Marriage Made in Hell *(1990).*

Colicos, if Greek, is likely from *kollix, kollikos* 'a long loaf of coarse country bread.' This surname would arise as the nickname of an ancestor who was a baker or whose height or shape reminded jesting friends of the breadloaf. Contrary to one venerable tome of Greek onomastics, it is not from the modern Greek *ho kolikós* 'the colic.' Surnames synonymous with diseases have an understand-ably brief tenure as names in every language. The country bread baked in a long loaf was familiar to ancient Greeks and to late medieval Greeks when surnames were forming. Classical Greek even had an adjective *kollikophagos* 'eating country bread.' Two other very remote possibilities exist. Colicos could be a dialectical altering of a modern word for share-cropper *kollegas* or it might be vowel gradation, also in a dialect, of *kolakos* 'flattering, of a flatterer.'

CONNORS

"Stompin' Tom" Connors 1936–

The folksy balladeer born in Saint John, New Brunswick, has composed Canadian standards like "Bud the Spud."

Connors is an Anglo-Irish version of *Ó Connor* which in Irish Gaelic means 'descendant of High Will' suggesting an ancestral nickname identifying a person of great resolution.

COON COME

Matthew Coon Come 1956–

An aboriginal leader, chief of the Mistassini Cree (1981–1986), and Grand Chief of the Grand Council of the Crees, he received an honorary LLD in 1998 from Trent University to acknowledge his continuing fight for recognition of his people's quest for survival, environmental respect, and basic human rights before the governing bodies of Canada and the world. He still hunts, fishes, and traps with his wife and five children near his home in Nemaska near James Bay. The place name Nemaska refers to a lake that abounds in namestek, Cree for 'fish.'

The chief's name is a translation of his Cree surname that will contain the Cree word for raccoon, *ocikomsis*. In Cree, a little raccoon is *pisiskis*.

COPPS

Sheila Maureen Copps 1952–

She is a Liberal politician, daughter of Victor Copps, longtime mayor of Hamilton. She has been a journalist with the Ottawa

Citizen *(1974–1976) and a federal Liberal leadership candidate in 1990, and has filled various posts in Chrétien's cabinet, including deputy prime minister, minister of the environment, and now minister of Canadian Heritage.*

Copps shows the common possessive *s* that makes the meaning 'descendant of Copp.' In Old English *cop, copp* meant 'top, summit, human head, hilltop, high place.' It thus can be a locative surname denoting a place the ancestor lived, or a last name based on the ancestor's nickname indicating a large head or cleverness.

COSMOS

Amor de Cosmos
adopted name of **William Alexander Smith 1825–1897**

The second premier of British Columbia (1872–1874) was one of Canada's true eccentrics. Born a colonist in Windsor, Nova Scotia, William Alexander Smith headed west early. By 1854 he was in California applying for an official change of name: "I desire not to adopt the name of Amor de Cosmos because it smacks of a foreign title, but because it is an unusual name and its meaning tells what I love most, viz.: order, beauty, the world, the universe." There is already in 1854 a Californian spiritual giddiness to his letters, as reported in a biography Amor de Cosmos *by Roland White (1958). He dabbled in the founding of communal paradises in the wilderness, but was also a practical and fervid "free Canada" advocate. After serving two years as premier of British Columbia, de Cosmos continued as a federal Member of Parliament for Victoria until 1882.*

In a wacky hybrid of Latin, French, and Greek, Amor de Cosmos means 'love of the universe.' But Smith coined his own moniker intending his new name to convey the more syrupy 'universal love.'

COUPLAND

Douglas Coupland 1961–

Generation X novelist who popularized the phrase in his 1991 fiction Generation X: Tales for an Accelerated Culture, *the British Columbian also wrote* Shampoo Planet *(1992), and* Miss Wyoming *(2000).*

In the British county of Northumberland lies Coupland, a town founded by Vikings who seem to have bought land to settle on rather than seize it by invasion. In Old Scandinavian it is *kaupaland* 'bought or purchased land.' But perhaps that real estate designation is merely the cover-up work of an early Viking spinmeister.

CREIGHTON

Mary Helen Creighton 1899–1989

The author was a folklorist and pioneer collector of Maritime folksongs and stories in long association with the National Museum of Canada. Her books include Bluenose Ghosts *(1957),* Bluenose Magic *(1968),* A Life in Folklore *(1975), and for children,* With a Heigh-Heigh-Ho *(1986).*

Creighton is a surname taken from the place an ancestor lived, here an old town in the English county of Staffordshire whose name is compounded of Old Welsh or Celtic **creig* 'cliff, big rock' whence English crag and craggy-faced and of Old English *tun* 'town, village.' Variants of the surname with the same meaning include Crichton, Crighton, and Chricton. The Scots surname Crichton stems from a place near Edinburgh where Crichton is made up of two roots that mean 'border' and 'town.'

CROMBIE

David Crombie 1936–

He taught political science and held administrative posts at Ryerson Polytechnic Institute until 1971. Then he was a popular mayor of Toronto (1973–1978), resigning to win a federal PC seat and fill various cabinet portfolios in the Clark and Mulroney governments, including secretary of state in 1986. In 1988, Mr. Crombie returned to his beloved Toronto to pursue government commission work including a study of the future of the Toronto waterfront and in 1994 involvement with the Raiway Lands Dispute, later playing a motive role in trying to attract the Olympic Games to Toronto.

Jonathon Crombie 1966–

David's son is a young actor who has appeared in the continuing role of Gilbert Blythe in the series Anne of Green Gables *broadcast on CBC-TV. His other television dramas include* The Killing Ground *(CBC, 1988) and* The Good Fight *(CBC, 1993).*

Crombie is a surname based on the Scottish town in which the ancestors lived, Crombie in Aberdeenshire. In Scotland the *b* is not pronounced. In the rest of the world, the *b* is spoken, saving the surname from sounding crummy, even though it shares the same origin as that English adjective. The Scottish place name contains the basic Gaelic root *crom* 'crooked, bent, curved,' which appears in words describing human form and topographical features. Compare German *krumm*, Welsh *crwm*, and Old British *crum* and **crumbo*, all meaning 'bend, bent.' The Old British root and its cognates show up in modern English words like crumb, crumble, and crumple. A more distant possibility is the Gaelic *crambach* 'quarrelsome.'

CROWFOOT

Isapo-muxika 1830–1890

A famous Blackfoot (Siksika) chief, he was born a Blood but raised a Blackfoot. He co-operated with whites when it seemed to be to the advantage of aboriginal peoples, but became angry at Ottawa after the Blackfoot were settled forcibly on their Alberta reserve in 1881.

Isapo-muxika means 'Crow Indian's Big Foot' in Siksika. Interpreters shortened it to Crowfoot. His ancestral honorific name was bestowed to celebrate his bravery as a teenager in a battle.

CUMMINGS

Burton Cummings 1947–

The Winnipeg-born rock musician was vocalist for the Guess Who (1968–1975). His hit songs include the group's only Billboard Number One "American Woman" (1970) and a solo Number Ten in 1977, "Stand Tall" along with "I'm Scared," and a contributing vocal on the 1985 famine aid recording "Tears Are Not Enough." In 1996 came a live CD of concert renditions of his hits, Up Close and Alone, *that sold more than 50,000 copies.*

Whether an Irish, Scottish, or English surname, Cummings was brought to the British Isles by Norman-French settlers. Various towns in France, like Comines near the French-Belgian border, may be the origin, or perhaps Bosc-Benard-Commin in the Eure where French surnames like Comin and Coumini appear in the twelfth century. Old Breton has Cunmin as a male first name in AD 895. All the surnames including Irish ones like Comyn, *Ó Coimín,* and *Ó Cuimín* may be diminutive forms of *cam 'bent, crooked' either as a topographical description or a nickname based on physique.

DA ROZA

Gustavo Uriel Da Roza 1933–

Born in Hong Kong of Chinese and Portuguese heritage, the influential Winnipeg architect's work includes the Winnipeg Art Gallery (1971). He taught at the University of Manitoba for years, continued to design houses, and in 1988 returned home to Vancouver to work there and to be closer to other commissions in transpacific China.

Da Roza is a Portuguese matronymic surname, a spelling variant of *rosa* 'rose.' The surname means literally 'from Rosa' which can be a woman's given name. Da Roza may also be a locative surname based on Rosa as the place of residence of the ancestor, namely, a locality of reddish soil or rock. Another possibility for the derivation of Roza is an ancestor's name based on a medieval Portuguese sign name: *da roza* 'at the sign of the Rose.' Street numbers did not exist in medieval Europe, and both houses and places of business were frequently referred to by the signs and symbols painted on the outer walls of the house.

DANBY

Kenneth Edison Danby 1940–

Born in Sault Ste. Marie, the popular painter of anonymous athletes and rural Ontario scenes counts among his most familiar images the masked goalie of At the Crease *(1972).*

Danby is a Yorkshire surname from one of three places in that county. In Old Scandinavian *Danaby* means 'Danes' farm or village.' The Old Scandinavian terminal *-by* appears in dozens of British place names and thence surnames like Appleby, Derby, Kettleby, Thursby, and Whitby.

DANDURAND

Anne Dandurand 1953–

This talented Québécoise quit a succeesful career as an actor in radio, television, theatre, and film in Montréal to become a novelist and short story writer whose works include L'assassin de l'intérieur *(1988),* Un coeur qui craque *(1990),* Petites âmes sous ultimatum *(1991),* La salle d'attente *(1994), and* La Marquise ensanglantée *(1996).*

Dandurand is a contraction of the southern French *D'Andurand* in which *de* is added to the surname to lend an aristocratic hue to *Andurand* which is itself an orthographical variant of *Endurant*, the present participle of the verb *endurer*. This was an ancestral nickname that meant 'patient' or 'stubborn.'

DARKES

Maureen Kempston Darkes 1947–

Toronto-born, this graduate of the University of Toronto has degrees in arts and in law. She joined General Motors' legal department in 1965, and fought her way up the corporate ziggurat to become the first female president of General Motors Canada in 1995.

Darkes is 'descendant of Dark,' a nickname usually descriptive of skin, hair colour, or complexion. The nickname existed in Old English too as *Deorc*.

Sometimes Darkes stands for Norman-French forms seen in eleventh- and twelfth-century names like Osbern de Arches and William de Arcis, indicating ancestors from northern medieval French towns like Arques-la-Bataille in the Pas-de-Calais or Argues, a town name in Eure and Seine-Maritime.

DAULT

Gary Michael Dault 1939–

The Toronto writer taught the history of art at several Canadian universities and was art critic at the Toronto Star *for five years. As a freelancer, he continues to write extensively on the lively arts for leading Canadian and international art magazines. Dault's masterly essays have graced many an artist's catalogue both in Canada and abroad. His newspaper work included a photography column for the* Globe and Mail *and for* Saturday Night *magazine, and a design column for* Canadian Art. *Gary Michael has been executive producer of CBC Radio's flagship morning show, and appears regularly on TVO to talk about art on programs like* Studio 2. *Among his books are* Barker Fairley Portraits *(1981),* Visions: Contemporary Art in Canada *(1983), and with Tony Urquhart,* Cells of Ourselves *(1989). His* Children in Photography: 150 Years *appeared in 1990.* Flying Fish, *a book of his intellectually sportive poetry, was published by Exile Editions in 1996. He was the editor and an essayist of* Architecture Canada 1997: The Governor-General's Awards for Architecture *from TUNS Press at Dalhousie University in Halifax. He reviews current gallery shows for the* Globe and Mail.

Dault is a French surname *d'Ault* 'from the town of Ault' in the Somme where *Ault* is a local variant of the Common Germanic *alt* 'old (place).' But in the specific instance of Gary Michael Dault's name, Dault is a variant of D'Aoust from *de* + *aoust* 'of August' where the ancestor's nickname arises from the fact that he was a seasonal worker (of August) and in medieval France that meant he was a harvester of cereal crops who hired out in August when such crops ripened. The French surname Laoust is of similar origin.

DAVIDSON

Florence Edenshaw Davidson 1896–1993

This Haida artist and teacher of her people's culture, born at Masset on Queen Charlotte Island, worked in basket weaving, ceremonial blankets, spruce-root and cedar-bark hats.

Her Haida names were *Jadalloz* and *g'egedngaá* 'Story Maiden.'

DAVIES

Robertson William Davies 1913–1995

One of Canada's greatest novelists was also a newspaperman, actor, playwright, humorous essayist, teacher and the founding master of Massey College at the University of Toronto. Among his outstanding novels are the Deptford Trilogy: Fifth Business *(1970),* The Manticore *(1972), and* World of Wonders *(1975). Other works of note:* The Rebel Angels *(1981),* What's Bred in the Bone *(1985),* The Lyre of Orpheus *(1988), and* The Cunning Man *(1994). A posthumous miscellany,* The Merry Heart, *appeared in 1996.*

Davies is the most frequent patronymic from the Biblical first name, David. It means 'descendant of Davy,' Davy being the common nickname. Davies is the standard Welsh spelling of the name, which is found widely in Cornwall and Devonshire.

The Hebrew name David began as an affectionate cradle word, something like a mother cooing "goody-woody" to a baby. From this general lullaby meaning of 'darling,' David then came to mean 'friend' in general. Its Welsh popularity stems from Saint David, patron saint of Wales; and two early Scottish kings bore the name. Many surnames sprang from it including Davis, Davis, Davy, Davitt, Dawes, Dawson, Dawkins, and the Scottish Gaelic McTavish. McTavish is not, as the *Penguin Dictionary of Surnames* states, from 'son of Tammas,' Lowland Scots for Thomas—for the simple reason that such a derivation does not explain the mysterious disappearance of the *m*. It is rather 'son of Tavy = Davy.' But some say that in the Gaelic spelling *Mac Tamhais* the *mh* accounts for the *v* in McTavish. Then let the wee woolywallocks have their say! Scots, of course, prefer Davidson, although the Irish McDevitt or McDade are also occasionally found.

DE BLICQUY

Lorna de Blicquy

A pilot for more than fifty years, the Canadian aviatrix was the first Canadian woman to fly over the Canadian high arctic and the first female civil aviation inspector. In 1993 she won the Trans-Canada

(McKee) trophy, Canada's oldest aviation award, that recognizes her achievements in air operations. In 1995 she was appointed to the Order of Canada.

Blicquy is a locality in Belgium that takes its name from the former Gallo-Roman territory of *Biliciacum = Bilius*, a male given name + *-acum* Latin locative suffix. *Bilius* is possibly related to a later word in medieval Latin **bilia* 'tree trunk,' thus *Bilius* would be a nickname for a man short and stout.

DEIGHTON

Captain John "Gassy Jack" Deighton *floruit* 1860–1880

The Vancouver saloon-keeper and owner of the Deighton Hotel gave his name to an early district of the settlement called Gastown. Vancouver was incorporated as a city in 1886 as a new terminus to the CPR and as a deep-sea port with accommodation for ocean-going vessels more capacious than the dockage at Port Moody.

Deighton is a surname based on the place an ancestor lived. The roots are Old English *dic* 'ditch' + *tun* 'farm, group of farm houses,' then 'town.' There are four towns in Great Britain with this name.

Dekanahwideh *floruit* 1600s

A fifteenth-century native statesman, he was the legendary (?) founder of the Five Nations (later Six Nations) Confederacy, still honoured today among the Iroquois Nations: Cayuga, Mohawk, Oneida, Onandaga, Seneca, and Tuscarora. Among the miraculous stories about "The Heavenly Messenger" was his stone canoe in which he brought his message of peace to the warring tribes, and in which he sailed away into the northern reaches of the Great Lakes, promising to return if the peoples broke their vows of mutual peace.

Dekanahwideh may be Wendat (Huron) for 'two rivers go together.'

DE KERCKHOVE

Derrick De Kerckhove 1944–

The writer and professor of French at the University of Toronto worked with Marshall McLuhan and became director of the McLuhan Program in Culture and Technology at the University of Toronto; his books include The Alphabet and the Brain *(1988) and* The Skin of Culture: Investigating the New Electronic Reality *(1995).*

De Kerckhove is a Flemish surname indicating the place an ancestor lived, namely, near the *kerckhove* 'churchyard.' Compare the Dutch *kerkhof*, the German *Kirchhof*, and the Scottish Gaelic *kirk* 'church.'

DE LA ROCHE

Mazo de la Roche 1879–1961

Her saga of the Whiteoaks who live at Jalna, stretched over many best-selling novels, is one of the great verbal depictions of a Canadian family. Many university English departments in Canada have never admitted de la Roche into their hoity-toity canon of the literary elect. Do not be put off by their snotty dismissal of Mazo de la Roche as a peddler of popular romance. She is mighty in familial portraiture. Try one of her novels like Jalna *(1927), all the while thinking of untenured English professors, wizened with envy, as they contemplate the nine million copies of the Jalna books sold, in ninety-two foreign-language editions.*

De la Roche is a French surname that probably began as a reference to an ancestor's residence, *la maison de la roche* 'the house on or near the big boulder or rock.' Mazo is a given name derived from a French surname like *Mazot* 'little mas' where *mas* was a medieval term in the south of France for a kind of feudal tenure in which one person held the right to farm a property. *Mas* derives from the Late Latin legal term for this tenure *mansus* 'consignment' or 'feudal transmission of land for temporary custody to an individual.' The surname Mazot began as a descriptive noun. *Un mazot* was the tenant who held a small *mas*.

DE LINT

Willem de Lint

The architect designed many unique buildings in Regina including the Norman MacKenzie Art Gallery. He is also the head of the Saskatchewan Boy and Girl Scouts movements. He was appointed to the Order of Canada in 1995.

De lint is Dutch for 'the ribbon' suggesting a surname based on the ancestor's occupation of draper or that his dwelling was on a ribbon of land or that he received some honour or decoration.

DEVINE

Donald Grant Devine 1944–

A farmer with a doctorate in agricultural economics, he taught at the University of Saskatchewan and was Progressive Conservative premier of the province from 1982, winning re-election in 1986 and 1991. As well as many accomplishments for Saskatchewan, he also had to observe several of his own cabinet ministers get involved with a million-dollar fraud case, the biggest in the province's history, a political scandal that by 1999 saw five people in jail out of the fifteen convicted. This was a sleazorama of the first magnitude, complete with fake expense accounts, numbered companies, and widespread incompetence.

Devine has two etymological strands. One Devine is Norman French (in English records from 1187) from Old French *devin* 'divine,' a nickname for an ancestor of exemplary religious character. The other is Irish Gaelic where the surname Devine is an anglicizing of *Ó Daimhín* 'descendant of Little Ox or Little Stag' or an

Englishing of *Ó Duibhín* 'descendant of Blackie,' that is, 'Little Black One,' a nickname referring to complexion, hair colour, or the 'black Irish,' a term of mild opprobrium used to describe Irish people of Mediterranean appearance.

DEWDNEY

Christopher Dewdney 1951–

Poet, artist, teacher, television commentator on TVO's Studio 2, *his works include* Fovea Centralis *(1975),* Predators of the Adoration *(1983),* The Immaculate Perception *(1986),* Concordat Provisio Ascendant *(1991) and, his most approachable poetry to date, the love poems in* Demon Pond *(1994).*

Sir Edgar Dewdney 1835–1916

The politician and civil engineer was surveyor-supervisor of British Columbia's Dewdney Trail constructed in the late 1860s to provide a route to the interior of British Columbia.

Dewdney is an orthographical transmutation of the Norman-French name *Dieudonné* 'God-given,' itself from a Late Latin Christian first name *Deodonatus* 'given by God.'

Compound names suggesting a newborn child is a gift of God are common in the naming vocabulary of many languages. Greek, for example, has *Dorothea* and *Theodoros* where the words *theos* 'god' and *doron* 'gift' are interchanged. Slavic has *bogdan* 'God-gift,' giving surnames like Bogdanovitch and feminine first names like Bogdana. Hebrew has Nathaniel 'God has given' with the verbal root *natan* 'give' and the Semitic root *el* 'god.' *El* appears in Hebrew words like Elohim (literally a plural form 'gods') and in Arabic words like *al-ilah* 'the god' which is conflated to *Allah*. The Hebrew version of the root appears as the prefix in names like Elijah, Elisha, and Elisheba, the later well known in its English form of Elizabeth.

DIEFENBAKER

John George Diefenbaker 1895–1979

The lively Progressive Conservative Saskatchewan defence lawyer became Canada's thirteenth prime minister (1957–1963).

Diefenbaker is a spelling variant of the German surname *Dieffenbacher* 'person from the Lower Rhine town of Dieffenbach.' The town was situated on the banks of a *dief* 'deep' *Bach* 'stream.'

DINGWALL

David Dingwall 1952–

A controversial Liberal politician from Nova Scotia who was federal minister of public works and government services (1993–96) and who also held the health portfolio in the Chrétien cabinet.

The surname Dingwall is part of the influx of Old Scandinavian words into English and Scottish Gaelic that began with the first Viking raids on northern Britain in AD 787. From that time until almost 1000, Scandinavian words like *sky, egg, law, riding, skin,* and *whisk* were all borrowed into Old English. Old Scandinavian is our modern label for the language spoken by the Vikings. Dingwall is a direct borrowing into Scottish Gaelic of the Viking word *thingvöllr*, which means 'meeting field.' A *völlr* was actually a round stake, several of which were hammered into the ground to mark off the field in which Vikings convened to squabble and vote about matters political and judicial. They were sea raiders after all, and many of their first settlements were mere temporary camps. *Thing* meant assembly, and the same root is the origin of our common English word *thing*—an example of a shift common in the semantic history of individual words, namely, the development of a word's meaning from the particular to the extremely general.

We know the piratical Norsemen liked to hold meetings in temporarily staked fields because *thingvöllr* shows up as a place name all over the Viking marauding territory. Both the Orkney and Shetland Islands have villages named Tingwall. In Iceland shivers the little town of Thingvellir. All of them are named after fields where Vikings convened.

Icelandic emigrants to Saskatchewan named the town of Thingvilla 'place where the local council meets.'

On the Isle of Man in solemn conclave sits the Tynwald, the Manx legislative assembly that meets once a year to proclaim new laws. Founded by Vikings who invaded the Isle of Man, the Tynwald consists of a governor, a council, and an elected assembly called the House of Keys. Tynwald is the Manx version of the Old Scandinavian word *thingvöllr.* Manx is a Celtic language now obsolescent but still in use for a few ceremonial occasions. Manx is even the subject of a favourite grim joke of linguists that appears in writer Thomas Pynchon's 1963 novel *V* wherein the hero of the story attends the most boring party ever held on earth. Among the guests is the world's last living Manx monoglot "who consequently spoke to no one."

Just north of Cape Breton Highlands National Park lies the little Nova Scotia village of Dingwall. Scottish emigrants to our Maritimes brought the name to Cape Breton Island and other Gaelic-speaking settlements of Nova Scotia. They were remembering Dingwall, a town in the Scottish county of Ross and Cromarty, often also cited as the origin of the family name. But Scottish settlers named Dingwall had also come to the Maritimes. And evidence in ancient deeds and wills shows that Dingwall existed as a surname before the Scottish town was founded.

But how did a person come to have a surname like Dingwall? Well, someone who dwelt beside a field where Vikings once met could be called Angus of the dingwall, and eventually Angus Dingwall.

DION

Céline Dion 1968–

The popular Québec singer's hits include "If You Asked Me To" and her duet with Peabo Bryson "Beauty and the Beast," as well as "Love Can Move Mountains," and "Des mots qui sonnent." At the end of the nineties, she recorded one of her biggest hit singles and a truly phenomenal best-seller, "My Heart Will Go On," featured prominently as the love theme in James Cameron's megahit movie Titanic.

Hon. Stéphane Dion 1956–

He was a political science professor at the University of Montréal, appointed to Chrétien's cabinet in January 1996 as intergovernmental affairs minister to deal with national unity policies.

Dion as a French surname has two sources. The ancestor may have lived in one of the half-dozen ancient French towns with names like Dion, Dions, Les Dyons, Dionne: all of them from early French *divonus*, from the Celtic word for god **devos*. The Dionne quintuplets' surname has this origin, too.

Dion may also be a surname based on the ancient baptismal name *Dido, Didonis* —not from the name of Aeneas's gal pal, the Queen of Carthage, but rather a Latinized form of the Germanic name *Thiodo, Diod* 'people.' The loss of the intervocalic *d* in *Didonis* to produce *Dion* indicates the word was borrowed at a very early date into French.

DONKIN

Eric Donkin 1929–1999

The versatile actor was associated with the Stratford Shakespearean Festival for many delightful seasons and is especially cherished for his Koko in Brian Macdonald's The Mikado *(1982–1987), a role he performed more than five hundred times. His film and TV work included a television version of* Waiting for Godot.

Donkin is a variant of Duncan (common in Scotland) and Dunkin. All stem from *Dunecan*, from Old Irish *Donnchad* 'brown warrior.'

DOUGLAS

Thomas "Tommy" Clement Douglas 1904–1986

One of my heroes, Mr. Douglas was a Baptist minister who became a politician, a Prairies socialist who helped found the CCF, precursor of the NDP, an incisive debater who could be warm and funny, the father of Medicare and the Canada Pension Plan, and premier of Saskatchewan (1944–1961). He was a plain, kind Christian, from the turn-of-the-century social gospel tradition, who had examined in his head and in his heart what exactly such a label might require of a man who found himself in the midst of the twentieth century. What it required of Tommy Douglas was compassionate action, something in very scant supply among the born-again haters who throng today's temples of brick and infest as well the sleazy television temples of instant, sound-bite salvation.

Douglas is a Scottish Gaelic topographical name made up of *dubh* 'black' and *glas* 'blue, water, stream.' It is the name of a very old settlement in Lanarkshire. But all over the Celtic world it was a common river name, showing up in England as Dawlish, Dowles Brook, Divelish; in Wales as Dulas; in Ireland and Scotland as Douglas. Black water might mean water in a peat bog or in a silted brook. In the late sixteenth century Douglas was used as the Christian name of a girl or a boy. Today it is a common first name for boys, and of course still the proud boast of the Clan Douglas.

DRABINSKY

Garth Howard Drabinsky 1948–

Lawyer and one of Canada's greatest showbiz impresarios whose nineties company Livent Inc. brought large musicals to Canadians and Americans, including the highly successful revival of Kern and Hammerstein's Show Boat *and the long-running* Phantom of the Opera. *Drabinsky's fiefdom imploded spectacularly at the end of the century in a litigious nightmare of suits and countersuits. His exit in fact resembled the old burlesque skit, "Fire in a Whorehouse," in which everyone in the theatre company rushes on stage screaming and ripping off their clothes. But Mr. Drabinsky has the entrepreneur's elan and crescent touch and I for one hope he will rise again.*

Drabinsky is a Polish surname from *drabina* 'ladder' + *ski*, a patronymic suffix in Polish that means 'son of' or 'descendant of,' thus Drabinsky means 'descendant of an ancestor named Ladder,' either because he was a renowned carpenter or because he was tall. But this surname can also mean 'son of a rabbi' to Polish Jews. Compare Slavic-Jewish names like Rabin and Rabinovitch. Drabinsky is an example of how Jewish surnames could slip past anti-Semitic officials by being disguised slightly, for there were many times in the Jews' European history when they were forbidden to call themselves by their true Hebrew names.

DRAINIE

Bronwyn Deborah Ann Drainie 1945–

John Drainie's daughter is a journalist, CBC broadcaster, and frequent contributor to the Globe and Mail. *Her books include* Living the Part: John Drainie and the Dilemma of Canadian Stardom *(1988) and* My Jerusalem: Secular Adventures in the Holy City *(1994).*

John Robert Roy Drainie 1916–1966

A Vancouver-born player who taught himself to be Canada's greatest radio actor, familiar to CBC Radio listeners from 1938 on, until his untimely death, in roles like Jake on the CBC Radio serial of W.O. Mitchell's Jake and the Kid. *Drainie recreated Stephen Leacock, reading his humorous works on stage, radio, and television. Many listeners will remember him from dozens and dozens of leading roles on Andrew Allan's CBC Stage series (1944–1956). Every year at the Actra Award ceremonies he is remembered in the giving of the John Drainie Award for Distinguished Contribution to Broadcasting.*

Bronwyn is a Welsh given name for females that means 'white breast,' really of course white upper chest, a token of beauty in the Middle Ages when white skin insured that the possessor was from quality folks, not certainly a field hand or outdoor worker. Such peasant underlings would have breasts tanned and brown from the sun.

Drainie is from the Welsh word *draen* 'thorn.' An ancestor nicknamed Thorny might have dwelt near a thorn-patch or had a prickly personality. Or, a founding ancestral Drainie may have lived in a house identified by a device or drawing of a thorn, much as some British pubs might blazon their location as being 'at the sign of the Thorn.' This method of differentiating dwellings was more common than we today assume; because centuries and centuries of western history elapsed, before street names and numbers became widespread.

DUCEPPE

Jean Duceppe 1923–1991

The popular Québec actor and director, best known outside of the province for his role as the long-suffering merchant in Claude Jutra's film Mon Oncle Antoine, *starred in many Québec television dramas and feature films and has a theatre named in his honour at Montréal's Place Bonaventure. He was a militant separatist who passed his passion on to his son, Giles Duceppe, the leader of the Bloc Québécois since 1997.*

Duceppe is a French surname that means 'descendant of the jailer' where *cep*, *ceppe* was the wooden stake to which the iron chains that bound prisoners were attached. Its Latin root is *cippus* 'post, pillar, stake.'

DUDEK

Louis Dudek 1918–

The Montréal-born poet is a literary critic, anthologist, founding publisher of Contact Press and Delta, *a literary magazine. A long-time professor of English at McGill University, his works include* Atlantis *(1967),* Epigrams *(1975),* Cross-Section: Poems 1940–1980, *and* The Birth of Reason *(1994).*

Dudek is Polish for 'piper' and refers specifically to one little piper, the hoopoe, a gaudily crested European bird, salmon-pink in colour, whose characteristic call has earned it the delightfully plosive ornithological name of *Upupa epops.* The Polish surname may have originated as a Jewish nickname for an ancestor who was a gaudy dresser or a show-off. In Yiddish it would be *fifer* and it was not a compliment. A *fifer* might be literally 'a whistler, a piper,' but it also meant 'a loudmouth, a braggart.'

The *dudek* could have been the bird on a shop sign. But Dudek also suggests a Yiddish cradle name for males *Dudel* or *Dudl* from the German and Yiddish verb *dudeln* 'to tootle, to play a pipe, to strum a stringed instrument.' A *dudel* in Yiddish also means 'a baby's fart.' The title character bears the name in Mordecai Richler's great Montréal novel, *The Apprenticeship of Duddy Kravitz* (1959).

DUFFY

Michael Dennis Duffy 1946–

Born in Charlottetown, P.E.I., Mike is an Ottawa-based television reporter on national politics first for CBC-TV and now for CTV, once called "Marzipan Cheeks" in the pages of Maclean's *magazine by a now deeply repentant junior scribe named Bill Casselman.*

Duffy is Irish and Scottish Gaelic 'black man of peace' where the Gaelic *dubh* 'black, dark' refers to hair colour or complexion. The Irish is *Ó Dubhthaigh*.

DUMONT

Gabriel Dumont 1837–1906

The Métis leader was Riel's adjutant general during the 1885 Northwest Rebellion.

Mario "Super Mario" Dumont 1970–

From 1994 to 1996, he was the young, charismatic leader of the separatist Parti Action Démocratique du Québec. As the member from Rivière-du-Loup, he won re-election to the Assemblée nationale in 1998.

Dumont is among the one hundred most common French surnames, taken from dozens of instances as a house name in medieval France, indicating a dwelling on an elevation, literally 'of the mountain' but usually meaning 'on the hill.'

DUNCAN

Sarah Jeannette Duncan 1861–1922

Born in Brantford, Ontario, the pioneer newspaperwoman was in 1886 the first female employed full-time by the former Toronto Globe. *She lived in India and England for most of her married life, but wrote one insightful novel about small-town Ontario life,* The Imperialist *(1904).*

Duncan is Scottish and Irish Gaelic from Old Irish *Donnchadh* 'brown warrior' < *donn* brown + *cath* warrior. *Donn* is cognate with OE *dunn* 'swarthy, dark, brown' from which modern English gets the adjective *dun*. Ireland has another familiar form of this name in the surname Donoghue and MacDonagh. The name occurs in England and Scotland in the forms like Dunkin, Donkin, and Duncanson.

$$\mathcal{E}$$

EATON

Timothy Eaton 1834–1907

He was a Toronto merchant and founder of the T. Eaton Company. The most familiar name in department-store retailing to several generations of Canadians, the company was founded in 1869 and went bankrupt in 1999.

There are at least twenty-nine villages in England named Eaton or Eton. Bearers of this surname had ancestors who lived in one of the hamlets. Eaton has one of two sources descriptive of locality in Old English, either *ea* 'river' + *tun* 'farm, small village' or *eg* 'island' + *tun*. But note that the second, an island settlement, could also describe a farmstead only partially surrounded by water or marsh.

EDDY

Ezra Butler Eddy 1827–1906

He was a manufacturer of friction matches and other wood and paper products at Hull, Québec.

Eadwig was a common Anglo-Saxon warrior name of typically Germanic compound form whose elements are Old English *ead* 'happiness, riches, wealth' + *wig* 'battle, war.' By the time of Middle English, Eddy had become a widespread surname. A familiar female given name in English that contains the same first root is Edith < OE *Eadgyth* = *ead* 'riches' + *gyth* 'strife.'

EDENSHAW

Charlie Edenshaw 1839–1920

Born at Skidegate on Queen Charlotte Island, B.C., he was among the earliest professional Haida artisans who worked in local media such as argillite and wood and in media imported by collectors such as gold, silver, and ivory.

Edenshaw is a borrowed white name. His true Haida names were *Tahaygen* 'noise in the housepit' and *Nngkwigetklals* 'they gave ten potlatches for him.' The potlatch was an important ceremony of many Pacific Coast peoples in which gifts were exchanged, chieftains invested with power, names given, spirits propitiated, and dances performed. The word came into English from Chinook Jargon from the Nootka word *patshatl* 'a giving, a gift.' But white busybodies did not understand the complexity of the potlatch and how its sociological strands were woven tightly into band and clan life. Thus the Canadian federal government outlawed the full ceremony in its 1884 Potlatch Law. By the time the ban was repealed in 1951 during revision of the Indian Act, serious clan disruption had resulted, permanently skewing tribal identities, ranks, and statuses.

ENGEL

Howard Engel 1931–

CBC Radio producer, cartoonist, and novelist, he was born in St. Catharines. Howard has used small-town Ontario settings for his detective fiction featuring sleuth Benny Cooperman, among which are The Suicide Murders *(1980)* A Victim Must be Found *(1988),* Dead & Buried *(1990),* There Was an Old Woman *(1993), and without Benny Cooperman,* Murder in Montparnasse *(1992),* Lord High Executioner *(1996),* Mr. Doyle & Dr. Bell *(1997), and* A Child's Christmas in Scarborough *(1997). For CBC he wrote teleplays based on* The Suicide Murders *and* Murder Sees the Light.

Marion Engel, née Passmore 1933–1985

Novelist and short story writer, married and divorced from Howard Engel, she wrote powerful and insightful novels about the muddled lives of some midcentury Canadian women: No Clouds of Glory *(1968),* The Honeyman Festival *(1970),* Monodromos *(1974),* Bear *(1976),* The Glassy Sea *(1977), and* Lunatic Villas *(1981). Marion wrote two collections of short stories:* Inside the Easter Egg *(1975) and* The Tattooed Woman *(1985). In September of 1973, CBC Radio's* This Country in the Morning *commissioned a fictional radio diary from Marion Engel that I produced and directed as a solo reading by Toronto actress Ann Anglin. During the production I got to know and like Marion, and making the radio serial was a happy time for all of us. In 1975 she published it as* Joanne: The Last Days of a Modern Marriage.

Engel as a Jewish surname can date back to the sign names of the medieval Frankfurt ghetto where German *Engel* 'angel' indicated an ancestor who lived in a house that bore an identifying sign depicting an angel.

Engel, meaning angel, derives from the Greek word for messenger, *aggelos*, in this case, messenger of God.

As a Germanic surname Engel can stem from the name of an early Germanic tribe, the *Angeln*, whose homeland was the narrow angle of land that separates Denmark from continental Europe. Thence came the Angles who invaded Great Britain with the Saxons and the Jutes and gave their name to words like Anglo-Saxon, Anglia, England, and English—originally *anglisc* or *englisc*.

Passmore is Norman French *passe mer* 'cross the sea,' hence a sailor. After some time in England the name became associated by folk etymology with *mere* 'lake' and *more* 'moor' so that the sense of this locative surname was 'one who had to cross the lake or the moor to reach his dwelling.'

ENRIGHT

Michael Enright

Journalist and broadcaster, Michael Enright has written for the Globe and Mail, *been* Maclean's *magazine correspondent in China, director of CBC Radio news, and host of the public affairs program* As It Happens. *When Peter Gzowksi retired from morning radio in 1997, Michael Enright took over as host of* This Morning *and brought a breeze of urbanity to CBC morning programming. Michael's tactful skepticism anchors his interviews and leaves many a hidden-agenda-toting spinmeister or Ottawa gasbag deflated with the gentlest of pins.*

Enright is a back-formation from McEnright, an Irish surname that means, claims Basil Cottle in the *Penguin Dictionary of Surnames,* 'son of Unlawful or son of Attack.' Begorra! Thank goodness it isn't both, as in 'son of unlawful attack.' For that would posit a familial origin steeped in bastardy!

ETROG

Sorel Etrog 1933–

A world-renowned artist who has put his mark upon the earth with genius and delight, the Romanian-born sculptor has lived in Toronto since 1963. Along with monumental bronze and sheet metal works, he designed the statuettes formerly handed out at the Canadian Film Awards, which were called the Etrogs.

Etrog is a Jewish surname derived from *ethrog* which is the Hebrew name of the fruit of a Middle Eastern tree, the *hadar*. The fruit has ritual importance in *Sukkot* 'little booths,' the Jewish Feast of Tabernacles, a harvest festival. In that celebration, the etrog—sometimes translated citron, but note that it is not a lemon—makes up part of the festive *Sukkot* bouquet along with a date-palm branch, myrtle boughs, and willow branches. The surname originates as the occupation name of a fruit-seller, as a house sign name, or as a simple name of respect. For, in rabbinical symbolism, the etrog, which should be ripe and fragrant for use in *Sukkot*, may represent the pious heart, seat of emotions. The etrog symbolizes also a person of kindness, courtesy, and wisdom. As a playful *shtetl* nickname it was given to someone as short and stout as an etrog.

Sorel is one of several affectionate short forms of the formal Jewish male name, Israel 'he who struggles with God.' Such pet forms include Sorel, Srul, Sroel, Iser, and Issur.

F

FAFARD

Joseph Fafard 1942–

Born at Ste-Marthe-Rocanville, Saskatchewan, this sculptor now based in Regina worked in plaster and papier-mâché portraits of people, went on to ceramic humans and animals, and in 1985 to The Pasture: *seven bronze cows at the Toronto-Dominion Centre in Toronto. One of Fafard's typically impish works is* The Candidate *(1987), a sculpture of Jean Chrétien in shirt sleeves sitting on a kitchen chair.*

Fafard is a French surname based on adding a diminutive suffix -*ard* to the indigenous and onomatopoeic French root *faf* whose general sense is 'fluff, trifle, object of little value.' The root is seen in terms like *fafiot* 'small banknote,' *fafie* 'trifle' and French school slang like *faffeuerie* 'a little mistake in a lesson.' Why a forebear would be called 'a little trifle' and then choose to perpetuate the remark by selecting it as a surname is a mystery.

FAIRCLOUGH

Ellen Louks Fairclough 1905–

The chartered accountant and city councillor at her birthplace of Hamilton, Ontario, became Canada's first female cabinet minister in the 1957 Diefenbaker government, and sponsored an early bill demanding equal pay for equal work on behalf of women.

Fairclough, a common name in Lancashire, is simply fair *clough* Middle English 'dell, hollow.' The crest of a pretty ravine was the site of a founding ancestor's house.

FERGUSON

George Howard Ferguson 1870–1946
This Tory lawyer was Conservative premier of Ontario from 1923 to 1930.

Maynard Ferguson 1928–
The Verdun-born jazz trumpet player worked early in his career in Montréal clubs, then moved to work with American big bands like Jimmy Dorsey, Charlie Barnet, Stan Kenton, and from the late 1950s to the eighties, a series of his own bands.

Max Ferguson 1924–
Versatile and sly as a CBC Radio satirist, Max was first on Rawhide *(begun regionally in 1946) and then on* The Max Ferguson Show, Max in the Morning, *etc. In later years, making one of Canadian radio's wittiest duos, Max worked with a sidekick, the wry and wonderful CBC announcer Alan McFee.*

Ferguson means 'son of Fergus,' a compound of two Irish and Scottish Gaelic roots that mean 'man' and 'choice.' Choice man? Probably. Ferguson is among forty most common names in Scotland.

FERRERAS

Sal Ferreras
A British Columbia drummer of Puerto Rican ancestry, in 1995 he headed the Vancouver Folk Music festival.

Ferreras 'son of the blacksmith' is a Spanish occupational surname related to Spanish words like *ferrería* 'foundry, ironworks' and *férreo* 'ferrous, made of or containing iron' and *ferrocarril* 'railway,' literally 'iron road,' all derived from Latin *ferrum* 'iron.' Compare the English noun 'farrier.' Spanish surname variants include Ferrer. Initial Roman *f* sometimes became *h* in Spanish and so another group of Spanish surnames from the same Latin root includes Herrado, Herrador, Herrero 'blacksmith,' Herreras 'son of the blacksmith' and Hierros 'son of Iron.'

FINDLEY

Timothy Findley 1930–

As an actor he was a charter member of the Stratford Shakespearean Festival, and then from the publication of his first book The Last of the Crazy People *(1967) he gained international repute and sales as one of Canada's leading novelists whose works include* The Butterfly Plague *(1969),* The Wars *(1977),* Famous Last Words *(1981),* Not Wanted on the Voyage *(1984),* The Telling of Lies *(1986),* Headhunter *(1993),* The Piano Man's Daughter *(1995),* You Went Away *(1996), and* Pilgrim *(1999). His short-story collections include:* Dinner Along the Amazon *(1985),* Stones *(1988), and* Dust to Dust *(1997). He has also written theatrical plays like* The Stillborn Lover *(1993) and television scripts like* The Whiteoaks of Jalna *(1971–1972) and with his lifetime partner Bill Whitehead,* The National Dream *(1974).*

Findley is a variant of Finlay—with what is called in linguistics the insertion of an 'excrescent' *d*, that is, the letter added for reasons of supposed euphony. In fact *d* is added here to represent the vivid glottal stop between the *n* and the *l* in some Scottish pronunciations of the surname. Finlay is Gaelic *fionn lagh* 'fair-haired hero.'

FLEMING

Donald Methuen Fleming 1905–1986

The lawyer from Exeter, Ontario, was federal minister of finance from 1957 to 1962 during the government of John Diefenbaker.

Sir Sandford Fleming 1827–1915

He was a civil engineer, inventor, and the scientist who proposed as early as 1875 the system of Standard Time zones still in use.

Fleming is Old French *flamanc* 'person from Flanders.' Flemish weavers migrated to various parts of England just before and during the time that surnames began to become well established in the thirteenth and fourteenth centuries.

FOLEY

David Foley 1963–

The Canadian comedian and actor gained fame on CBC-TV as part of the comedy group The Kids in the Hall *and later as a star of NBC-TV's sitcom* Newsradio.

Foley is Folly or Folley with one *l* removed in an attempt to disguise the underlying French origin of the surname, namely *folie* 'madness, craziness.' The English surname also arises from various compound English place names whose second element is Folly. To make one up: Smith's Folly might be a house or field name for a property that was a financial or agricultural disaster for its original owner. Foley may also be an Irish warrior surname from a Gaelic form like Ó Foley 'descendant of Plunderer.'

FOLLOWS

Megan Porter Follows 1971–

The daughter of actors Ted Follows and Dawn Greenhalgh rose to fame early in her career starring in the CBC television serial of

Anne of Green Gables. *The versatile actress has played several seasons at the Stratford Shakespearean Festival, and starred in feature and television films like* Deep Sleep, Terminal Station, Back to Hannibal, *and* Inherit the Wind.

Follows is an alteration of Fallows from Old English *falu* 'pale brown' then, by its colour, land that is left unploughed for a season or two to increase its fertility, that is, fallow land. The naming ancestor dwelt near 'the fallows,' fallow fields. When fallow came to mean 'barren, not pregnant' and have other negative nuances, some forebears changed the spelling to Follows.

FORSEY

Eugene Alfred Forsey 1904–1991

A Rhodes Scholar educated at McGill and, of course, Oxford, he was an expert on the Canadian Constitution. As a Liberal Senator from 1970 to 1979 he was a witty and learned debater on Canadian public affairs.

Forsey is a variant of Fursey from the Old English field name *fyrs + (ge)hæg* 'furze fence.' The ancestor lived on or near a field enclosed by a living fence of spiny gorse bushes. Furze is a synonym for gorse. The botanical name is *Ulex europaeus* and this prickly legume still makes a deterrent hedge on the heaths.

FOWKE

Edith Margaret Fowke, née Fulton 1913–1996

She was a collector of Ontario folklore and folksongs, and a writer on Canadian folk music, as well as a teacher and longtime CBC Radio hostess whose books include Tales Told in Canada *(1986).*

Fowke is an Anglo-Norman form of the Old French *Fouques,* itself from Old German *fulco, folco* 'people.' Compare modern German *Volk* and English 'folk.'

FRASER

Blair Fraser 1909–1968

The journalist was Ottawa editor of Maclean's *(1943–1960), and then for two years its editor and finally its London correspondent with many appearances on CBC radio and television as political commentator.*

Brad Fraser 1959–

The Edmonton-born playwright's most popular drama is Unidentified Human Remains and the True Nature of Love *(1989). Denys Arcand directed a film version of it in 1994. Other plays include* The Ugly Man *(1992),* Outrageous *(1994), and* Poor Superman *(1994).*

Graham Fraser 1946–

Blair's son is also a journalist who has been Washington bureau chief for the Globe and Mail *and is the author of* Playing for Keeps: The Canadian Election of 1988 *(1989).*

John Anderson Fraser 1944–

A music and dance critic for the Toronto Telegram *and the* Globe and Mail, *he was also a foreign correspondent. Being China correspondent for the* Globe *gave him the background for his best-selling 1980 book* The Chinese: Portrait of a People. *From 1987 to 1994 he was editor of* Saturday Night *magazine. He is now master of Massey College at the University of Toronto and writes a weekly column for the* National Post.

Simon Fraser 1776–1862

The fur trader and explorer founded early settlements in what became British Columbia.

No plausible etymology of the surname Fraser has ever been put forward. The first person whose name is so spelled to be mentioned in Scottish records, Sir Simon Fraser (died 1306), is also named as Simond Frysel. If one wished to join the puzzled chorus, one might toss in this suggestion—although it has no textual support—of an origin in Old French *fraseur* 'one who hulls' in a kitchen, hence apprentice cook from *fraser* 'to shell beans.' Basil Cottle's nonsense about strawberries (French *fraises*) in the *Penguin Dictionary of Surnames* is the result of the rapid onset of acute polycottleglottosis or many-tongued British dictionary fever, an infection of the upper etymological tract, a malady that at times overcomes the best of onomasticians. It presents with symptoms that include not being able to close a dictionary and reshelf it, and the utter inability to type on the keyboard of one's word processor the words, "We don't know the origin of this surname."

FROBISHER

Sir Martin Frobisher 1539–1594

The explorer who discovered Frobisher Bay was knighted, not for digging up several tons of worthless ore on the shores of Warwick Sound, but for his marine gallantry against the Spanish Armada in 1588.

Frobisher from Old French *forbisseor* is a variant of furbisher and furber, a medieval occupational surname describing one who polished armour and burnished swords. Its Germanic root is probably related to German colour and dye words like *Färber*, *Ferber* 'dyer' and *Farbe* 'colour.' German and Yiddish *Ferber* meant not only dyer, but painter in general, while *furber* in Middle English was applied to a person whose job was general cleaning-up. The Italian verb *forbire* seems borrowed early from the same Germanic source.

FRUM

Barbara Frum, née Rosberg 1937–1992

She was an astute interviewer on CBC Radio's As It Happens *(1971–1981) and then on CBC-TV's* The Journal.

David Frum 1960–

The National Post's *controversial journalist of neoconservative hue is the son of Barbara and Murray Frum.*

Murray Frum 1931–

Dentist, real estate mogul, chairman of the Frum Development Group, vice-president of the Art Gallery of Ontario, he is also past president of the board of directors of the Stratford Festival.

Frum is a Jewish surname from the German adjective *fromm* 'pious' but standing probably for an ancestor named Avrom, short for Abraham. The *v* was pronounced *f* in some Yiddish dialects. The root was also part of pet names in Yiddish like Fruma Sarah 'pious Sarah.'

FRYE

Herman Northrop Frye 1912–1991

A professor of English at Victoria College and then chancellor of Victoria University, Dr. Frye was one of Canada's most internationally respected literary critics whose works include Fearful Symmetry *(1947),* Anatomy of Criticism *(1957), and* The Great Code *(1982).*

Frye is a common name in the southern counties of England. Its source is Old English *frig* 'free-born.'

Fulford

Robert Marshall Blount Fulford 1932–

A quick analyst of whatever the Zeitgeist proffers, he began as a brilliant liberal explicator of popular culture, then like so many middle-aged literati slowly turned to the neoconservative dark side and became "proudly elitist" (his words). Mr. Fulford has been a critic for the Toronto Star, *the* Globe and Mail, *editor of* Saturday Night *magazine, and radio and television host. Selections from his journalism have been published as books. His most captivating study is* Accidental City: The Transformation of Toronto *(1995). In 1999 Fulford published* The Triumph of Narrative: Storytelling in the Age of Mass Culture. *He is now a columnist at the* National Post.

Fulford is the name of four places in England all derived from Old English *ful* 'foul, dirty' + ford 'place in a stream or river where domestic animals and humans may cross.' Perhaps a foul ford is one that is not shallow, and therefore much silt and muck are stirred up each time the water is forded?

G

GABEREAU

Vicki Gabereau 1946–

The popular CBC Radio interviewer conducted her own network afternoon show from 1988 to 1997 and then began Gabereau, *her successful television program for CTV, still thriving in 2000.*

Gabereau is a part of a French surname group with many variant spellings: Gabareau, Gabarot, Gabreau, Gaboreau, Gabbarot, Gabarret. There are two different etymological sources. The Gabereau group with a single *b* are likely to derive from the early Norman verb *gaber* 'to make fun of, to joke about,' itself brought to northern France by the Vikings whose Old Scandinavian had *gabb* 'a joke.'

With the double *b* of Gabbarot we slip south to Gascony, a former French province in the foothills of the Pyrenees, where a word in the Gascon dialect is *gabarro* 'gorse, furze' making Gabbarot a locative surname arising from the fact that an ancestor's house was in a place full of gorse, a spiny shrub that abounds on the coastal heathlands of southern France.

Is the English *gab* 'chat, idle lip-flap' also a monosyllabic borrowing from *gabb,* the Old Scandinavian word for joke? I think so. Others say gab is a back-formation from gabble or related to an Irish Gaelic word for mouth *gob* as in "Shut yer gob, yuh dirty-faced bastard!" Gab's first appearance in print meaning 'idle chat' is in eighteenth-century Scotland where one thousand years earlier Scandinavian borrowing into Scottish Gaelic was extensive.

GAGLIARDI
Reverend Phillip Arthur "Flying Phil" Gagliardi 1913–1995
This colourful Kamloopsian—the correct designation for a resident of Kamloops, British Columbia—was minister of highways in Wacky Bennett's Social Credit government from 1952 to 1972. Gagliardi earned his nickname from his overuse of government airplanes—even to fly his family on vacations to Dallas. It also referred to his driving habits which caused the minister to be ticketed frequently by police. In 1988, at the age of 75, the ordained Pentecostal minister won a mayoralty race in Kamloops.

Gagliardi is an Italian surname 'descendant of the robust one' where *gagliardo* is an Italian adjective used as a nickname. The originally northern Italian word is not from Latin, but from a Celtic root **galia* 'strength, vigour.' Compare the similar French word *gaillard*. The root named a vigorous fifteenth-century dance in triple time, the galliard (Fr. *gaillarde*, Ital. *gagliarda*).

GALBRAITH
John Kenneth Galbraith 1908–
Born at Iona Station, Ontario, the economist and writer, professor of economics at Harvard, and liberal adviser to Democratic presidents

counts among his works The Affluent Society *(1958) and a child-hood memoir of southern Ontario,* The Scotch *(1964).*

Galbraith is Scottish Gaelic from Old Gaelic *Gall-Bhreathnach* 'stranger-Briton' where the term denoted a Welsh settler who had moved north into Scotland. What a pleasant, welcoming name for a newcomer!

GALT

Sir Alexander Tilloch Galt 1817–1893

He was a railway mogul and developer of coal fields near Lethbridge, Alberta, minister of finance in the first federal cabinet (1867), and first Canadian High Commissioner to London (1880–1883). As minister, Galt helped assure confederation by attending the Charlottetown, Québec, and London Conferences.

John Galt 1779–1839

He founded the town of Guelph. Galt, Ontario, now part of the city of Cambridge, was named after this Scottish novelist and promoter of immigration to Canada.

Galt is both an English and a Scottish surname. Middle English *galte, gaute, gault* 'boar, hog' was used as a nickname, either derisive or occupational for a swineherd or operator of a piggery. The root is Old Scandinavian *goltr* 'pig.' But some Scottish etymologists want to see it as a variant of Gall, Gaul, or Gaw, all from the Celtic word *gall* 'stranger,' which was used abusively to denote lowland immigrants to more northerly parts of Scotland.

GANONG

Gilbert White Ganong 1851–1917

He founded with his brother James Harvey Ganong the well-known candy company still in New Brunswick.

William Francis Ganong 1864–1941

This son of James Ganong became a professor of botany, historian, cartographer of New Brunswick's waterways, and collector of the province's folk ways.

Ganong stems from a Latinized form of a Germanic warrior name *Wano,Wanonis* 'one who waits' which contains Old High German *wân* 'a waiting' and may have been the nickname of an army officer who deployed delaying tactics. It recalls Quintus Fabius Maximus Verrucosus, the Roman consul who gained the Latin nickname *Cunctator* 'delayer' because of his defensive strategy of avoiding pitched battles with Hannibal's forces and thus saving Rome from one of Hannibal's invasion of her territory.

GARNEAU

François-Xavier Garneau 1809–1866

He was the most influential writer and historian of nineteenth-century Québec, whose major work was Histoire du Canada *(1845–1852).*

Hector de Saint-Denys Garneau 1912–1943

Called by some the first modern poet of Québec, he wrote two important works: the collected poetry, Regards et jeux dans l'espace *(1937) and the posthumous* Journal *(1954).*

Marc Garneau 1949–

With a doctorate in electrical engineering, he was the first Canadian astronaut in space (1984). In May 1996, he took part in a U.S. space-shuttle mission and played a key role in several Canadian experiments, including use of the Canadarm in satellite retrieval, all part of testing procedures involved in the eventual construction of an international space station.

Raymond Garneau 1935–

The economist and Liberal politician was Québec's minister of finance (1970–1976) and was elected federally in 1984 and retired from politics in 1988 to become president of a life insurance company.

Garneau is a pet form of Garnaud, itself from the compound Germanic warrior name *Warin-wald* 'protection-ruler' suggesting one who was a captain of the guard, but just as likely to be the typical pairing of Germanic name elements, where the elements sound impressive and do not need to make semantic sense.

GILMOUR

Clyde Gilmour 1912–1997

The popular film and music critic in 1996 celebrated forty years as host of CBC Radio's Gilmour's Albums, *the longest-running one-man show in Canadian radio history.*

David Gilmour 1949–

Novelist and former arts critic on CBC-TV's The Journal *and Newsworld's* Gilmour on the Arts. *Back on Tuesday (1986) and* How Boys See Girls *(1991) are deftly and delightfully written end-of-our-century novels of rueful male confession about failed marriages and botched love affairs.*

Gilmour in Scottish Gaelic is 'servant of Mary' where the Gaelic word *gille* 'servant' implies religious affection, so that the full meaning is 'devotee of the Virgin Mary' indicating an ancestor whose favourite saint was Mary. There is an entire class of Scottish Gaelic surnames that stem from such religious first names. Compare:

• Gilbride   'servant of Saint Bridget'
• Gilchrist   'servant of Christ'
• Gilfillan   'servant of Saint Fillan'
• Gilfoyle   'servant of Saint Paul'

- Gillanders 'servant of Saint Andrew'
- Gilmartin 'servant of Saint Martin'
- Gilmichael
- Gilpatrick

The *gille* root is reduced to a lonely *l* in McLean = Mac + Gille + Ian = 'son of the servant of Saintt John.' Note, however, the literal serving status of the ancestor indicated in names like Gill 'servant,' Gillespie 'servant of the bishop,' and Gilroy 'servant of the redhaired one.'

GLASSCO

John Glassco 1909–1981

He was a poet, translator, and autobiographer whose works include Complete Poems of Saint-Denys-Garneau *(1975) and* Memoirs of Montparnasse *(1970). These witty musings on the state of his own being during three years he spent during the 1920s in Paris are for me the best autobiography ever written by a Canadian.* Memoirs of Montparnasse *was first published in 1970, although written in 1932. A few years after its publication, I directed a dramatized reading of Glassco's memoirs with actor Colin Fox for CBC Radio's* This Country in the Morning. *Colin Fox was brilliant, both in editing the memoir for radio and then as an actor recreating Glassco's sophistication and intelligence. It is CBC Radio work I am most proud of. If you have never ridden Glassco's surf of foaming language, I urge you to it.*

Glassco is a respelling, Victorian or earlier, to disguise the too dowdy and plain Glasgow, indicating where the ancestor lived. Glasgow is a Gaelic place name that means 'grey-green hollow,' suggestive of its original site on the River Clyde. But Glasgow came to have unsavoury connotations for many Scottish people as a centre for crime and the ugliest poverty in Scotland, thus the impulse to change a surname like Glasgow could be powerful, especially in a family whose economic status was on the rise.

GOMEZ

Avelino Gomez 1928–1980

The fondly remembered Cuban-born Canadian jockey won 4,100 races in his career and earned his place in the Sports Hall of Fame. Gomez was a favourite athlete of many racetrack regulars.

Gomez is a typical Spanish surname with the patronymic terminal Spanish *ez* representing genitive *s* to give a meaning 'son or descendant of Gomo.' Gomo, a pet form of Gomesano, originated in the Spanish mountains of Burgos and Santander as Gome in the time of the Visigothic invasions of Spain. *Gome* seen in early records as *goma* stems from the Gothic word *guma* 'man,' so that Gomez means 'son of a complete or total man' with the implication of machismo. Gomez is now one of the most widely distributed Spanish surnames in the world.

Avelino is a Spanish given name from the name of an Italian Saint Andrea Avellino, himself named from Avellino, in the Italian region of Campania, which even in the days of ancient Rome was noted for the many hazelnut trees that grew there. Compare Italian *avellano* 'hazelnut tree' and the international botanical name of the hazelnut *Corylus avellana*.

GOTLIEB

Alan Ezra Gotlieb 1928–

The Rhodes scholar and lawyer has served in the Department of External Affairs, deputy minister posts, and as Canadian ambassador to Washington.

Phyllis Fay Gotlieb, née Bloom 1926–

She is a literary critic, poet, and internationally published science-fiction novelist whose works include Sunburst *(1964),* O Master Caliban *(1976), and* The Kingdom of Cats *(1985).*

Sondra Gotlieb, née Kaufman 1936–

A newspaper columnist and novelist whose humorous work often reflects her experience as the wife of diplomat and public servant Alan Gotlieb. She is the author of First Lady, Last Lady *(1981) and* Wife of. . . *(1985).*

Gotlieb is a variant of the German surname Gottlieb 'God love.' Ashkenazic Jews sometimes took the name as a translation-surname from the Hebrew given name of the father, Yedidyah 'beloved of God' (Biblical English: Jedidiah). 'Beloved of God' could also produce a surname translated into Slavic roots, one like Bogolub. Gottlieb was also sometimes shortened to Lieb, then later lengthened to produce surnames like Liebman, Lipman, and Lipkin. Patronymic forms include Lipis and Lipes.

GOULD

Glenn Herbert Gould 1932–1982

The most brilliant classical pianist Canada has so far produced gave up live performance in 1964 to concentrate on recordings and CBC Radio documentaries. Among his award-winning radio works was The Idea of North *in which words and natural sounds were blended with genius. Although his literary output was small, Gould was a genius, too, at wielding the English language. Read his articles and reviews.*

Gould is a variant spelling of Gold found as a British surname in the west Midlands and the southwest of England generally. As an English surname derived from an ancestor's nickname, Gold is simply 'blond, yellowhaired.' The Anglo-Saxons used it as a first name for boys and girls. Gould is also used as a spelling of the Jewish surname Gold which was not always occupational for a goldsmith, but, far more often, a matronymic meant to honour a mother with the Yiddish name Golda 'yellowhaired.'

GRAHAM

Florence Nightingale Graham, a.k.a. Elizabeth Arden
1878–1966

The Canadian-born cosmetics mogul changed her name to Elizabeth
Arden, selecting Elizabeth for its queenly resonance and borrowing
Arden from the eponymous hero of Tennyson's 1864 narrative poem,
Enoch Arden, *about unrequited love.*

Graham, a common Scottish surname, was brought to Scotland by
a Norman, William de Graham in AD 1127. Graham was a Norman
spelling of his natal town, Grantham, a place in Lincolnshire whose
name in Old English means 'village of an Anglo-Saxon named
*Granta.' This male personal name meant 'one who snarls or com-
plains.' Old English **grantaham* can also support a meaning like
'gravel farmstead.'

GWYN

Richard John Philip Jeremy Gwyn 1934–

This political journalist, the Toronto Star's *national affairs columnist,*
is a frequent guest as analyst on CBC-TV and TVO. Richard Gwyn,
as a writer on Canadian politics, is a refreshing analyst of compas-
sionate liberal-socialist bent who combines kick-ass insights into
rightwing foolerie with a style among the best in Canadian papers.

Gwyn is a Welsh surname from Old Welsh *gwyn* 'white.' Like
all the given and last names in world languages that stem from a
root meaning 'white,' it refers to relative fairness of hair or complexion, that is, the ancestor possessed fairer than normal hair or
skin for a particular small community. Gwyn is also a Welsh male
given name. The element is found in female given names like
Gwendolyn. Consider too King Arthur's wife, Guinevere, with its
Cornish version Jenifer. *Gwynedd* is the Welsh name for North
Wales used as a female given name Gwyneth.

H

HADDAD

Claire Haddad 1924–

The Toronto-based fashion designer of women's clothes was a founding member of the Fashion Designers' Association of Canada and was created a member of the Order of Canada in 1979.

Haddad is an Arabic surname from the occupation of the ancestor. *Haddad* in Arabic means 'blacksmith, ironmonger.' The verbal root is *hadd* 'hone,' so that the *haddad* is literally and originally 'one who sharpens' (knives and swords).

HAMILTON

Francis Alvin George Hamilton 1912–

He was a teacher who became a politician and leader of the PC Party in Saskatchewan from 1949. By 1957 he was idea man in Diefenbaker's cabinet, serving as minister of northern affairs.

Robert Hamilton 1753–1809

He was an Upper Canada land speculator and politician whose son George founded Hamilton, Ontario.

All the surnames, including the Scottish ones, derive ultimately from the town of Hamilton in Leicestershire. Old English **hamel* 'cut off, maimed' + *dun* 'hill.' Compare modern English 'dune' and 'down.' It aptly describes a hill that had its top sliced off by a retreating glacier.

HANDELMAN

Stephan Handelman 1948–

A journalist and writer on international affairs, his postings included chief European correspondent for the Toronto Star, *1981 until 1987.*

Handelman is a German-Yiddish surname formed to look like *Handelsmann* 'tradesman' but is actually a matronymic based on the mother's Hebrew name Hanna, which among Jews living in medieval Germany could become *Hannel* or *Handel*. Biblical Hannah, mother of the prophet Samuel, is a shortened version of *Hanani* 'God has favoured me.' In its Greek form, the familiar given name *Anna*, it gave birth to all the European and Slavic variants of Anna like Ann, Ännchen, Annette, Anja, Anya, Aña, Anita, Anushka, Nana, and Nanette.

Hanomansing
Ian Hanomansing
The popular CBC-TV news reporter and host, with the most mellifluous and dulcet voice among Canadian announcers, has been based in British Columbia, although he has covered new stories in Ottawa and many other parts of the country.

This sonorous surname originated in India. Hanuman is a Hindu demigod who appears on earth in the form of a sacred monkey. Hanuman leads a band of simians who help Rama, one of the forms of Vishnu the Preserver. As a personal given name and as a surname, Hanuman continues to be popular in India. It means literally in Sanskrit 'large-jawed' and is the nominative of the compound adjective *hanumant*. The common grey monkey of India, a slender, long-tailed langur, is called a hanuman and is held holy by Hindus.

During the sixteenth century, a group of followers of Hinduism splintered off from the main body of believers and became Sikhs, that is, disciples (Sanskrit, *sisya*) of Guru Nanak, a Punjabi holy man. Sikhs believed in one god and combined various tenets from Islam and Hinduism into a new religion. At puberty, when a Sikh boy joins the *khalsa* or inner circle of warriors, he is permitted to add Singh as the last element in his surname. This is the origin of the compound surname Hanuman Singh. As the family moves across the world to new lands, it unites into Hanomansing. *Singh* means 'lion' in Punjabi.

HANSEN

Rick Hansen 1957–

A wheelchair athlete, Hansen raised more than $20 million for spinal cord research with his Man in Motion tour (1985–1987) through more than thirty-four countries.

Hansen sports a typical Scandinavian patronymic suffix *-sen* 'son' and can be a Norwegian or Swedish surname meaning 'son of John.'

HARCOURT

Michael Harcourt 1943–

He was mayor of Vancouver, then NDP premier of British Columbia whose scandal-plagued administration caused him to step down in February 1996.

Harcourt, if of Norman-French origin, is a surname from the natal town of the ancestor. France has two little towns named Harcourt, in Calvados and in Eure. The *har* stems from early Germanic *hari-* 'army' and *court* 'large manor' or from Old French *hare* 'cry used to incite hunting dogs.'

There are two places in Shropshire named Harcourt, and Cottle says they mean 'falconer's cottage' and 'harper's cottage' or 'cottage where there was a salt harp.' A salt harp was used to sift salt.

HARNOY

Ofra Harnoy 1965–

Born in Israel, Canada's most internationally renowned cellist began her mastery of the instrument under her father Jacob's tutelage at the age of six just before the family immigrated to Canada in 1972. From the Royal Conservatory of Music in Toronto she has gone on to perform to great acclaim as soloist with most of the major orchestras and in solo recitals all over the world. Ms. Harnoy has recorded thirty-eight solo albums, and received many prizes including two of Canadian music's Juno Awards and other honours like the Order of Canada in 1995.

Harnoy originates as a Russian-Jewish surname. The Russian noun denoting the colour black may be transliterated as *chornoi*. Although the name in some instances was adopted freely by Jewish families during their dispersion through northern Europe, in many more cases the name is the result of anti-Semitic local laws that forced Jewish people to assume permanent family names in the language of the national authorities who ruled over them. In some Russian *shtetlach* (Yiddish 'little towns') this was accomplished by ordering Jewish residents to congregate in the town square while some functionary divided them—men, women, and children—into four groups differentiated by the hair colour or stature of the father: darkhaired, lighthaired, tall, and short. Then various Russian words for these attributes suffixed with Slavic patronymics became the legal surnames of these Jewish families. A darkhaired or dark-complexioned ancestor may lie behind such Slavic-Jewish surnames as Harnoy, Charnoy, Chorny, Charnin, Charnis, Chernoff, and Chernovsky. Fair-skinned ancestors might have been given surnames containing the Slavic root for white *byelo-*, names such as Belsky, Byelov, and Byelin. When such divisions for forced naming happened in Germany, the resulting Jewish last names were Schwartz 'dark' or 'black,' Weiss 'white' or 'lighthaired' or 'with pale skin,' Gross 'tall,' and Klein 'short.' This happened in other European countries as well. Consider some Hungarian Jews whose surname is Fekete, the Hungarian word for black or darkhaired. One proviso must be repeated: some families did get to choose their goyish sur-names. But many did not.

Ms. Harnoy's given name is the beautiful Hebrew Ofra, perhaps the feminine of *ofer*, the Hebrew word for fawn. Both male and female words for young deer are still popular today in Israel as first names. Curiously, Ofra appears in the Old Testament as a man's name (First Chronicles 4:14). This has led some scholars of Hebrew etymology to suggest that Ofra may derive instead from a different Semitic root and may mean 'she who turns her back.' I suggest that these meanings are simply the same radical in different reflexes, that is, that the root meaning of *ofer*, the Hebrew word for fawn, is 'creature that turns or shows its back.' What is more memorable about young fawns than their beautifully flecked backs, evolved by nature as camouflage?

HARRON

Donald Hugh Harron 1924–

Comic actor, writer, and creator/performer of Charlie Farquharson, the word-mangling rube of Parry Sound, Don Harron has performed on Broadway, in the West End, during the first three seasons of Canada's Stratford Shakespearean Festival, and on Canadian and American radio and television. He has published many books of Canadian humour, as well as the libretto for the longest-running Canadian stage musical Anne of Green Gables, *which has brightened the Charlottetown Festival every summer for thirty-five years.*

Mary Margaret Harron 1953–

Born in Bracebridge, Ontario, and educated at Oxford, the screenwriter and film director ruffled politically correct feathers in 2000 with the release of her satiric horror movie American Psycho, *based on the notorious 1991 novel by Bret Easton Ellis. She co-wrote and directed this stunning close-up of a modern, urban alpha male in whose mind lack of affect collides with greed to so deaden his senses that murder is all that reminds him he is alive. Both the bizarre but insightful novel and the film of* American Psycho *were roundly condemned—especially by sniffish philistines who had neither read nor seen them. No stranger to controversial themes, Harron had earlier directed the interesting 1996 biopic* I Shot Andy Warhol. *Mary is the daughter of Canadian humorist Don Harron and his first wife, Gloria (Fisher) Vizinczey. To the flabbergastment of some Don Harron fans, father thought daughter's* American Psycho *script was "very funny."*

Harron has two possible roots. It stems either from a nickname that's for the birds or from something fishy.

As a bird nickname, Harron, Herron, Hairon, or Heron began as an affectionate tag for an ancestral male who was thin and long-legged, like the wading bird, the heron. French also has last names for long-legged family founders that compare them to herons, for example, Héron, Hairon, and Airon. Norman-French surnames appear early after the conquest, recording the legal affairs of such persons as William Herun in 1212 and Roger Heirun in 1221. Hern is a thirteenth-century Middle English variant of the word *heron*.

As a surname that began as the occupational name of a fishmonger, one who sold herrings and other fishes, it appears as Harron, Herrin, Hering, or Herring. The same occupational name appears in Old French surnames like Haran and Harent, both of which mean seller of herrings (French *harengs*). So, too, do German surnames like Heering, Haering, and Hering. Among the French families who came to Britain after the Norman conquest in 1066 there are printed records of surnames such as Ralph Hareng (1166), Peter Harang (1210), Nigel Haring (1275). Then much later, during various wars between England and France—in some cases centuries later—*her-ring* surnames appear in official documents where the *g* has been elided in an attempt to disguise their French origin, and the names are written as Herrin and Harron.

HEALEY

Jeff Healey 1966–

He's a Toronto-based rock guitarist, composer, and singer.

Healey is a variant of Irish Gaelic *Ó Healy* 'descendant of Clever' or 'descendant of Claimant.' It is still among the one hundred most common names in Ireland.

HÉBERT

Anne Hébert 1916–2000

One of Québec's most influential novelists, also a poet and play-wright, she was the author of Kamouraska *(1970), filmed by Claude Jutra, and* Les Fous de Bassan *(1982), filmed by Yves Simoneau. Ms. Hébert was one of the great wordsmiths of Québec French. Her* mots justes *were French words that rang like precise bells on the ear and on the page. Her French had none of the flabby wobble of much of twentieth-century French fiction and expository prose. She was a superb editor of her own writings and was able, perhaps better than any other writer of her century, to flench off the blubbery excesses to which French is prone and so to produce a lean, fatless tendon of prose that flexed to permit thought and emotion to reside cleanly together in the same sentence, neither quality overwhelming the other.*

On her mother's side of the family, Madame Hébert is related to two famous figures in Québec literary history: nineteenth-century historian François-Xavier Garneau and the influential twentieth-century poet Hector Saint-Denys Garneau, her cousin and her friend.

When Saint-Denys Garneau died of a heart attack while canoeing alone on a lonely Québec river in 1943, it deeply affected Anne Hébert's life and her calling to literature. Her first novel was Les Chambres de bois *in 1958. Her influential volumes of poetry include* Les Songes en équilibre *(1942),* Le Tombeau des rois *(1953), and* Mystère de la parole *(1960). A collection of poetry,* Le jour n'a d'égal que la nuit, *appeared in 1993. Her other novels include* Héloïse *(1980) about ghostly vampires haunting the Paris subway system. Hébert lived in Paris for more than thirty years because, she said, "Montréal is too American; Québec City is too small; and Paris is very, very beautiful." Three years before her death doctors told her she had cancer, and Ms. Hébert returned to Québec City to live out her life at home. Among her later works were* L'Enfant chargé de songes *(1992),* Aurélien, Clara, Mademoiselle et l'officier anglais *(1995),* Est-ce que je te dérange? *(1998), and her last book,* Un habit de lumiére *(1999).*

Hébert is a variant of Herbert, a French surname based on an ancestor's given name, Old German *Hariberht*, made up of *harja* 'host' and *berhta* 'bright.' After the Norman Conquest, Herbert spread widely throughout Great Britain as a male given name.

HENRY

Frances Henry 1931–

An anthropologist at York University with a special interest in black studies, he is the author of The Caribbean Diaspora in Toronto: Learning to Live with Racism *(1995).*

Henry began as a Norman-French variant of the Old Germanic warrior name *Haimirich*, a compound of *haimi* 'house' and *ric* 'ruler.' In dozens of languages it has spawned thousands of surnames, a few of which are Fitzhenry, Harriman, Harrison, Hawkins, Heinrichs, Henderson, Hendriksen, Hendry, Herriot, Parry, and Perry.

HENSON

The Reverend Josiah Henson 1789–1883

An American-born slave who escaped to Canada in 1830 and founded the Black settlement at Dawn in Upper Canada. He was said to be the model for Harriet Beecher Stowe's hero in Uncle Tom's Cabin *(1852).*

Henson is an English surname, a patronymic based on the Middle English given name *Hendy* 'courteous, kind.' This adjective, *hendy,* illustrates vowel gradation as it occurs across various English dialects. *Hendy,* meaning kind, is originally 'handy,' that is, literally giving people one's hands in gestures of assistance.

HENSTRIDGE

Natasha Henstridge 1975–

Born in Springfield, Newfoundland, she grew up in Fort McMurray, Alberta. The beautiful young actress starred in the horror film Species *(1995) and in a later sequel, as well as other films.*

Henstridge is the name of a town in Somerset, in Old English *Hengest-hrycg* 'stallion-ridge' either because stallions were kept on the ridge or because it belonged to an Anglo-Saxon with the then common male given name *Hengest* 'stallion, stud-horse.'

HEPPNER

Ben Heppner 1956-

Born in Murrayville, British Columbia, the Canadian operatic tenor has risen to international prominence singing the major tenor roles in Wagner and Strauss.

Heppner is a German and Flemish surname that means 'person from Heppen' which is a town in Belgium, itself named after a founder with the Germanic male given name *Heppo* related to Old High German **helfan* 'help.' Thus Heppo was a helper.

HERRNDORF

Peter Herrndorf 1940–

He is an efficient and innovative mover and shaker in the adminis-trative realms of Canadian culture. As a CBC-TV executive he helped start The Journal, *sat on the board of governors of the Stratford Shakespearean Festival, was publisher of* Toronto Life *magazine, then head honcho at TVO, Ontario's educational television author-ity, and now is the chief executive at The National Arts Centre in Ottawa.*

Herrndorf as a European village name is an example of folk ety-mology where the German *Herrendorf* 'village of men' stands for a much earlier *Harindorf* 'army town' or *Erindorf* 'town of a per-son named *Eri* 'honour.'

HEWITT

Angela Mary Hewitt 1958–

She received a Bachelor of Music degree from the University of Ottawa at the age of eighteen and in 1985 took first prize at the International Bach Competition in Toronto. The Ottawa-born pianist who now lives in London, England, returns frequently to Canada to perform the classical and modern piano repertoire, especially her prime interest, the music of Bach. Ms. Hewitt has made five record-ings of the Bach oeuvre including a 1997 Hyperion recording of the Six Partitas. In 1998 her CD of Messiaen piano pieces was released to critical acclaim.

Foster Hewitt 1902–1985

The fons et origo *of hockey broadcasting, Mr. Hewitt spoke one of the first play-by-play descriptions of a hockey game using an upright telephone as a radio microphone on March 22, 1923. Foster did the first game from Maple Leaf Gardens in 1931, raising an already high voice to an excited scream of "He shoots! He scores!" and borrowing from Italian the word* gondola *to name his broadcast booth high over the ice. In the 1950s Hewitt easily made the transition to televised hockey commentary. Through the CBC's broadcasting of* Hockey Night in Canada, *he is indelibly linked with Saturday at home in the minds of several generations of Canadians.*

In 1969 my first job in Toronto at CBC Radio on Jarvis Street required me to disembark at the College Street subway and then walk along Maitland Street behind Maple Leaf Gardens and so enter the CBC Radio building from its back door. One brisky and snappy day early in November soon after I began my first CBC assignment, I was trotting along Maitland when out of the Gardens came a red-faced little figure bundled up in a very expensive winter coat. My jaw dropped. It was Foster Hewitt! Now I have never asked anyone for an autograph in my life. I don't faint when movie stars are discovered nibbling shrimp at the next table. But I did grow up listening and watching Foster Hewitt. I greeted him and told him how much a part of my childhood and of our family Saturday nights he had been and still was. He was in person a shy and modest man. But he took the time to chat amiably with a fan, asked me what in particular I was doing at the CBC, and spent some ten minutes with me telling with some relish a few CBC anecdotes not for general publication. I may have encouraged this, as I began our conversation by relating several tales-out-of-school myself. Afterward, as I walked on to work, I finally felt "big city" for the first time since moving to Toronto. I was a kid from the boonies and now I had truly arrived in the city. That night I phoned home and told my dad I'd met Foster Hewitt. "Try to keep your head now, Bill," Dad said.

Hewitt is a very old English surname that originated in the county of Kent. Last names—as we discovered in the introduction to this book—arise from four basic sources: the first names of ancestors, the places ancestors lived, the nicknames of ancestors, and their occupations. Hewitt belongs to the class of English surnames that originated as the name of the place where the founding ancestor lived.

At Hewitts in Chelsfield and at Hewitts in Willesborough (Kent) lived a family named de la Hewatte whose first appearance in printed records occurs in the year 1270. Nearby occur records for de la Hewett (1301) and atte Hewete (1338). Note that the variation in spelling was great until English orthography was standardized through the widespread use of dictionaries at the end of the seventeenth century. The Old English word *hiewett* 'place hewed' or 'cutting' referred to a farmstead or acreage where trees had been cut down, that is, a clearing.

Individuals had one name to begin with. As population density increased, with the rise of towns and villages, a method was needed to differentiate clearly between two or more persons both with the same single name. For example, a village might have two persons named John. In the parish register of births and deaths, one might be a John whose father's name was Robert. He would be entered as John, son of Robert, and eventually his patronymic surname would be John Robertson. Another John might dwell at a clearing in the woods, at a *hewitt* in Old English, a place prominent and known to all local folk. He might be first styled John at the hewitt; and soon his name was shortened to John Hewitt and became hereditary.

HIRSCH

John Stephen Hirsch 1930–1989

A brilliant theatre director, he was a founder of the Manitoba Theatre Centre in Winnipeg, director and artistic director at the Stratford Shakespearean Festival, and head of drama at CBC-TV.

As Jewish migrants during the diaspora spread up the Rhine Valley into medieval Germany, they often were forced to adopt Germanic names. There they also created their own Germanic dialect, which became known as Yiddish. After settling, some Jewish merchants took last names based on the signs on their shops. Hirsch is such a surname. It's German for 'deer.' The founder of the name may have had the painting of a deer above the door of his shop or place of business. Among the most famous Jewish surnames to originate in this manner is that of the banking family, Rothschild. *Rot + Schild* meant the founding ancestor could be found 'at the sign of the *red shield*.'

Such a deer sign meant that the owner's true first name in Hebrew was Naphtali. Certain Biblical names like Naphtali had symbols associated with them. This symbol was called a *kinnui*. For example, in the Bible, Jacob blesses Naphtali and calls him "a swift-footed deer." Thus deer becomes the *kinnui* of the male personal name Naphtali. So it was often used to represent any Naphtali. In Biblical Hebrew, Naphtali means 'one who struggles for something.'

As so often happened in their history, Jews were forced to assimilate by adopting non-Jewish names. Thus a Naphtali might become Hirsch, as a first name to begin, as a surname later.

All the following Jewish first names and surnames arise from the Naphtali-*kinnui*-Hirsch nexus: Herschenhorn and Hirschhorn (deer antler), Hersch, Herschel, Herz, Herzog, Hirschfeld, the French Cerf, and the Slavic Jellinek, Jellin, and Yellin. Herz and Herzog arose from dialect pronunciations.

HNATYSHYN

Raymond "Ray" John Hnatyshyn 1934–

Lawyer and Progressive Conservative politician, he has held various PC cabinet posts including minister of justice, and was governor-general of Canada.

Hnatyshyn is Ukrainian, a variant of *Hnatyshak* 'descendant of Hnat, Ihnat, or Ignatius,' the first name derived from one of the saints named Ignatius (see *Ignatieff* entry). There is also a folk etymology that the name is related to the Ukrainian verbal stem *hnatesh* 'pursue, chase.' This is spurious.

HORN

Kahn-Tineta Horn 1940–

This member of the Mohawk Wolf Clan of Kahnawake, Québec, has been a fashion model, political activist, and civil servant, promoting the causes of aboriginal peoples outside and inside the federal Department of Indian Affairs.

Kahn-Tineta is a Mohawk name that means 'she makes the grass wave' implying she goes like the wind and is speedy. Horn is a borrowed English surname or a translation. Grass is important in aboriginal myth, and sweetgrass *(Hierochloe odorata)* is the chief ceremonial herb.

HOWE

Clarence Decatur Howe 1886–1960

An engineer, he built grain elevators across Canada and the world, then entered politics to become the great Liberal power-broker of the thirties and forties. As minister of transport for Mackenzie King in 1936 he created what became Air Canada. During World War II as minister of munitions and supply he turned Canada into an efficient producer of war materials, and then he helped the economy after the war return rapidly to free enterprise and expansion.

Gordon Howe 1928–

He was one of our finest athletes and hockey players during thirty-two record-breaking seasons.

Joseph Howe 1804–1873

The fiery reform journalist and politician was premier and lieutenant-governor of Nova Scotia and always a great defender and proponent of his province.

Howe as a surname and place-name element common all over northern England has a variety of origins. Sometimes the ancestor lived near a hill or tumulus, an ancient burial mound, and this is Old Scandinavian *haugr* 'mound.' In other instances it is Old English *hoh* 'heel, projecting spur of a hill, steep ridge' also indicative of the location of an ancestor's dwelling. An orthographical kaleidoscope of formal variation sees Heugh, Hoe, Hoo, Hoof, Houf, Hough, How, Howe, Howes, Huff, Hughf, and even Hughff !

HURTIG

Mel Hurtig 1932–

Edmonton-based founder of Hurtig Publishers and creator of The Canadian Encyclopedia, *he is a fervent nationalist whose passion for his country has taken many forms including trying to start a new political party. He is the author of the best-selling* The Betrayal of Canada *(1991),* At Twilight in the Country: Memoirs of a Canadian Nationalist *(1996), and in 1999 a study of poverty and homelessness in Canada. Mel Hurtig is an ornament to his country, and a living rebuke to those right wingers who say that one cannot be a good man of business and a compassionate patriot at the same time. Would that some of our greedier entrepreneurs could take a page or two from Hurtig's diary.*

Hurtig is a German surname based on the nickname of an ancestor. The adjective *hurtig* means 'quick, speedy, agile, nimble.' However, it is likely that the founding ancestor bore the single Hebrew name of Naphtali, and that Hurtig was a translation and *kinnui* for Naphtali.

Certain Biblical names like Naphtali had symbols associated with them. This symbol was called a *kinnui*. For example, in the Torah, Jacob blesses his son Naphtali and calls him "a swift-footed deer." Thus 'deer' or 'swift' becomes a *kinnui* of the male personal name, Naphtali. So it was often used to represent any Naphtali. Thus a Naphtali among German-speaking peoples might become a Hurtig (quick) or a Hirsch (deer), as a first name to begin, as a surname later. In Biblical Hebrew, Naphtali means 'one who struggles for something.'

HUTT

William Ian deWitt Hutt 1920–

One of Canada's leading actors, associated with the Stratford Festival from its founding in leading Shakespearean roles and all of the modern canon as well, Hutt has starred on Broadway in Albee's Tiny Alice *(1964), and appeared memorably as John A. Macdonald in CBC-TV's* The National Dream *(1975) and in the film of Timothy Findley's* The Wars *(1984). Timothy Findley wrote a play specifically for William Hutt and Martha Henry and they appeared in* The Stillborn Lover *(1993) to great acclaim.*

Hutt is a dialectical variant in Buckinghamshire, Lancashire, and Leicestershire ofHudd, a pet form of the male given name Hugh. Hutt may also be a severe vowel shortening in speech of one of the many Norman-French diminutives of Hugh such as Hewet, Hewit, Huitt, or Huot, all meaning 'Little Hugh.'

HYLAND

Frances Hyland 1928–

One of the treasures among Canadian actors, she has played Stella in A Streetcar Named Desire, *acted with Gielgud in* The Winter's Tale, *and was invited to our Stratford Festival by Tyrone Guthrie in*

1954 where her many memorable performances include an out-standing Ophelia opposite Christopher Plummer. Television, radio, and film work have kept this officer of the Order of Canada busy. In 1994 she received the Governor-General's Award for the performing arts. Among the plays she has directed are Othello *at Stratford in 1977 and* Driving Miss Daisy *at the Neptune in Halifax in 1991.*

Hyland is a surname based on the ancestor's place of residence, being either High Land or, more probably, a dialectal pronunciation of Hayland, Old English *heg-land* 'hay-land.'

HYSLOP

Jeff Hyslop 1951–

Singer, dancer, choreographer, theatre director, he is perhaps best known to Canadian audiences for the title role in many performances of Andrew Lloyd Webber's Phantom of the Opera. *Other roles were in such musicals as* A Chorus Line, Godspell, The Fantasticks, *and* The Pirates of Penzance *(CBC-TV). Younger television viewers know him as Jeff the Mannequin on the series* Today's Special. *As director and choreographer, he's staged* Peter Pan, Irma La Douce, *and many revues.*

Hyslop is one of many variants (Haslop, Haslup, Heaslip, Heslop, Hislop) of the Old English *hæsel-hop* 'hazeltree-valley' describing one who lived in such a vale.

𝓘

IGNATIEFF

George Ignatieff 1913–1989

A Canadian diplomat who served as Canada's United Nations ambassador, he was president of the Security Council in the 1960s. Later he was chancellor of the University of Toronto (1980–1986).

Michael Ignatieff 1947–

The writer and historian has written such books as The Needs of Strangers *(1984),* The Russian Album *(1987),* Asya *(1990),* Scar Tissue *(1993),* Blood and Belonging: Journeying into the New Nationalism *(1993),* The Warrior's Honour: Ethnic War and the Modern Conscience *(1998), and also in 1998 a biography of the Oxford philosopher and historian of ideas, Sir Isaiah Berlin.*

Ignatieff is a Russian patronymic surname whose literal meaning is 'son of or descendant of Ignatius.' The Russian Orthodox Church approved of the first Jesuit, Saint Ignatius of Loyola (1491–1556), founder of the Society of Jesus. Ignatia, Ignatz, and variants were given names at certain times in Russian history. But also Ignatius was a popular Latin name for saints—at least four Christian worthies were so dubbed—doubtless because of the name's meaning in street Latin: *ignatus = in* 'not' + *natus, gnatus* 'born.' However, the literal meaning of the elements must be added to, since the adjective did not mean 'not born' but 'low-born, of humble birth.' And so when *Ignatius* came to be a male given name in postclassical Latin, its humility made it an apt one for early Christians. There was also a Roman family name, a variant of Ignatius, Egnatius.

Saint Ignatius of Loyola took his name from an apostolic church father, Ignatius, bishop of Antioch who wrote seven letters to various Christian communities around AD 125 that give us useful portraits of Christian life in the years immediately after the age of the apostles. Ignatius is shown in Koine Greek as *Ignatios*. A far-fetched but intriguing suggestion is that one orthographical variant of the Greek version of the name, *Iknatos*, might be a much later Greek borrowing of the ancient Egyptian king's name Ikhnaton (1375–1358 BC), the XVIII Dynasty ruler who introduced monotheism into a polytheistic muddle of deities with his worship—exclusively—of Aten, the Egyptian sun-god. Ikhnaton or Akhenaten means 'Aten is pleased' or 'he who serves the Aten' in ancient Egyptian. Ignatius itself has contributed to last names in dozens of tongues.

IMLACH

George "Punch" Imlach 1918–1987

Joining the Toronto Maple Leaf organization in 1958 after a low-lustre career with the Québec Aces, Punch went on to coach the Leafs when they were NHL champions in 1962, 1963, 1964, and 1967. It was said his specialty was that of a taskmaster who could squeeze hockey talent from aging players.

Imlach is a German surname indicative of where a forebear lived, namely, *im Lach* 'at or near the lake.' There is a subgroup of such phrasal surnames in German. *Imlach* is similar to *Imbach* 'near the stream,' *Imburg* 'at the fortified town,' *Imholz* 'in or near the woods,' and *Imhaus* 'in the house' with the implication that the ancestor was a live-in servant.

INNIS

Harold Adams Innis 1894–1952

At the University of Toronto he taught political economy and what today we might call communications theory, applying it in new modes in his ground-breaking books The Fur Trade in Canada *(1930),* The Cod Fisheries *(1940), and* Empire and Communications *(1950), all of which influenced Canadian scholars, including Marshall McLuhan.*

Innis indicates a Scottish ancestor's residence. Scottish Gaelic *Innis* 'island' is the name of a specific place in Scotland. Variants of the surname include Ennis. The Gaelic element appears widely (Innisfree, Inniskillen) in the place names of Britain and Ireland. Compare modern Irish *inis* 'island' and modern Welsh *ynys* 'island.'

J

JELINEK

Maria Jelinek 1942–

The Czechoslovakia-born figure skater with her brother Otto won the world figure-skating championship in 1962, then turned professional. Another brother Henry wrote a book about this remarkable family entitled On Thin Ice *(1965). Her father owned a cork manufacturing business in Bronte, Ontario, and her brother Frank, a sports equipment plant.*

Otto Jelinek 1940–

A champion figure skater, and successful politician elected to the House of Commons first in 1974 and again in 1979, 1980, 1984, and 1988, the Conservative MP held many federal portfolios in his long career.

Jelinek is a Czech surname meaning 'descendant of a man nicknamed *Jelen*, 'deer,' usually because of quick-footedness. How apt a surname. It may also refer to an ancestor who was a deerhunter. The same Slavic root for deer appears in Polish *jelen* and Russian *olyen* to give surnames like Jelinski, Olyenov, Olin, and Olinsky.

JONES

_____ Jones

This entry concerning one of the most widespread surnames in English is for everyone named Jones.

Jones has been the commonest surname in Wales for more than a hundred years, and so it is mildly surprising that it is ultimately Hebrew, not Welsh. Some true Welsh personal names like Morgan, Owen, and Meredith did become early established as last names in Wales, but true surnames were rejected by Welshmen until they were imposed on Wales by Henry VIII, and then the surnames adopted were usually Norman in origin, giving Welsh last names like Hughes, Williams, and Jones. The true ancient Welsh form of a man's name looked like this example: *Ioan Ap Gryffyd Ap Jorweth Ap Madog* and so on. It means: John, son of Griffith, son of Jorweth, son of Madog. And there were Welsh speakers in this century who could list their male ancestors back centuries with long lists of male names connected with *ap* 'son of.'

Jones derives from one of the Welsh forms of the personal name John: Ioan. That spelling reflects the Welsh and the medieval English pronunciation of the Biblical name John, which sounded exactly like the way we today say 'Joan.' The earliest Welsh forms for John were Ieuan or Evan, but Ioan was chosen when the Welsh Authorized Version of the Bible was first printed, hence the vast popularity of Jones as a surname. John is Hebrew, from *Johanan* which means 'God has favoured,' implying that God has favoured the parents by giving them a child. Made popular by John the Baptist, it is the most widespread personal name in the Christian world, with versions found in more than one hundred languages. The *s* in Jones makes it a patronymic, so that it's literal meaning is 'son of John.' And so Jones has a noble history that takes us back to ancient Hebrew.

JUTRA

Claude Jutra 1930–1986

Montréal-born film director of Mon Oncle Antoine *(1971), the best Canadian feature film so far about life in a small company town, and, before his suicide in the throes of Alzheimer's disease, direc-tor of several superb TV features including* Dreamspeaker *(1977) and* The Wordsmith *(1979).*

Jutra is a French surname based on an ancestor's nickname. *Jut* is a popular contraction of the male given name *Just, Juste* from the very common Roman Christian name *Justus* 'just man.' Among the diminutive forms of *Jut* from which Jutra might be derived are Jutard and Juttard, both of which also produced French surnames. A much remoter possibility is a contraction of the nickname-surname *Jottereau* 'little *jote*' where *jote* is 'cabbage, beet, vegetable.'

$\mathcal{K}$

KIDDER

Margot Kidder 1948–

The Yellowknife-born actress in films and television gained fame as Lois Lane in Superman *(1978) and* Superman II *(1981). She starred in Canadian director Don Shebib's* Heartaches *(1981) and in many made-for-TV movies and feature films since.*

Kidder may be occupational from Middle English *kidde* 'bundle of twigs,' hence 'wood-seller, faggot-seller.' It can also be *kidder* 'goatherd.'

KILLAM

Thomas Killam 1802–1868

A rich shipowner and merchant of Yarmouth, he became the first MP for Yarmouth County in 1867.

Izaak Walton Killam 1885–1955

Named after the English author of The Compleat Angler, *the Yarmouth-born financier became one of Nova Scotia's richest men, with networks of holdings in paper, publishing, utilities, and construction. His wife left multimillion-dollar bequests to many universities and hospitals (e.g., the Izaak Killam Hospital for Children in Halifax) and the estate inheritance tax of $50 million helped begin funding of the Canada Council.*

Killam stems from the ancestral residence in one of three English towns named Kilham, all from an Old English dative of location *cylnum* 'at the kilns.' At such large ovens and furnaces, bricks were baked, pottery was fired, grain and hops were dried, and lime was calcined.

KOFFMAN

Morris "Moe" Koffman 1928–

Master of jazz saxophone and flute in widely popular modes on many commercial recordings, Moe is also a composer of instrumental hits (his biggest: "Swinging Shepherd Blues" in 1957). His own jazz bands and combos have delighted Canadians, particularly Torontonians. His sax is one of the mellow assets of Rob McConnell's Boss Brass.

Koffman is an occupational surname, a variant of the German and Yiddish *kaufmann* 'merchant, shopkeeper.' Some of the many variants include Kauffmann, Kaufler, Koffler, Koifler, and Kuffman.

KRALL

Diana Krall 1964–

In 1999, this Canadian jazz pianist and vocalist recorded one of the best-selling Canadian jazz CDs of all time. Under the CD title When I Look in Your Eyes, *Ms. Krall and her trio, with some silvery and soulful strings courtesy of Johnny Mandel, brought new life to old standards like "Let's Fall In Love," "Do It Again," and "I'll String Along With You." Ms. Krall won a Grammy for her jazz performance on that CD, and it was nominated for best album. In Canada she won a Juno for best jazz album. Her earlier CDs include* Love Scenes, *also replete with sweetly swung classics. Ms. Krall continues to tour in Canada and abroad.*

Krall is a Sorbian surname from Lusatia in the northwest of Germany. Lusatia is a small German province between the Oder and the Elbe rivers. Sorbian is a Slavic language in which *kral* means 'king.' Compare the Czech word for king, *král*, and the Polish *król*. The reflex of this Slavic root appears in Russian as *korol*. The name first appears in print as Crol in 1369, then as Kral in AD 1374. Merely for the purposes of onomastic comparison, consider too a great Canadian football player from the first half of the twentieth century, the Toronto's Argonauts mighty triple-threat player, Joe Krol. He could run; he could pass; he could kick. His nickname? "The King."

Sorbian is a living language with some 100,000 speakers today and two very distinct dialects, although some linguists would say that Lower Sorbian and Upper Sorbian are separate languages because of the vocabularic and phrasal differences. The Sorbian surname Krall was early borrowed into German, usually as *Krahl* and is widespread throughout Germany and Europe with that spelling.

Does the surname mean that a founding ancestor was a king? Almost never! But, of the perhaps one dozen different origins, all are connected with the regal meaning of the word. *Kral* or king begins in many a family record as the nickname of the founding ancestor. He might have been called, let's say, Ivan Kral (John the King) because he swaggered like a king or displayed some other regal bearing in his person. He might be Ivan of the *kral*, because he was a servant in a royal household. In medieval times, even someone who played a king in a pageant or play might be a *kral* or king. At certain holidays, especially the medieval Feast of Fools, a King of Misrule was elected from among the townsfolk in many parts of northern Europe including places where Slavic-speaking peoples lived. This Ivan too might be called *kral* thereafter. A jousting tournament also had an official called a king. Ivan, *kral* of the joust, might proudly bear this nickname for the rest of his life and then see his descendants adopt it and turn it into an inheritable surname. Sorbian parents are also recorded in legal documents as having christened a male child with an additional or byname of *Kral*, in hopes that he might attain royal qualities later in life.

Finally, let us return to the north German plain and Lusatia, land of Sorbian speakers. They call themselves *Serbja* and, yes, that's the same word the Serbians of the former Yugoslavia use. Perhaps these two peoples, the Sorbians and Serbians, were once branches of one ancient Slavonic tribe, one branch settling in Lusatia, the other pushing southward to what would be Yugoslavia (literally 'south-slav-land'). Another older name for Sorbian is Wendish. These Wends or Sorbs have left permanent marks on the map of Germany. Near Lusatia is the great German city of Leipzig, whose parks and fairgrounds have filled with trade fairs for seven or eight hundred years. Leipzig is just a German attempt at the city's original name, Lipsk, which is Slavic for 'place of the *lipa*,' that is, lime or linden tree. A few kilometres away is bombed old Dresden, also wearing a German version of its original Slavic name, *Drezdzane* 'boggy woods people' aptly named for the impassable marshlands encountered by early Slavic settlers. Russian *t* becomes *d* in some southern Slavic languages, so we can compare *drezdzane* with *tryasyenye* 'boggy' in Russian.

KRIEGHOFF

Cornelius David Krieghoff 1815–1872

The Dutch-born but German genre painter of nineteenth-century scenes in rural Québec left a valuable historical record of daily life, even if he romanticized the lively, everyday incidents. Still his detractors opine that his Canadian canvases illustrate only a sticky, heavy-handed Germanic kitsch.

Krieghoff is a locative German surname which signifies that the ancestor lived near a parade square where troops mustered and drilled. The *Krieghof* 'war-courtyard' was a feature of many larger towns in German-speaking Europe. Compare the *Paradeplatz* in Zürich, Switzerland.

KURELEK

William (Wasyl) Kurelek 1927–1977

A visionary Roman Catholic idealist, he painted the modern Canadian prairies and our country as a paradise that had slipped from our grasp because of moral lapse. His illustrations for W.O. Mitchell's Who Has Seen the Wind *(1976, 1991) and his own children's books are masterpieces of charged folk art.*

Kurelek is a Ukrainian occupational surname possibly meaning 'descendant of the censer,' the thurifer or incense-bearer in the Russian Orthodox Church. Compare the general Slavic and Russian root *kurel* 'smoke.'

L

LAMARSH

Julia "Judy" Verlyn LaMarsh 1924–1980

Lawyer, politician, broadcaster, writer, she was Liberal Member of Parliament for Niagara Falls from 1960 to 1968 and an important member of Lester Pearson's cabinet, helping to introduce the Canada Pension Plan and Medicare. In 1967 she headed Canada's centennial festivities, and the next year published Memoirs of a Bird in a Gilded Cage.

LaMarsh can be a locative surname from Lamarsh, a village still in Essex listed in the Domesday Book for AD 1086 as *Lamers,* and so from Old English *lam* 'loam' + *mersc* 'marsh.' Or, if Norman

French, it's from Lamarche, the name of three localities in France which were on or near an Old High German *marca* 'frontier, border.'

LANG

k.d. (Katherine Dawn) lang 1961–

Born in Consort, Alberta, the popular singer of awesome range and beautiful voice has recorded such albums and CDs as A Truly Western Experience *(1984),* Angel with a Lariat *(1986),* Shadowland *(1988),* Absolute Torch and Twang *(1992),* Ingenue *(1992),* Even Cowgirls Get the Blues *(1993),* All You Can Eat *(1995), and* Drag *(1997).*

Lang is a German adjective for 'long.' It was a common medieval German nickname for tall, thin persons. It is also a Scottish surname with variants like Laing.

LAUMANN

Silken Laumann 1964–

The champion Canadian rower won a gold medal in single sculls at the 1987 Pan-American Games, a 1991 world championship at Vienna, a bronze medal at Barcelona in 1992, and another World Cup in single sculls in Switzerland in 1991 and 1994.

Laumann is a German locative surname, a variant of Lohmann, which means 'one whose house is in the woods.' It is thus semantically related to German surnames like Imlau and Imloh 'in the woods.'

Silken may be the English adjective, but it echoes a Low German and Frisian given name for females, *Silke*, a very popular pet form of Celia or Cecilia.

LAURENCE

Margaret Laurence, née Jean Margaret Wemyss 1926–1987

She was one of Canada's most talented and compassionate novelists whose masterworks include The Stone Angel *(1964),* A Jest of

God *(1966),* The Fire-Dwellers *(1969), and* The Diviners *(1974).* Other interesting early works include The Tomorrow-Tamer *(1963),* The Prophet's Camel Bell *and* This Side Jordan *(1960). Margaret Laurence's protagonists were immensely important to a whole generation of Canadian female readers.*

Wemyss is the name of two places in Scotland, one in the former Scottish county of Fife, the other in Ayrshire. The word is Scottish Gaelic for 'caves' with the addition of a supernumerary English possessive or plural marker, *s.*

Laurence and its many variants (Lawrence, Lauritz, Lavrens, St. Lawrence River, etc.) in all the languages of the West owes its ubiquity to the popularity of five saints who bore the name Laurentius 'from the town of Laurentum' named because it abounded in bay trees (Latin *laurus*). A triumphant crown of fragrant bay leaves is a laurel. A versifier crowned with such a token of honour is a poet laureate.

The most notable of the holy men who bore this name was St. Lawrence the Deacon who was martyred in Rome in AD 258. A Roman administrator demanded that St. Lawrence surrender all the valuables in his church. He gathered the poor and the sick in front of the Roman bureaucrat and said, "Here is the church's treasure." The Roman official did not appreciate even the broadest irony, and ordered that St. Lawrence be roasted to death on a gridiron. He was extremely popular among medieval Christian paupers and is one of the saints mentioned in the canon of the Roman Catholic mass. There are 237 churches dedicated to St. Lawrence in England alone. Laurence was a popular name in Ireland also from the days of St. Laurence O'Toole, Archbishop of Dublin (1130–1180). Among the many international surnames that stem from the saint's name are De Laurentiis, Larkin, Larry, Laurenceau, Laurent, Lavrens, Lawrie, Lawson, Lorençon, Lorent, Lorenzi, and Lowrie.

LEACOCK

Stephen Leacock 1869–1944

From 1915 to 1950 he was Canada's best-known writer (more than sixty books) and one of the best writers of humorous essays in the English-speaking world. He wrote Elements of Political Science *in 1906 and it became an early standard college textbook. His funny books are still funny—even when their sometimes politically incorrect biases are acknowledged—and they include* Nonsense Novels *(1911),* Sunshine Sketches of a Little Town *(1912), his comic masterpiece* Arcadian Adventures with the Idle Rich *(1914),* Winnowed Wisdom *(1926),* Short Circuits *(1928), and his posthumous and uncompleted autobiography* The Boy I Left Behind Me *(1946).*

Leacock, a variant of Laycock, is a surname based on the location of an ancestor's home. Either of two English villages, Lacock in Wiltshire or Laycock in Yorkshire, gave rise to the surname. Both are Old English **lacuc* 'small stream' compounded of OE *lagu* 'pool, marsh, lake, creek' + *uc* a diminutive suffix. The OE root is akin to Latin *lacus* and Gaelic *loch* as in Loch Ness. The Germanic root, slightly modified, shows up in OE *leax* 'salmon' and German *Lachs* 'salmon.' The German word earlier travelled through the dialect filter of Yiddish to give *laks* 'salmon' and thence bagels and *lox* 'smoked salmon.'

LÉVESQUE

René Lévesque 1922–1987

A compelling television commentator in the mid-fifties, he went on to help found the separatist Parti Québécois *in 1968 and won power in 1976, staying on as premier of Québec until 1985.*

Lévesque is a variant of *L'évêque* French 'the bishop.' This meant the ancestor worked for a bishop or in his household. Old French *évesque* stems from ecclesiastical Latin *episcopus*, a Roman transliteration of the Koine Greek *episkopos* 'over-seer' which was the term for religious superintendent or bishop among early Greek-speaking Christians. Even the word *bishop* derives from the same Greek word, after a series of alterations: Old English *bisceop* > Middle English *bischop* > modern English *bishop*.

LIGHTFOOT

Gordon Meredith Lightfoot 1939–
One of Canada's most successful folksingers and composers, he wrote, among many others, the hit songs "Early Morning Rain," "For Lovin' You," and "If You Could Read My Mind."

Lightfoot—refreshingly in English onomastic study where modern spellings disguise the meaning of so many surnames—is just what it looks like: the ancestor was agile, nimble, and quick-of-foot. Similar phrasal nicknames produced these English surnames: Lightbody, Lightburn ('nimble child' but also as a locative 'bright stream'), Lightfellow, and Lightlad.

Lingenfelter

Hon. Dwain Matthew Lingenfelter 1949–
First elected to the Saskatchewan legislature in 1978, this grain farmer from Shaunavon has held many senior provincial portfolios including minister of Crown Investments Corporation, minister of social services, and in 2000, minister of agriculture. Mr. Lingenfelter has been deputy premier of the province and Opposition and Government house leader. He was in the national news during 1999 and 2000 calling for federal aid to Saskatchewan farmers to the tune of one billion dollars.

Lingenfelter as a German surname is a dialectic, phonetic variant of Lindenfelder, that is, 'person from a place called Lindenfeld,' in turn meaning 'field enclosed by linden trees.' It does not have to refer to a town or village. Lindenfelder may also signify that the founding ancestor of the family owned land or fields (German *felder*) whose prominent feature was a grove of linden or lime trees.

LOMBARDO

Gaetano "Guy" Alberto Lombardo 1902–1977

He was born in London, Ontario. His dance band, the Royal Canadians, played "the sweetest music this side of heaven" and sold 300 million records over fifty years. Lombardo's New Year's Eve radio and television broadcasts became a North American tradition for more than forty years. For many, the new year had not dawned until they heard Guy Lombardo and His Royal Canadians playing "Auld Lang Syne" at the stroke of a frosty midnight.

Lombardo as a surname arises from the Italian adjective that tags an ancestor from Lombardy. But the story does not end there, for it has roots that sink deep into European history. Lombardy, or *Lombardia*, is one of *le regioni dell'Italia*, a region like Calabria or Puglia. This central northern region of the republic has as its hub the busy, industrial city of Milan. Lombardy is the origin of one of the most common words in English, *lumber* (see below).

The Lombards were a Germanic tribe living in northwest Germany by the first century of this era. They skirmished with the imperial legions of Rome from time to time, but were usually peaceful, successful farmers. The Roman historian Tacitus mentions them and calls them Langobardi.

The German roots of their name are *lang* 'long' and *Barte* 'axe.' The Langobardi then had a properly ferocious Germanic clan name "men of the long axe." Ancient word studies suggest the less frightening Germanic root *Bart* 'beard.' So they might be The Long Beards. And, instead of axes, they carried sickles? Like Father Time? I don't think so. And neither does modern etymology. There is no written evidence whatsoever that they called themselves *Langbarden* 'long-beards,' though you will see this supposititious flapdoodle in some continental dictionaries.

Population growth and pressure from the barbarian Huns forced the Langobardi to migrate during the fourth century into most of what is now Austria. And then they crossed the Alps and invaded northern Italy. By 572 they held every major city north of the Po.

The Kingdom of Lombardy lasted for more than two hundred years, and its power extended over much of Italy, including for a time, Rome. In southern Italy they were *langobardi* or *longo-bardi.* The word survives today as a Sicilian surname, *Longobardo*. But in the north the first element of their name was modified and they were *lombardi*.

Eventually Lombard greed for new territory forced Pope Adrian I to form an alliance with the king of the Franks. In 774, Charlemagne smashed their armies and became king of Lombardy. The middle ages saw the region as a hornet's nest of quarrelsome city states. Then Spain ruled for almost two hundred years followed by a century of Austrian dominance. France had a fling from 1796 to 1814. And finally *Lombardia* became a part of Italy in 1859.

In the middle ages, the Lombards were great bankers. From about 1400, immigrants from Lombardy spread through Europe as money-changers and bankers. In London, England, they set up money-changing shops, pawnshops, and banks, and gave their name to Lombard Street in central London, which is still the chief avenue of large British banking firms. Lombard became an English word for any merchant or banker.

Since the early 1800s there has been a common saying in British betting slang to indicate long odds, that is, a sure thing. To the question, "What are the odds, mate?" the reply was "Lombard Street to a China orange." Lombard Street was solid real estate. It would always be there in London. On the other hand, an orange imported from China and still edible was a rarity and an uncertainty. A China orange might be a breakable one made of porcelain.

Then in Middle English "lombard" changed to "lumber." Even Lombard Street, though the spelling remained, may have been pronounced differently. In 1668, the great British diarist Samuel Pepys writes Lumber Street for Lombard Street. Many current dictionaries do not support my derivation of 'lumber'—but the iffy derivations they offer are not supported by me!

For 150 years in English a lumber was a pawnshop, a place for used goods. Lumber also came to mean the goods themselves, goods no longer useful to the owner, or items he had to pawn for financial reasons. For that meaning, compare this couplet, from that great master of the English satirical couplet, Alexander Pope, in his *Essay on Criticism* of 1711:

> "The bookful blockhead, ignorantly read,
>   With loads of learned lumber in his head."

The lumber room in a British house is still a spare room filled with unused wooden furniture and household junk. Then British colonists who immigrated to America began to use the word to mean unfinished planks, cut timber, and pieces of wood in general. And soon the medieval Italian word *lombardo* was wearing full Yankee dress as a lumberjack!

Lombardy, as the place of origin of many Italian families, gives its name to several locative surnames. Among them are:

• Bardello
• Bardi
• Lombardelli
• Lombardi
• Lombardini
• Lombardino

• Lombardo
• Longobardo

In Sicilian dialect, a *lombardo* is a shopkeeper, because, at various times in history, small merchants from Lombardy migrated south, and set up shops in Sicily. In Genoa, which was a rival of its neighbour many times in Italian history, a *lombardo* is a stupid person.

Americans remember the fighting football coach, Vince Lombardi (1913–1970), who took the soggy Green Bay Packers and shaped them into a gridiron squad who bulldozed their way to five NFL championships. Under head coach Lombardi they also won the first two Super Bowl games.

Art lovers know Pietro Lombardi, great sculptor and architect of fifteenth-century Venice. He and his sons, Tullio and Antonio, planned and built Santa Maria dei Miracoli, a splendid Venetian Renaissance church. Pietro sculpted Dante's funeral monument at Ravenna in 1482, and later completed his masterpiece, the Zanetti tomb in Treviso cathedral.

The nineteenth-century German art critic Friedrich von Schelling said, "Architecture is frozen music." Lombard builders have been making sweet music for centuries.

M

Note: The Gaelic names in Mac- and Mc- are in this listing placed first under the letter *M.*

McARTHUR

Kim McArthur 1953–

Born in Brantford, Ontario, this Canadian publishing executive began her publishing career at McGraw Hill and Methuen before starting Little, Brown Canada in 1987. After Little, Brown Canada was closed in May of 1998 by Time Warner, Kim founded her own publishing enterprise, McArthur & Company. Many of the Canadian and international authors she had nurtured for the American company came with her happily to this new venture, and under her Canadian aegis they have flourished together.

Kim's part of the McArthur clan hails from the Scottish island of Islay, southernmost of the Inner Hebrides, and probably the place where whisky was first made in Scotland. Islay a was stronghold of the Lord of the Isles and is home of fine malt whiskies like peaty Laphroaig, named after a place on the south coast of Islay, and smoky, exquisite Lagavulin. Charles MacLean in his *Pocket Guide to Scotch Whisky* writes, "Laphroaig is an old tar, a salty dog, among whiskies—not a drink for the faint-hearted, but its mighty flavour is unique." Famous blends like Islay Mist began here too.

The family name in Scottish Gaelic is *Mac Artair* and means 'son or descendant of Arthur.' The first record of the surname in Scottish documents is in a register from the year 1569 where we see listed a gentleman with the musical name of Gyllemechall M'Carthair.

Whoever the founding *Artair* was, he was likely named after King Arthur, a possibly legendary Celtic king of sixth-century Britain about whom the sweet tales of Camelot were told. The etymology of the name *Arthur* is disputed. Recorded history offers no firm evidence. But we do have hints. First and importantly, the spelling with *th* does not appear until late in the sixteenth century, and so is nothing but a bored scribe's filigree. The first mention of King Arthur is as Artorius, possibly a Latinized version of a true Celtic name, Artos, which meant 'bear.' For fifteen hundred years before surnames became fixed around 1600, members of bear clans took the name of their totem animal as their personal name. People did this from northern Russia to Persia, from Ireland all the way east to India. So a Celtic king named Bear, that is, King Artos, is not in the least unusual in Indo-European naming history. The Celtic word *artos* is cognate with the Greek word for bear, *arctos*. Both languages belong to the larger Indo-European language family. Our arctic regions were so called because they lie under the most conspicuous constellation of the northern hemisphere, one that Canadians usually call the Big Dipper, also known as the Plough, Charles' Wain, the Great Bear, Ursa Major to the Romans, and *Arctos* 'The Bear' to early Greek astronomers. Our adjective and noun, *arctic,* derives from the Greek adjective *arktikos* 'pertaining to the earth under or the sky around The Great Bear constellation.'

McClung
Nellie Letitia McClung, née Mooney 1873–1951
The Canadian pioneer for women's economic rights wrote sixteen books including an early Canadian best-seller Sowing Seeds in Danny *(1908). She raised five children, campaigned as a suffragist across Canada, was a Liberal MLA for Edmonton from 1921 to 1926, sat on the first CBC board of governors, and was a delegate to the League of Nations in 1938.*

McClung is Gaelic *mac* 'son of, descendant of' + *long* 'ship, boat' where Ship was the nickname of a fisherman or sailor.

MacDonald
Brian Macdonald 1928–
An inventive choreographer and director of musicals, he was a founding member of the National Ballet of Canada, worked with Hair *composer Galt McDermott on the pioneering 1957 satirical revue* My Fur Lady, *staged at McGill University and then toured*

across Canada. He has created dance works for ballet, directed TV, opera, and stage productions, notably a series of Gilbert and Sullivan operettas at Stratford, one of which, his Mikado, *enjoyed a long run on Broadway.*

Flora Isabel MacDonald 1926–

She began as PC Party secretary, ran successfully as MP for Kingston and the Islands and held ministerial portfolios in the Clark and Mulroney governments.

Sir John Alexander Macdonald 1815–1891

Lawyer, businessman, and nation builder, he was the first prime minister of Canada.

Macdonald is Gaelic 'son of Donald' and Donald is ultimately the Gaelic *Dhómhnuill*, a compound warrior name from Proto-Gaelic **dubno* 'world' and **valos* 'mighty.' It is among the ten most common surnames in Scotland.

MACEWEN

Gwendolyn MacEwen 1941–1987

She was a versatile writer of poetry, fiction, short stories, and a wonderful travel volume Mermaids and Ikons: A Greek Summer *(1978). Her poetry collections include* A Breakfast for Barbarians *(1966),* The Shadow-Maker *(1969), and* Afterworlds *(1987).*

MacEwen is Gaelic 'son of Ewen.' Ewen is a very early borrowing into several Gaelic languages of the Greek saint's name Eugenios. In Gaelic it gives Ewen, in Welsh Owen. Many minor saints bore the name; the most famous was Saint Eugenius of Carthage (died AD 505). The Greek adjective *eugenios* 'well-born, noble' also produces the given name Eugene and the sometimes abused science of eugenics.

MacIsaac

Ashley Dwayne MacIsaac 1975–

Growing up in Inverness county on Cape Breton Island, he was step-dancing and playing the fiddle before he was nine. The agile Maritime folk and rock fiddler and composer (first CD, Close to the Floor*) combines many musical traditions in a breezy style that delights all ages and won him among other plaudits the 1996 Juno Awards for best new solo artist and for best roots and traditional solo CD* Hi How Are You Today? *In 1996 the sequel CD was* Fine Thank You Very Much. *He also seems to have mastered the art of gaining publicity by means of controversial statements and outlandish behaviour.*

MacIsaac is Gaelic 'Isaac's son.' The surname also shows up with the Scots variant MacKissack, and, contracted, as the Manx surname Kissock. In Genesis, Isaac is the son of the patriarch Abraham and his wife Sarah. When she hears the birth of Isaac foretold, Sarah laughs. This story is an example of Biblical folk etymology, explaining to readers and hearers of the Torah the meaning of her son's name. The Hebrew verbal root in the name is indeed *tsehook* 'laugh' but the Biblical form of the name itself, which might be transliterated *yitzchaq*, translates as 'May He (God) laugh, smile, or look with favour upon (this child).'

McKenna

Frank Joseph McKenna 1948–

The New Brunswick Liberal lawyer won every seat in the province in his 1987 clobbering of Richard Hatfield. McKenna kept his campaign promise to quit as premier of New Brunswick after he had been in office for ten years, and he did so in 1997.

McKenna is originally Irish Gaelic *MacCionaodha* 'son of Cionaodh,' with the possible meaning of 'loved one.'

Maclean or McLean

John Angus MacLean 1914-2000

For twenty-eight years, MP for Queen's County, he won victory in 1979 and was premier of Prince Edward Island until 1981.

John Bayne Maclean 1862–1950

The magazine publisher created Maclean's *and Maclean-Hunter.*

John Duncan MacLean 1873–1948

The politician was premier of British Columbia in 1927–1928.

James Stanley McLean 1876–1954

He created Canada Packers Ltd. in 1927 and ran it until 1954.

Robert "Bob" McLean 1933–

Windsor-born Canadian talk show host and broadcaster with a long and varied career in Canadian radio and television and, briefly, in the United States where he replaced Tom Snyder at Philadelphia's KWY-TV. Bob hosted radio talk shows at CKBB in Barrie, CKO in Vancouver and Toronto, and CKXM in Edmonton. He was host of The Bob McLean Show *and* McLean at Large *on CBC-TV, riding the network noon hour for eight years. He then hosted* McLean & Company *at CKCO-TV in Kitchener, Ontario, for many years. His wife, Willa, has produced his shows for the last twelve years. Bob and Willa McLean have been good friends to Canadian books and their authors, having interviewed every ink-stained wretch who ever stumbled into a television studio clutching his or her latest volume, and that includes your humble deponent.*

MacLean as a Gaelic surname combines Mac + Gille + Ian to mean 'son of the servant of John.' All that remains of the *gille* root is the el. The most famous gillie in history was probably a personal servant of

Queen Victoria who, after the death of Prince Albert, accompanied the grieving queen on so many occasions that scandal-mongering whisperers suggested the old queen might indeed be amused and perhaps aroused by the presence of the handsome, burly Scot. But let us abandon that coarse rumour, leaving it to echo down the imposing corridors of Windsor and Balmoral. Gillie could also mean 'devotee,' one devoted to a saint. So it is probable that the originating MacLean ancestor was the son of an early Christian who held pious regard for St. John the Baptist. Ian or Eoin or Iain are Gaelic variants for John.

MCLUHAN

Herbert Marshall McLuhan 1911–1980

One of the pertest minds to ever saunter into the groves of Canadian academe, McLuhan taught us that the form in which information is delivered deeply affects our perception and interpretation of it. The medium, McLuhan argued, rather determines than transmits meanings (messages). The popular slogan "the medium is the message" marks an extension of this basic principle. His seminal, still vibrant books are: The Mechanical Bride *(1951),* The Gutenberg Galaxy *(1962),* Understanding Media *(1964),* The Medium Is the Message *(1967), and* From Cliché to Archetype *(1970).*

McLuhan is an alternative Anglo-Irish spelling of MacLoon. Early members of the family changed their surname because they didn't like the loony look of it. McLuhan is a Galloway name, in Irish *Mac Giolla Éoin* 'son of the servant of (St.) John' and thus a semantic variant of MacLean.

MCNAB

Archibald McNab 1781–1860

A felonious scalawag, crooked as a dog's hind leg, the seventeenth chief of Clan Macnab fled to Upper Canada in 1822 to evade debts owed in Scotland. Groups of MacNabs had already emigrated to Canada and more came after their chief arrived, lured by his promise of a new life in McNab Township (1824) on the Madawaska River in what became northern Ontario. McNab cheated his own kin, hauled them into court for protracted and vexatious litigation brimming with abuse of process, and, driven by soul-rotting greed, the dour crook might have left them to die penniless in the snowbanks, had they not been Scottish. After trying for fifteen years to end his depredations, the settlers of McNab Township petitioned the Upper Canada council for his removal and they won finally. Archie fled again, this time to Hamilton, Ontario, where he spent a decade attempting other scams amd failing at them too. McNab died in disgrace and exile in France, leaving two bastard children.

The Scottish Gaelic surname McNab or MacNab or Macnab means 'son of the abbot.' Concerning the etymology of MacNab, two questions arise. How does that *n* get in front of the *ab* in MacNab? That's because the Gaelic form of the name was *mac an aba* 'son of the abbot.' Second query: How could celibate abbots have offspring and thus found families? Unlike most other Catholic abbacies, those held by Celtic abbots were lay positions and the office was hereditary. In Glendochart, the MacNab homeland in Perthshire, Scotland, stood a great monastery where the first chiefs of the clan were lay abbots. Some Scottish families with the name Abbott are actually disgruntled MacNabs who, at several points in the long, troubled history of the clan, grew so angry at clan leaders that they changed their names, and translated MacNab back into English as Abbott!

MACNEIL, MCNEIL
Rita MacNeil 1944–
The popular singer from Big Pond, Nova Scotia (pop. 175), beginning in 1995–1996 hosted Rita & Friends, *her own musical variety*

show on CBC-TV. She has received the Order of Canada and many Juno and Canadian Country Music Awards. Among her best-selling albums are Flying on Your Own *(1987),* Reason to Believe *(1988),* Now the Bell Rings *(1988),* Home I'll Be *(1990),* Porch Songs *(1995), and* Music of a Thousand Nights *(1997).*

Bill McNeil 1924–

Cape Breton Island's gift to CBC Radio, Bill was a Glace Bay miner when he finally won an audition as announcer at CBI in 1950. His long and generally happy career included years of hosting Assignment *and the Ontario regional program* Fresh Air *until the early nineties.*

MacNeil is Scottish Gaelic 'son of Neal.' But Neal as a given name for more than one thousand years has had a whirligig circumnavigation of northwestern Europe that might have made Erik the Red himself too pooped to pillage. It began as Old Irish *Níall*, an affectionate diminutive of *niadh* 'champion.' The early Viking raiders of Ireland carried the name to Iceland where it shows up in *Njálssaga*, the title of the best Icelandic family saga, called also *The Saga of Burnt Njál*, probably compiled late in the thirteenth century. The invading Norsemen introduced the given name into Norman French as Nel or Nele where it produces later French and Flemish surnames like Neelen, Neilz, Nel, Nélat, Nelet, Nelis, Nelles, Nellon, Nesle, Nieloux, Niles, and Nille. These names are not *all* pet forms of Cornelius, as Marie-Thérèse Morlet states in her usually brilliant *Dictionnaire étymologique des noms de famille* (1991). Even the Italian surname Nelli comes from this root. But that is not the terminus of Neil's travels, not by a long oar. Among Latin-writing Norman scribes who re-introduced Neil to the British Isles, the name, when recorded in official documents, was turned into Latin *Nigellus*, because their folk etymology thought of it incorrectly as a diminutive of the Latin adjective *niger* 'black.' That spelling produced the given name Nigel. English surnames from the root include Neal, Nelles, Nelson, and Nielson. In the Scandinavian languages one sees forms like Nielsen, Nielsholm, and Nilquist. The modern Irish version is still Niall.

Magnussen

Karen Diane Magnussen 1952–

The Vancouver-born athlete won many figure-skating and free-skating championships, including Olympic medals and the world championship in 1973.

Magnussen is Scandinavian 'son of, descendant of Magnus.' *Magnus* is the Latin adjective for 'big, great' and has been a popular given name in Norway and Denmark for almost one thousand years, ever since Magnus I was king of Norway and Denmark (died AD 1047). The king's father, St. Olaf, admired Charlemagne whose Latin name was Carolus Magnus 'Charles the Great.' St. Olaf may have found the name there.

Maillet

Antonine Maillet 1929–

Born in Buctouche, New Brunswick, the foremost Acadian playwright and novelist counts among her masterworks La Sagouine *(1971),* Pélagie-la-Charrette *(1979),* Le Huitième Jour *(1986), and* Évangéline Deusse, *her new play that debuted in 1996, reuniting a Maillet script and the great Québec actress Viola Léger who first created La Sagouine, Maillet's famous Acadian washerwoman.*

Maillet is a pet diminutive form of Maille, a French surname that arose either as a nickname "Chain mail" or an as occupational descriptive for one who made chain mail, that is, an armourer. A medieval tax was collected on armour made of these linked metal

rings and the French surname Maillard names such a tax collector.
A maillard might also be a blacksmith.

MANNING

Ernest Charles Manning 1908–1996

*A protegé and student at "Bible Bill" Aberhart's Prophetic Bible
Institute in Calgary, he went on to a powerful position in the
provincial Social Credit party and then became Alberta's longest-
serving premier from 1943 to 1968, maintaining fiscal and social
conservatism and deep suspicion of "the left." At the end of his pre-
miership, on the eve of Canada's centennial, Manning wrote an
influential book,* Political Realigment: A Challenge to Thoughtful
Canadians *(1967) calling for a regrouping of right-wingers into a
new social-conservative political party. His son, Preston, researched
the book for his father, and went on to found a version of the political group called for in the book, the Reform Party of Canada.*

Preston Earnest Manning 1942–

*As smiling Brian Mulroney, with pipes atoot, banners awave, and
blarney afroth, led the Progressive Conservative lemmings scurry-
ing toward the Cliff of Quick Death at the end of the 1980s, Preston
Manning created the Reform Party (founding convention,
Winnipeg, 1987). Reform became a haven for all manner of
Canadian conservatives, from wacko hate-mongers and lunatic
fringeoids who pined to establish all-white utopias under plastic
bubbles in the lee of the Rockies to good-hearted Christian social
conservatives. Manning had several good innings leading the
proud do-badders, including 1993, when Reform's federal electoral
success in the West effectively fired the coup de grâce into the mori-
bund noggin of the Progressive Conservatives. In 1997, Manning
led Reform to 60 seats and the status of official opposition. Manning*

had already tried to unite disgruntled PCs with Reform in what he called a United Alternative. Claiming ultimate conversion of the Reform multitude, Manning finally united the right (again?) at yet another founding convention in Ottawa in January of 2000, when CCRAP was born. The Canadian Conservative Reform Alliance Party hoped to be known as the Canadian Alliance and not by its fecal acronym. But too many journalists made jokes about the short form and so, a few days after the convention, the official name was altered to The Canadian Reform Conservative Alliance Party.

Manning was already a personal, first name in Old English where it meant 'descendant of a servant,' that is, of a *Mann*, a varlet, a vassel. It was also an early byname where *manninga* after an Anglo-Saxon first name might mean 'of the family of a person named Mann' or 'of the followers of a chief named Mann.' There was also a variant Anglo-Saxon first name, Manna. *Mann*, as well as meaning a male person, had also an exemplary sense in Old English nomenclature; that is, it could mean 'a true man,' describing a manly hero, a tough stud, a hunk at whose feet fragile maidens swooned and dragons simply fainted away without so much as a fiery hiccup. CBC Radio comedian Rod Coneybeare invented a wonderful character who personified this type and dubbed him Manny Mann. The personal name also lies behind English village names like Mannington and Manningford.

Mirvish
David Mirvish
Founder of his own gallery and creator of a wonderful bookstore that specialized in art books, he also partnered with his father as owner-manager of London's Old Vic Theatre where he presented the world's best productions, including several Canadian companies, from 1982 until sale of the Old Vic to Britain's Royal National

Theatre in 1998. That same year he received the Olivier Award, along with his father, for their lifetime contributions to British theatre. In 1993 David Mirvish and his father built and opened the exquisite Princess of Wales Theatre in Toronto.

Edwin "Honest Ed" Mirvish 1914–

Toronto department store entrepreneur and theatre owner-producer of the Royal Alexandra and The Princess of Wales theatres in Toronto, Honest Ed is also once-upon-a-time possessor of the Old Vic in London, England.

Mirvish is a variant of the Yiddish Mervitz or Mervis from a place name, *Mierzwica*, which occurs with spelling variations dozens of times throughout Russia and Lithuania. If the settlement was Slavic, the components of the place name are lexical items like Russian *mir* 'hamlet, small community in pre-revolutionary Russia' + descriptives like *vika* 'vetch, tares' to give 'little place where vetch grows.' Vetch was then a common fodder crop used to feed domestic animals. If the place was founded and named by Jewish settlers, one may look for *shtetl* names transformed by Slavic spelling coventions. Then the initial component may be the founder's name Meir (variants: Meyer, Mayer, Meier) from Hebrew *me-ir* 'one who shines.'

MOSKOVITZ

Jason Moskovitz

As CBC-TV's amiable senior political correspondent, Mr. Moskovitz is finally reaping his reward after years spent nobly in the television news trenches. To this CBC viewer at least, the well-informed and brisk Moscovitz excels.

Moskovitz or Moskowitz looks on the surface like a Slavic locative surname meaning 'descendant of one from Moscow.' But the

Moscow locative surname is usually Moskovsky. In fact, Mosko is a pet name among Polish Jews for Moses. The suffix *-ko* and *-ka* is an affectionate diminutive tacked to the end of many given names in Polish, Russian, Ukrainian, and several other Slavic tongues. In Slavic words that are not surnames, the suffix operates as a true lexical diminutive. So Moskovitz is actually 'descendant of Mosko.' In English, for Mosko, we might say Moze or Moe.

MUNRO

Alice Munro 1931–

She is the best writer Canada has ever produced. Certainly Munro writes short stories as well as any living English author. Her collections, often themed, include Dance of the Happy Shades *(1968),* Lives of Girls and Women *(1971),* Something I've Been Meaning To Tell You *(1974),* Who Do You Think You Are? *(1978),* The Moons of Jupiter *(1982),* The Progress of Love *(1986),* Friend of My Youth *(1990),* Open Secrets *(1994), and* The Love of a Good Woman *(1998).*

Munro is one rare example where linguistically accurate family history has preserved the precise meaning of a complex surname. Munro details the founding ancestor's place of residence. The Munroes came from Ireland from the foot of the river Roe in County Londonderry. Irish Gaelic is *Bun-Rothach* 'man from the foot of the Roe.' In Scottish Gaelic, in the county of Ross, the family name was altered to *Mun-rotha* because of known linguistic transformations that need not concern us here.

MURRAY

Anne Murray 1945–

The popular singer from Springhill, Nova Scotia, had hits with "Snowbird," "Danny's Song," "You Needed Me," and many others.

Murray is a variant of Moray, a province of Scotland. Aptly enough, Gaelic *Moray* means 'seaside settlement.'

N

NAISMITH

James A. Naismith 1861–1939

The doctor and physical education director who invented basketball in 1891 was born at Almonte, Ontario.

Naismith is an Anglo-Saxon occupational agent noun, *knif-smith* 'cutler, one who makes knives.'

Nanook (Nanuq)

Nanook was an Inuit hunter of the Canadian Arctic who "starred" in American explorer Robert Flaherty's silent film Nanook of the North *(1920). It is often called the first documentary film. But scenes were rehearsed over and over again, and Flaherty did retake after retake. Thus artifice and flim-flam shroud even the earliest examples of this so-called truthful mode of cinema and now television. Truth is compromised by editing, and the other falsifying paraphernalia of recording. Flaherty's years in our Arctic were financed by Revillon Frères, a French fur company. Nanook came to a bad end in his dealings with southern whites. Meanwhile, Flaherty, ever the itinerant con man, sailed off to the south seas to film more tropical truths.*

Nanuq (a better transliteration than *nanook*) means 'bear' in Inuktitut.

NASH

Cyril Knowlton Nash 1927–

The writer and broadcasting administrator is best known as a CBC-TV journalist and newsreader. His many books include

History on the Run *(1984)*, Kennedy and Diefenbaker *(1990)*, Prime Time at Ten: Behind the Camera Battles of Canadian TV Journalism *(1987)*, and The Microphone Wars *(1994) about protracted management follies at the Canadian Broadcasting Corporation, as well as* Cue the Elephant *(1996) and* Trivia Pursuit *(1998)*.

Nash is from an ancestor's homestead or a place name which in Middle English was the phrase *atten asch* 'at the ash tree' where the initial *n* was actually the old dative case ending of *at*, which became attached to *asch* so that newcomers to such a community thought it was called Nash and perhaps never knew that the place was founded amid a stand of ash trees. There are half a dozen British hamlets called Nash.

NUNZIATA

John Nunziata 1955–

He was elected to the House of Commons for York South-Weston in 1984, 1988, and 1993, where he has proven himself among other roles an excellent Opposition critic. In April of 1996 he was expelled from the Liberal caucus for voting in the House of Commons against the government's budget proposal and he now sits as an independent, while contemplating a run in the next mayoralty race in Toronto.

Nunziata is an Italian surname based on a familiar Italian epithet of the Blessed Virgin Mary, *L'Annunziata* 'Our Lady of the Annunciation.' The angel Gabriel who made known to Mary news of the Incarnation is also known as *l'angelo annunziatore.* These terms and the office of papal *nunzio* and the English words *announce*, *announcer*, and *announcement* all derive from Latin *nuntiare* 'to report, to bring a message.' The earlier noun *nuntius* 'messenger' is possibly a contraction of **nouentius* from two roots **nou* 'new' and *uentum* 'having come' so that a *nuntius* was someone who came with new things (like news?).

O

O'LEARY

Michael Grattan O'Leary 1889–1976

He was a political reporter, then the Progressive Conservative editor of the Ottawa Journal. *Prime Minister John Diefenbaker tossed in the reward of a senate seat in 1962.*

O'Leary is an occupational surname from the Irish *Ó Lao-ghaire* 'descendant of calf-keeper.'

OLLERENSHAW

Duncan Ollerenshaw 1964–

The actor is currently a member of the acting company at the Stratford Shakespearean festival. He was a memorable Ephesus in the 1995 Stratford production of Shakespeare's bawdy The Comedy of Errors.

Ollerenshaw 'a small stand of alder trees' is the name of a place in Derbyshire where the surname is common. *Shaw*, a dialect word for wood, copse, thicket, is from Old English *sceaga* 'small woods.' Olleren is a modern spelling of the Old English word *aloren* 'alder trees.'

OSLER

Sir William Osler 1849–1919

One of the greatest clinicians Canada has produced, Osler helped establish current postgraduate training methods for physicians, published widely, and was the author of a standard textbook The Principles and Practice of Medicine *(1892, many revisions). A Victorian of daunting energy, he also knew the value of humour in education and in patient care: "The chief thing that separates human beings from animals is the desire to take pills."*

Osler is a medieval occupation name from Old French *oiseleur* 'fowler, bird-catcher' or Old French *oiselier* 'seller of game birds.'

OUZOUNIAN

Richard Ouzounian 1950–

"Ouz" is a witty writer of revue songs, director, producer, and general gadfly of the Canadian theatre scene, who has run Theatre Manitoba, theatre companies in Vancouver and Toronto, and also been a drama critic for CBC Radio and a television administrator in charge of the arts at TVO (1995–2000). He has also written musicals with composer Marek Norman including Dracula *(1998) that played to great acclaim at Stratford and then was telecast on TVO and CBC-TV, and* Emily *(1999) based on Lucy Maud Montgomery's Emily trilogy.*

Ouzounian is an Armenian surname with the standard Armenian patronymic suffix -*ian* 'descendant of, son of' borrowed from the Hellenistic Greek surname suffix -*ianos*, itself from a common Latin adjectival suffix -*ianus*. In Armenian *ouzon* means 'tall' and Ouzounian 'descendant of the tall man' refers to a specific heroic ancestor who defeated a Turkish foe in times past. But it is also similar to English surnames like Lang, Longman and Tallman.

P

PALLISER

John Palliser 1817–1887

He explored western Canada from Lake Superior to the Okanagan Valley as leader of the Palliser Expedition (1857–1860) and his reports and maps were invaluable to planners of the Canadian Pacific Railway and others opening our West. Palliser's Triangle of semi-arid prairie and Palliser's Pass are named after him.

Palliser is a medieval occupational surname widespread in north-east England's County Durham. A palliser was one who made fences or palings. Compare the word *palisade*.

PALMER

Daniel David Palmer 1845–1913

The popularizer of chiropractic manipulation of the joints, especially of the spine, was born in Port Perry, Ontario. In 1898 he opened the Palmer School of Chiropractic in Davenport, Iowa, to teach his techniques. An early patient of Palmer, a Reverend Weed, coined the word chiropractic, *which has the general sense from its Greek roots of 'doing things with the hands.'*

Palmer is an early medieval honorific that harks back to the times of the Crusades when a pilgrim returning from the Holy Land always brought back a palm-branch because of its association with the story of Jesus. In Old French, a *palmer* was also one who set out on one of the Crusades.

PARIZEAU

Jacques Parizeau 1930–

He joined the Parti Québécois in 1969 and worked his way to party president by 1988. The reward? Premier of Québec from 1994 to 1996.

Parizeau is a pet form of Patrice, and so it's similar to Patty or Paddy. The name was popularized by *Saint Patrice*, Saint Patrick.

PELLETIER

Gérard Pelletier 1919–1997

A lifelong enemy of Québec Premier Duplessis, he gained attention reporting on the 1949 Asbestos Strike for Montréal's Le Devoir. As a labour activist, he helped Pierre Elliott Trudeau and Jean

Marchand found Cité libre *magazine and then entered Liberal politics to hold cabinet portfolios under Trudeau, and later ambassadorial posts.*

Un pelletier was a medieval French occupation, the name of one who made and sold prepared animal skins and furs, from the Late Latin *pelletarius*. Compare the English word *pelt.*

PICKERSGILL

John Whitney "Jack" Pickersgill 1905–1997

A very influential policy wonk—as we might say today. He was right-hand man to two Canadian prime ministers, Mackenzie King and St. Laurent, and his written history of that era is still of value.

A Yorkshire surname, Pickersgill means almost literally 'den of thieves.' Pickersgill Lane is a place in Killinghall in the west riding of Yorkshire. Gill is from Old Scandinavian *gil* 'ravine' and a picker in Middle English was a petty thief who stole things easily picked up. This ravine of the cutpurses must have been a dangerous dell indeed. Perhaps the founding ancestor lived up on the ridge of the ravine whence he could observe the robbers below at their nefarious deeds.

PRATT

Edwin John Pratt 1882–1964

A boy of the Newfoundland outports, he became through twelve volumes of verse one of Canada's most anthologized poets and a professor of English at Victoria College (1920–1953). His best narrative poetry is steeped in Newfoundland and Canadian history.

John Christopher Pratt 1935–

Art Critic Joan Murray calls this austere stylist "one of the great classicists of contemporary Canadian painting."

Mary Pratt, née West 1935–

A painter of what one critic called "domestic photo-realism tempered by lush delight in surfaces," she was married to artist Christopher Pratt.

Pratt is an ancestor's nickname from an unattested Old English adjective **prætt* 'cunning, tricky, astute.' However, the noun *prætt* 'guile, a trick' is in print from AD 1000. It is highly unlikely that the surname derives from the British slang term *pratt* 'buttocks' since this does not appear in print until 1567, and Pratt as a surname shows up in a document dated 1179. Still, this does not prevent British children with the name from having to abide a certain amount of schoolyard joshing.

ℛ

RAE

Robert "Bob" Keith Rae 1948–

The leader of the Ontario NDP from 1982 (MPP, York South), after he resigned his federal seat. He was leader of the Opposition in the Ontario legislature (1987–1990) and then NDP premier of Ontario (1990–1995).

Rae is a Scots variant of Roe from Old English *ra* 'deer, roe.' The ancestor might have received the nickname because of his hunting ability, his swiftness-of-foot, or even for certain bashful, retiring ways.

RANKIN

The Rankin Family, a popular family of five singers (Cookie, Heather, Jimmy, John, and Raylene) from Mabou on Cape Breton Island with a background in the Celtic music of our Maritimes, they have recorded CDs that include The Rankin Family *(1989),* Fare Thee

Well Love *(1992),* North Country *(1993),* Grey Dusk of Eve *(1995),* Endless Seasons *(1995), and* The Rankin Family Collection *(1996). In 2000 they suffered the loss of a family member when John was killed in an auto accident.*

Rankin was a popular first name for men in medieval England. *Ran-kin* is a pet or diminutive form of the compound Old English first name Randolph, from *Rand-wulf* 'shield-wolf.' The first and last name Randal is from the same source.

RASKY

Harry Rasky 1928–

Co-founder of the news-documentary department at CBC-TV (1952–1955), he is the maker of award-winning television documentaries and biographies, shown on CBC-TV and internationally, whose subjects include Marc Chagall, Robertson Davies, Northrop Frye, William Hutt, Yousuf Karsh, Raymond Massey, Arthur Miller, Christopher Plummer, George Bernard Shaw, Teresa Stratas, and Tennessee Williams. He has published books based on his television documentaries and been honoured with many international awards.

Rasky appears Slavic but is a Jewish matronymic surname honouring a mother named Rachel. A common nickname for Rachel in Russian Yiddish is *Raske* (in German Yiddish it's *Reichel*). *Rachel* 'ewe' is a very ancient Hebrew given name for women.

RASUL

Firoz A. Rasul 1952–

Developer and promoter of a fuel cell for car and truck engines—indeed for any size vehicle engine—Mr. Rasul is the president and CEO of Ballard Power Systems of Burnaby, B.C. which, since 1982, has been working with major automobile manufacturers to perfect a fuel cell that uses hydrogen and produces no emission other than pure water. Let us hope it spells the end of the gasoline-powered internal combustion engine which has spewed so much pollution and disease upon this smoggy old planet.

Firoz is an Arabic adjective meaning 'successful, properous.' It is an honoured Muslim name for it was borne by one of the companions of the Prophet Muhammed. Rasul is a surname based on a noun that can also be used and was first used as a given name. Rasul is a Muslim honorific, one of the names of the Prophet. *Rasul* is Arabic for messenger, with special reference to the supreme messenger of Allah, Muhammed. Its Arabic plural *rusul* would be, for example, the term to use if one were translating English plurals like apostles, delegates, or emissaries. The Arabic root *r-s-l* has a basic, primordial meaning of 'to be long, to flow (like long hair)' and developed meanings like 'to send forth, to dispatch, to communicate, to get in touch.'

REEVES

Keanu Reeves 1964–

The handsome actor has become a superstar of Hollywood films. He is Canadian though born in Beirut to an Hawaiian father and an English mother. His feature films include River's Edge *(1987),* Point Break *(1991),* My Own Private Idaho *(1991),* Bram Stoker's Dracula *(1992),* Much Ado About Nothing *(1993),* Speed *(1994),* Johnny Mnemonic *(1995),* The Devil's Advocate *(1997), and in 1999* Matrix. *In a rare theatrical outing Reeves played Hamlet in 1994 at the Manitoba Theatre Centre in Winnipeg.*

Keanu is Hawaiian and means 'cool breeze.' *Ke-ahe-anu* is literally 'the breeze cool.'

Reeves is a possessive surname from the medieval occupation of reeve, who at various times and places could have been a bailiff, an overseer, or a magistrate. Reeves 'of the reeve' could also denote one who worked in the house of a reeve, or who was the son of a reeve.

ROHMER

Ann Rohmer

Pert host of Breakfast Television on CITY-TV in Toronto, Ann is Canadian television's most amiable morning presence, cheerful, bright, and simpatica*! CITY ought to share Ann Rohmer with the rest of Canada. If one was ever teaching a class of student hosts how to be warm and gracious while efficiently conducting a television magazine program, one would obtain tapes of Ann Rohmer. Of course, the instructor would be duty-bound to tell each class that Ann is married. She and her sister Catherine are daughters of Richard Rohmer.*

Richard Rohmer 1924–

This writer and lawyer is a retired major-general whose country has showered him with honours that include the Distinguished Flying Cross in 1945 for his service as a fighter pilot in the RCAF. Mr. Rohmer invented the idea of the "Mid-Canada Corridor" and the University of Canada North and promoted them along with other innovations in his many non-fiction books. He has also authored ten works of fiction such as 1973's best-seller Ultimatum *and the 1995 historical fiction* John A's Crusade*. A recent entry in the non-fiction sweepstakes was his 1997* Golden Phoenix: The Biography of Peter Munk.

Rohmer, Röhmer, or Römer are surnames that arose in various parts of Roman Catholic Germany, and were originally bynames given to those who had made a holy pilgrimage to Rome and then returned to their native villages and towns. Pious trips to Rome were also undertaken as acts of penance and atonement for various sins. Several English surnames stem from ancestors who made similar trips, surnames like Romer and Roomer. The Elizabethan pronunciation of Rome rhymed with modern room, for Shakespeare rhymes Rome with doom and groom. The pronunciation lasted well into the eighteenth century. John Donne and Alexander Pope both used it.

The German surname Rohmer less frequently derives from a dithematic Germanic warrior name that appeared in Old High German as *Hruodmari*, and in Old English as *Hrothmar*. The two "themes" of this double-decker name are *hruod* 'fame' + *mari* 'brave.' Even less frequent is a derivation from *romer*, a Low German noun of the Middle Ages equivalent to modern German *Rühmer* 'one who praises.'

ROMANOV

Roy John Romanov 1939–

A successful NDP politician in Saskatchewan, he has been premier of the province since 1987.

Romanov is a Slavic patronymic surname meaning 'descendant of an ancestor named Roman.' For more than eight hundred years, Roman has been a popular male given name in many Slavic languages, including Ukrainian, Polish, and Russian.

ROSS

James Sinclair Ross 1908–1996

Born on a farm near Prince Albert, Saskatchewan, the novelist and short story writer worked all his life as a banker. His major novel As For Me and My House *(1941) is a great, subtle, bleak portrait of the bound souls and evasive hearts of a minister and his wife, a married couple isolated in a small Prairie hamlet in the midst of the Great Depression and cut off from one another too, each wrapped solo in the sticky, dead cocoon of the self. Ross shows how the wife is alive to her natural Prairie landscape, but incapable of probing the inner mindscape of her husband or herself. The novel is for me among the best Canadian works of fiction written so far. But* As For Me and My House *resists synopsis. Instead, it compels perusal. It was a seed in the loam of the work of Margaret Laurence who acknowledged her debt to Ross many times. In 1992 Ross was made a member of the Order of Canada and won the Lifetime Achievement award of the Saskatchewan Arts Board in 1993. Among his other works are a novel,* Sawbones Memorial *(1974) and* The Lamp at Noon and Other Stories *(1968), a collection of his short pieces edited by Margaret Laurence.*

Ross as a Scottish surname is locative, taken from the former county of Ross, which in turn was named from the Scottish Gaelic *ross* 'isthmus, promontory.' That word was borrowed into Gaelic from Celtic **ros*, a topographical word that referred to heath-covered uplands, moor country, and also the spur of a hill. In 1958 Ross was the twenty-second commonest name in Scotland.

RUBEŠ

Jan Rubeš 1920–

The Czech-born operatic bass has contributed hugely to the development of opera in Canada, chiefly through his work with the Canadian Opera Company. He has directed theatre and opera, and as an actor he has been memorable playing an Amish farmer in the Hollywood thriller Witness *(1985) directed by Peter Weir. He has acted in many Canadian television features including* Charlie Grant's War *(1984).*

Rubeš is a locative Slavic surname based on an ancestor's house being located on a boundary or border. Compare Russian *rooBESHCH* 'border' and Ukrainian *ruBEEZH*. It may also be a locative surname from Czech *rub* 'reverse side, other side, wrong side.'

S

SCHREYER

Edward Richard Schreyer 1935–

Born at Beauséjour, he entered the Manitoba legislature at age twenty-two, becoming by 1969 NDP provincial premier. In 1979 Trudeau made him governor-general of Canada, a post he held until 1984, when he became Canada's high commissioner to Australia for four years, before returning to private life. While premier, he encouraged Manitoban bilingualism and favoured a powerful federal government.

Schreyer is a German name denoting the important medieval occupation of *Schreier* 'town crier,' one who walked through the central streets of a town declaiming the latest news and government bulletins. There are also German records indicating the noun was sometimes the humorous nickname of an ancestor who was a loud-mouth, a real windbag.

SHAMAS

Sandra Shamas

Born in Sudbury, the brilliantly funny stand-up comedienne based in Toronto is of Lebanese extraction. One of her early gigs was as puppeteer for the CBC/Jim Henson television series Fraggle Rock *(1984–1986). After comic monologues at Toronto venues like the Back Room at the Rivoli, Ms. Shamas has had national and international success with one-woman shows like* My Boyfriend's Back & There's Gonna be Laundry *and* Wedding Bell Hell.

Shamas is an occupational, religious surname from Arabic *shammas*. The shammas can be a layperson who performs duties similar to a sexton, or, in Middle Eastern Christian rites, the shammas may be an acolyte or liturgical cantor.

STRATAS

Teresa Stratas, née Anastasia Stratakis 1938–

A world-renowned opera diva, the soprano, who is a superb actress as well, has sung with most of the West's great companies, including important premieres such as her 1979 Lulu *at the Paris Opera that featured the first complete production of Alban Berg's masterpiece.*

The Greek surname Stratakis is usually considered locative, from an ancestor who lived on or beside an important road, Modern Greek *strata* 'way, road' itself borrowed into Greek from a Roman engineering term, the Latin *stratum* 'a road coated with a layer or stratum of gravel.' A more purely Greek origin may lie in *stratos* 'army.' To either of these roots add the common Greek adjectival then surname suffix *-akis* 'descendant of.'

Anastasia is a pious female given name in the Greek Orthodox Church meaning 'female associated with the Anastasis,' which is the Greek word for the Resurrection. Anastasis is the rising or literally the up-standing from *ana* 'up'+ *stasis* 'act of standing.' Anastasia was popular in the west because it was the name of a fourth-century martyred saint. Then during the middle ages a legend grew up that the Blessed Virgin Mary had the help of a midwife when she gave birth to the baby Jesus. This putative midwife was called Anastasia, and of course there is a pun in the name, since a midwife stands up in front of the woman whom she is assisting in childbirth.

TATANGA

Tatanga Mani 1871–1967

The Stoney Indian leader, statesman, and philosopher, born in the Bow River Valley of Alberta, had the English name of George

McLean. His thoughts on world peace are worth fresh consideration.

Tatanga Mani in the Stoney language is literally 'buffalo walking.' Canadian aboriginal actor Graham Greene has a memorable scene in the film *Dances with Wolves* trying to guess the charade as the Kevin Costner character imitates a buffalo—badly—but Greene's character does understand and says, "Tatonka!" which is the similar word for 'buffalo' in the language of the Lakota Sioux.

TENNANT

Veronica Tennant 1947–

Her great technique and intensity made the ballerina one of the greatest stars of the National Ballet of Canada.

The popularity of Veronica as a female given name is due to Saint Veronica, a woman of Jerusalem whom pious legend states stood along the *via dolorosa* and took pity on Jesus and his suffering as he was led to his crucifixion. Veronica stooped down and wiped Christ's sweating brow with her veil. Later she noticed that the cloth now bore a true image of the face of Christ. At St. Peter's in Rome such a cloth, claimed to be the original veil of St. Veronica, may be seen among the holy relics in the Vatican collection. July 12 is St. Veronica's feast day, and girls born on this date are sometimes baptized with the name in the Russian Orthodox, Greek Orthodox, or Roman Catholic Churches.

One standard but dubious etymology of Veronica arises from this story, and is the origin found in many, poorly researched "names-for-your-baby" books. Monkish folk etymology posits that the name is a contraction of the Latin phrase *vera iconica* meaning 'true image,' from the same Greek root that gives us the word for a religious painting, icon. Such a derivation is linguistically unlikely, and, frankly, just plain silly.

Much more probable is the derivation of Veronica from a medieval Latin adjective *veronicus* meaning 'person from the Italian city of Verona.' Veronica would mean a woman of Verona, a suitable name for a girl because the women of that city were considered to be among the most beautiful in all of medieval Italy. Shakespeare places Romeo and Juliet "in fair Verona where we lay our scene." But Verona also claimed to possess the veil of St. Veronica at one point during the Renaissance! Sixteenth-century Italian referred to this as *la veletta veronica* 'the Veronese veil.' This, I believe, is the origin of the feminine first name. Véronique is the French spelling. In some Slavic tongues, it is Veronika or Beronika. The fact that one of the Catholic Stations of the Cross commemorates St. Veronica's kindness to the suffering Jesus insures the name's continued popularity in all languages of the Western world.

Another doubtful source of the given name Veronica is the female first name Berenice (often shortened to Bernice), originally a Macedonian form of the Greek *Pherenike* 'bringer of victory.' The vowel shiftings and interlingual gradations necessary to support this bizarre transformation may happen on Mars, but have not so far occurred on earth, except in the frantic noggins of certain desperate etymologists.

Tennant as an English surname originates as tenant. A putative ancestor might have been called John the tenant, a man who held land in one of various forms of feudal tenure. In form, it's *tenant,* a Norman-French participial form from *tenir* 'to hold.' By the end of the period of Middle English, about AD 1500, when some British surnames had assumed their final form, tenancy came to refer to renting a piece of land for a specified time by lease. The spelling *Tennant* is not, of course, an attempt to disguise the fact that the founding ancestor did not own any land outright. It merely reflects how variable English spelling was, before the rise of dictionaries and widespread literacy combined to regularize orthography. The surname appears as Tennant, Tennent, and Tennents. Tennant is common in Yorkshire and southern Scotland.

TILLEY

Alexander Tilley 1938–

Inventive Canadian designer of outdoor and travel clothing and originator of the Tilley hat

Leonard Percy de Wolfe Tilley 1870–1947

The New Brunswick lawyer and politician was premier of the province from 1933 to 1935. He was the son of the Father of Confederation listed next.

Sir Samuel Leonard Tilley 1818–1896

Born at Gagetown, New Brunswick, he began in the drugstore business and rose to political fame as a staunch advocate of New Brunswick's inclusion in Confederation. He was Macdonald's politically astute point man in the province and held many cabinet portfolios in both Macdonald governments.

The origins of Tilley as an ancient British surname are complex. The earliest form of the name appears as Ralph de Tilio in the Domesday Book of the English county of Derbyshire in AD 1086. This man was of Norman-French extraction, and a recent arrival from France—remember the Norman Conquest of 1066 a few years before. The founding ancestor of this family took his name from the place he lived in France. There are five little towns in northern France that may be the locality of origin: Tilly-sur-Seulles in Calvados, Tilly in Eure, Tilly in Seine-et-Oise, one in Meuse, and one in the Pas-de-Calais. Only a rigorous genealogical search might determine the precise locative origin of the family.

This Norman Tilley has many spelling forms both in England and in France, among which are: Tillie, Tilly, Tiley, Tily, Tylee, Tyley, Tilhet, Thillet, and Thiellet! Why is this particular name and its variants so widespread over northern France? Because it belonged to a Teutonic tribe who controlled much of the area, even long before the Romans conquered northern Gaul. The area was known to Gallo-Romans as *Tilliacum* and that term was based on the tribe's name in Old Germanic *Tielo,* short for *Theod-ilo*, and that word contains a Germanic rootword *theod* that means 'the people.' So Tilley harks all the way back to a word at least two thousand years old and means 'the people.'

Is that it then, for Tilley? Unfortunately no. Several hundred years later in England, Tilley was coined as a new matronymic surname based on the nickname of an ancestral mother. Till and Tilly were pet forms of Matilda. Some English Tilleys also stem from Middle English *tilie* 'one who tills the fields,' a forebear who was a husbandman.

TOBIN

Brian Vincent Tobin 1954–

The feisty Newfoundland Liberal made a big splash as Chrétien's minister of fisheries, and then in 1996 he quit federal politics to return to his native Newfoundland where he won a huge majority to become premier of the province in February of 1996. He was re-elected in every election and is still in office in 2000.

Tobin can be a Norman-French surname or an Irish one. In both cases the name harks back to Normandy. If Norman French, it stems from *Tob-in* 'little Tobias' or 'Toby.' Tobias is the Koine Greek and hence New Testament form of the Hebrew male name Tobiah 'Yahweh (God) is good.' As a Christian first name, Tobias is the source of surnames like Tobey, Tobin, and Tobyn. For the

Semitic root at work elsewhere, compare a modern Hebrew female given name like Tova 'good female' and the familiar Hebrew salutation of good luck, *mazel tov*, literally 'luck good' with the adjective postpositive in Semitic languages.

If Tobin is of Irish provenance, it derives from a Norman surname St. Aubyn or St. Aubin, originating in Brittany. The *t* of saint is slurred to the beginning of Aubin in everyday speech. Aubin stems from a Roman surname, Late Latin *Albinus*, ultimately from *albus* 'white, fair, with white complexion.' Aubin as a name was popularized by a beloved sixth-century bishop, Albinus of Angers.

TREMBLAY

Michel Tremblay 1942–

He is the leading French-Canadian playwright of the second half of the twentieth century whose vivid, joual-flecked dialogue sparkles in such plays as Les Belles-Soeurs *(1968),* À toi, pour toujours, ta Marie-Lou *(1971),* Hosanna *(1973),* Albertine en cinq temps *(1984), and* Le gars de Québec *(1985). In the mid-seventies Tremblay turned increasingly to fiction in a series of continuing novels under the series title* Plateau Mont-Royal, *which nevertheless move through the same world as his plays, the working-class neighbourhoods of Montréal. He did not abandon theatre however, as shown by* Messe solennelle pour une pleine lune d'été *'High Mass for a Full Summer Moon' which debuted early in 1996 at Montréal's Théâtre Jean Duceppe. His recent theatre piece* For the Pleasure of Seeing Her *has also played in English Canada.*

Tremblay beats out Smith as the most common surname in Canada. In 1995, there were 180,000 Canadians with the last name Tremblay. One out of every fifty Québécois is named Tremblay! Many families with the surname settled early in *la Nouvelle France*. At least six towns in France are called Tremblay or Tremblais. The place name stems from the Gallo-Roman adjective *tremuletum* 'place abounding in trembling aspen trees.'.

TRUDEAU

Joseph Philippe Pierre Yves Elliott Trudeau 1919–

The constitutional lawyer and Liberal writer became the fifteenth prime minister of Canada and the first born in the twentieth century. Holding the prime minister's office from 1968 to 1979 and again from 1980 to 1984, Trudeau became one of the most influential figures in modern Canadian history.

During his years of political power, a hoary folk etymology, very common and very wrong, made the rounds about Trudeau. You could ask anyone on the street in Québec and be told that Trudeau was, *bien entendu*, from *trou d'eau*, a supposed old term for water-hole. And of course there were vulgar jokes told that depended on this spurious etymology. Trudeau as a surname goes back to an ancestor who bore the Germanic warrior name *Trudo*. The root is Old High German *drud* which meant 'strong, hardened, tough, mighty.' So frequent a first name was it in very early French that we even find it in ancient church records with a full Latin declension: *Trudo, Trudonis*, etc. Quite the opposite with our little water-hole *trou d'eau* which is **never** found in print. *Trou* was simply not used like this in early French. *Trou* indicated always an absence, a hole that was empty. Even in the most recent French coinages using the word, this holds true. For example, the English astronomical term *black hole* is translated in current French by *trou noir*.

TWAIN

Eileen "Shania" Twain 1965–

The million-CD-selling country-and-western singer-composer grew up in Timmins, Ontario, as Eileen Twain and got her start singing at Ontario's Deerhurst Inn. She has won many awards for her work, for example, Junos, Country Music Awards, and Grammies. Her first CD The Woman in Me *(1995) has sold more than eleven million copies. Her 1997 CD* Come On Over *was also a smash hit.*

Her adoptive father, Jerry Twain, is full-blooded Ojibway. Shania was the name of a girl she worked with at the Deerhurst Inn, and, when it came time to confect a show-biz name, she changed it to Shania (pronounced sha-NYE-a) which is Ojibwa for 'on my way.'

There seems to be no mention of Twain as a surname in print until the American satirist Samuel Langhorne Clemens (1835–1910) used it as his pseudonym and called himself Mark Twain based on the shout of a Mississippi riverboat deckhand who called out water depth from a sounding line sunk in the turbid waters of the river. When the line showed a depth of two fathoms, the mate shouted out to the pilot of the boat, "Mark twain!" that is, the mark is twain, i.e., 'two.' Twain is listed in some dialect dictionaries as a local pronunciation of Dwayne.

U

URQUHART

Anthony "Tony" Morse Urquhart 1934–
No artist's work can be summed up in a phrase, but this southern Ontario painter, sculptor, and draughtsman had a well-titled retrospective that toured Canada in 1988–1989. It was called Worlds Apart: The Symbolic Landscapes of Tony Urquhart.

Jane Urquhart, née Carter 1949–
Born in Geraldton, Ontario, this novelist of warm, poetic insight counts among her works The Whirlpool *(1986), her greatest storytelling to date,* Away *(1993), and* The Underpainter *(1997).*

Urquhart is the name of half a dozen places in Scotland. The linguistic origin of the name is not clear. It may be Old Celtic, a pre-Roman language of the British Isles, and it may mean 'on the woodside' denoting the habitation of an ancestor who dwelt on the forested slope of a hill. Onomastician Basil Cottle says the places in Fifeshire named Urquhart have a Scottish Gaelic root that means 'cast' or 'shot' and that refers to some lost incident in history that was memorable enough to name the place in which it happened. Professor Reaney's contention that all the Urquhart surnames go back to the barony of Urquhart in Inverness is, simply, unsupported.

ν

VANDERHAEGHE

Guy Vanderhaeghe 1951–

Born in Esterhazy, Saskatchewan, the novelist and short story writer has published such works as Man Descending *(1982), which won the Governor-General's Award for fiction,* My Present Age *(1984),* Homesick *(1989),* Things As They Are? *(1992), and* The Englishman's Boy *(1996).*

Vanderhaeghe is a Dutch surname of a familiar topographical type in the Netherlands. *Van der haeghe* means 'of the hay(field)' in Dutch. Such a locative tag named the position of an ancestor's house within a small community. The locative tag began to be written down in registers of marriage, birth, and death, and soon became an inherited surname.

VANIER

Georges-Philéas Vanier 1888–1967

A lawyer, soldier, diplomat, and a great Canadian citizen, he served as founding officer of the Royal 22e Regiment, the famous

Vingt-Deux's (a.k.a.Van Doos), and as Canada's ambassador to France during the Second World War. From 1959 to his death in 1967 his moral dignity and compassion made him one of the best governors-general Canada has ever had.

Jean Vanier 1928–

The son of Georges Vanier founded L'Arche *(the ark), a series of homes for handicapped men that now stretches over Canada, France, India, Africa, and the United States. He is also the author of several books of spiritual guidance including* Community and Growth *(1979).*

Vanier is an occupational French surname. A *vanier* or *vanneur* made *vans*. In medieval French a *van* was a sort of flat basket in which grain was sold.

W

WALSH

Mary Walsh 1952–

Satirist and comedienne on Maritime stages and on CBC TV's This Hour Has 22 Minutes.

Walsh begins as a word expressing Anglo-Saxon xenophobia. In Old English it was *wælisc* 'foreigner, stranger.' The invading Anglo-Saxons called any Celtic peoples they found in Britain by this adjective, in particular the Welsh who dwelt in Wales, Old English *Wealas* 'land of the foreigners.' The Welsh call themselves *Cymry* and their land *Cymru*. This insulting adjective gave rise to a number of common surnames. But the adjective became obsolete in late Middle English, and so the surnames survived without any obvious semantic opprobrium attached to them. These surnames include Wallace, Walles, Wallice, Walch, Walsh, and Welsh. Wallace is the Scottish form, while Walsh is Irish and is still one of the fifteen most common names in Ireland.

Z

ZOLF

Larry Zolf 1934–

Larry Zolf is the major gift of Winnipeg's North End to Canadian life. A longtime CBC host and producer of public affairs television programs, Larry is also the author of a wonderfully satiric look at Canadian journalism, a 1989 novel entitled Scorpions for Sale, *and now a new collection of ageless Zolfiana entitled* Zolf. *Zolf is a laugher. Zolf is smart and funny. So seldom does this trio of felicities occur together that many of his friends have long since declared him a Living National Treasure. A furtive campaign exists to promote Zolf to the Canadian senate. Yes!*

Zolf is most likely a Yiddish variant of the Polish *żólw* 'turtle.' In strict Polish orthography the *z* is surmounted by a dot, indicating a sound for this dotted *z* much like the *si* in vision. And note that Polish *w* is pronounced like English *v*, except at the end of a word where it is almost as hard as English *f*. An ancestor might adopt a surname like Turtle because it was an identifying sign on his house or his shop. Does that mean he sold turtles? No, it probably indicates he was a jeweller, who would have used tortoise-shell inlays in making personal adornments and ornamental boxes. For this use, compare the German and Yiddish surname Schildkraut or Shyldkrot which meant 'turtle' and 'tortoise-shell.'

Three other remoter possibilities exist as origins for the surname Zolf. *Zol* was a variant for Saul among Polish and Russian Jews. Zolf could be a later contraction of a surname that began as Zolov 'descendant of Saul.'

In the Volkovysk district of Grodno, near Bialystok, in what became known as the Pale of Settlement, was a little *shtetl* called Zel'va. This gives Jewish surnames of place like Zelvensky, Zelvin, Zelfin, Zelver, and Zilvin. Note the gradations of the first vowel in these names. A form like Zolfin with a short *o* could arise from such gradation.

The final possible derivation of Zolf is from Zelfman, a person who made soap, from a Yiddish word *zeyf* 'soap.' This root produced Jewish occupational surnames like Zelfman, Zelfin, and Zeyfman. Zolf could be a shortened variant of one of these names.

Envoi

I was just sitting here by the fireside enjoying some light reading, but now find I can put aside for the night Franz Bopp's *The Conjugation of the Sanskrit Verb*. For I know how to say in Sanskrit: "The water oxen are calfing noisily beside the alarmed holy man." While my studies in foreign languages continue, perhaps yours are about to begin? I hope perusal of my little book has fired your curiosity about the origins of your own and others' last names. The bibliography of this book gives clues about where to start digging.

This has been my admittedly selective romp through some Canadian surnames whose origins provoked my interest. Any conclusions to be drawn? Yes. Our tolerance of racial difference should increase. Look at all the fiercely French surnames that turn out to be Germanic warrior names. Look at the given and last names of certain anti-Semites whose very names spring from Biblical Hebrew! The contemplation of this wonderful, tangled root mass of human names behooves all of us to smile more often upon our neighbours and to dismiss ignorant extremists who blat of racial and linguistic purity. In the naming habits of the chief languages of the Western world there is no such purity. All names blossom from much-hybridized seed. So have we.

Autobiohagiography

The *curriculum* of my *vitae* zigzags in a most uncool pattern. I coined the jawbreaker title of this piece to make ironic comment on how autobiography can't help but render its writer in saintly hues. Nothing saintly, alas, about your humble deponent, *moi*. I think Peter Ustinov invented the truest title ever slapped on an autobiography, *Dear Me*. That said however, several readers of my six books have wondered in letters how I could possibly have attained my present state. They don't say state of what? It's tricky to put who I am into words. But if you really want to know, meet me tonight out behind the old rink and I'll act it out for you with sock puppets. In your hand you hold my seventh book and, frankly, I think it's time to permit a biographical sketch of myself.

Born in Dunnville, Ontario, in 1942, I am a writer and broadcaster. Les Nirenberg bought the first prose I ever sold. A nervous nerd uncertain of any life direction, I was in Grade 11 at Dunnville High School in the late 1950s. Les was the editor and sole proprietor of *The Panic Button*, a Canadian satirical magazine of the late fifties and early sixties, that he published out of a variety store on Weston Road in Toronto called The Co-existence Candy Shop. Les paid me twenty dollars for a funny piece about eight hundred words long, and more for subsequent submissions between 1959 and 1963. On the day *The Panic Button* arrived in the mail and I saw my first column, I was ecstatic. I carried that issue around with me for months and kept a dog-eared copy in my high-school locker to show friends.

After university where I chose the academic rigour of courses like Learn Bomb Disposal While You Sleep, my first media job was as story editor and then producer for the CBC Radio Current Affairs department, especially one of their daily programs called *Matinee with Pat Patterson* where I worked from 1968 to 1971. Pat Patterson and the wonderful CBC Radio technicians taught me more about editing, tightening, and shaping material than any grammar teacher I ever had. During this freelance production gig, I was allowed to do occasional features and on-air scripts for other programs, including a short series on linguistics for the CBC Radio series *Ideas* in 1969.

In the early 1970s I spent three great years as senior producer at *This Country in the Morning* (predecessor of *Morningside* and *This Morning*) helping put Peter Gzowski on the radio every weekday. The production team who made *This Country in the Morning*, including executive producer Alex Frame, gave me the most enjoyable teamwork experience of my life. After Peter Gzowski left for an attempt at live television, I stayed on under the delightful leadership of executive producer Ann Gibson with hosts such as Michael Enright, perhaps the smartest and most likeable person I ever met in journalism or broadcasting and Judy LaMarsh, perhaps the most unpleasant person I ever met.

In 1975, at the invitation of Jack MacAndrew, head of the CBC-TV Variety Department, I left radio to try television, as executive producer of *The Bob McLean Show,* a network noontime talk show. I also appeared weekly with Bob as The Plant Nut to deliver cock-eyed horticultural advice. Out of this early interest in plants was to come one of my later books, *Canadian Garden Words* (1997).

During 1977 I accepted an offer from Daryl Duke and Norman Klenman to move to British Columbia to my first job in private television where I was executive producer of *The Vancouver Show* at CKVU-TV. While living in Vancouver, I was television columnist for *Maclean's* magazine (1978–1979) and daily television columnist for a feisty but short-lived newspaper, the *Vancouver Courier*. I was a panelist for one season on *Conquest*, a CBC Radio quiz show conducted by the delightful Chuck Davis. Then, in 1979 I returned to Toronto where executive producer Gary Michael Dault of *Morningside* asked me to write and direct comedy skits for CBC Radio's flagship morning show. I also wrote and hosted a satirical news broadcast, "Large News," weekly on *McLean at Large* on CBC-TV between 1979 and 1980.

My happiest time in broadcasting was the decade I spent from 1979 to 1989 as word nut and movie reviewer on *Jack Farr's Radio Show,* which was heard across the country Saturday afternoons on CBC Radio. Jackie was the best wacky host CBC Radio ever had. He helped me loosen up on air because Farr never let the regular guests on his show get away with even a minute of pomposity. CBC Radio was extremely short-sighted in letting Jack Farr fold that show. They have never been able to replace him. But Jack and I remain the best of friends to this day. And I await some enterprising producer's call to return Farr to the national airwaves where he belongs.

During this time I did occasional editorials for *Commentary* on CBC Radio, and between 1982 and 1987 occasional film reviews for *The Journal* on CBC-TV.

During four years (1990–1994), I conducted a weekly radio item called "Word Clout" on CBC's *Later the Same Day* with superb host Kathryn O'Hara. For the 1995–1996 season of CBC-TV's *What on Earth?* I did a series of interviews with host Bruce Steele about regional expressions from Vancouver Island to Newfoundland. I was a panelist on linguistic topics on the TVO program *Imprint* between 1990 and 1995 when it had an exceptional host, Daniel Richler. As a columnist for *Canadian Geographic* magazine from 1995 to 1999 I wrote "Our Home & Native Tongue" in every issue, exploring our national word-ways.

In the fall and winter of 1996, I tried my hand as a comic actor in CBC-TV's six-episode comedy *Newsroom.* Ken Finkleman, the writer, director, and star, chose me for the part. I was a principal on the series, but it's only a small role. It was a hoot to shoot, and is still very funny to watch. Ken has developed from Hollywood gag man to maturing artist, and I think he's a living national treasure of Canadian satire—and I say that only because he hired me for so many of his projects! His sallies have teeth and are not couched in typical sitcom gag lines. That and his unique comic view set Ken's work far above blander Canuck comedy fare on television.

Many hundreds of times I have guested on local radio phone-in shows and on television shows across the country, talking about my books and receiving fabulous information from listeners and readers.

In September 1995, I published *Casselman's Canadian Words: A Comic Browse by Bill Casselman through Words and Folk Sayings Invented by Canadians.* The book spent ten weeks in the top ten of the *Toronto Star* National Best-seller List for paperback non-fiction, including two weeks at Number One. The book reappeared on the national best-seller list the next summer, reaching sixth place on August 3, 1996.

In October of 1996 was published my second book, *Casselmania: More Wacky Canadian Words & Sayings,* featuring sections that examine our weather rhymes, our use of Eh?, and a satiric tour of my very own *Canadian National Museum of Bafflegab & Gobbledygook.*

The Nelson Canadian Dictionary, published in the fall of 1996, contains a full page of "Canadian Folk Expressions collected and annotated by Bill Casselman."

In September 1997, came my third popular word book, *Canadian Garden Words*, subtitled: *The Origin of Flower, Tree, and Plant Names, both wild and domestic, entertainingly derived from their sources in the Ancient Tongues, together with Fancy Botanical Names & Why You Shall Never Again Be Afraid To Use Them.*

My textbook about medical vocabulary, *A Dictionary of Medical Derivations: The* Real *Meaning of Medical Words* appeared in June 1998, published by Parthenon Publishers in England and the United States. I wrote it with the editing assistance of my urologist brother, R.C. Casselman, M.D., F.R.C.S.(C) and his wife, Judith Dingwall, R.N., D.P.H.N. Both Ron and I were born and grew up in Dunnville, attending Dunnville Public School where our father Alfred Casselman was principal for many years. We both graduated from Dunnville High School, as well. The medical dictionary has been placed on introductory courses in scientific vocabulary at Yale University, Johns Hopkins School of Medicine, and appears to have been ordered for medical reference libraries wherever in the world medicine is taught in English.

My examination of Canuck kitchen lingo, *Canadian Food Words: The Juicy Lore & Tasty Origins of Foods that Founded a Nation,* was published by McArthur & Company of Toronto in October 1998, and sold out its first printing by Christmas of 1998.

July of 1999 saw the publication of my first original mass-market paperback: *Canadian Sayings: 1,200 Folk Sayings Used By Canadians, Collected and Annotated by Bill Casselman*. Published by McArthur & Company, the book stayed in the top ten on Canadian best-seller lists for eight months, all through the summer, fall, and winter of 1999 and well into 2000 to become the best-selling book I've written so far. For the year 2001 I have written a calendar based on *Canadian Sayings*. If I had to name the *amigo de mi corazón* of the six books I've written, it would be that little paperback.

Looking back, well past the halfway point of my life, it might seem to have been a jumpy affair with occupational hops and skips every nanosecond. It may well have been. To be honest, I've been too busy to notice. Life can slip through our fingers like silken sand. If we are not careful, we can stand mesmerized by the shoosh of those temporal sand grains, and miss what is all about us on this blessed earth. I hope I have not done that. My work has taken me to every province and territory of Canada, where I always try to find time to pursue my chief delight and hobby, the study of words, particularly words and sayings that Canadians have added to the mighty hoard of English. I have travelled in Europe, Africa, and Central America. But my favorite *posto al sole* is an old stone farmhouse in Italy which I rent now and then. This little place in the sun, where lemon trees bloom in the garden, has a splendid perch on a hillside overlooking the Bay of Naples near Sorrento. When I'm there, I am.

Selected Bibliography

Avis, Walter S., C. Crate, P. Drysdale, D. Leechman, M.H. Scargill, and C.J. Lovell, eds. *A Dictionary of Canadianisms on Historical Principles.* Toronto: Gage, 1967.

Bahlow, Hans. *Deutsches Namenlexicon.* Munich: Suhrkamp Taschenbuchverlag, 1972.

Bardsley, Charles W. *A Dictionary of English and Welsh Surnames, with Special American Instances.* Baltimore, MD: Genealogical Publishing Co., 1968.

Barney, Stephen A., with Ellen Wertheimer and David Stevens. *Word-Hoard: An Introduction to Old English Vocabulary.* New Haven, CT: Yale University Press, 1977.

Baugh, Albert C., and Thomas Cable. *A History of the English Language.* 3rd ed. London: Routledge & Kegan Paul, 1978.

Beauvillé, Guillemette de. *Les noms de famille en France tirés des noms de métiers, de charge et de dignités.* Paris: 1957.

Bélisle, Louis-Alexandre. *Dictionnaire nord-américain de la langue française.* Reprint of 1979 edition. Laval, QC: Éditions Beauchemin, 1989.

Bergeron, Léandre. *Dictionnaire de la langue québécoise.* Montréal: VLB Éditeur, 1980.
———. *The Québécois Dictionary.* Toronto: Lorimer, 1982.

Black, G.F. *The Surnames of Scotland.* New York: New York Public Library Reprints, 1946.

Canadian Encyclopedia. 4 vols. Edmonton: Hurtig, 1988.

Canadian Encyclopedia: Year 2000 Edition. James H. Marsh, editor-in-chief. Toronto: McClelland & Stewart, 1999.

Canadian Oxford Dictionary. Katherine Barber, ed. Toronto: Oxford University Press, 1998.

Canadian Who's Who 1999. Elizabeth Lumley, ed. Toronto: University of Toronto Press, 1999.

Chambers, J.K., ed. *Canadian English: Origins and Structures.* Toronto: Methuen, 1975.

Cottle, Basil. *The Penguin Dictionary of Surnames.* 2nd ed. Harmondsworth, UK: Penguin Books, 1978.

Cowan, David. *An Introduction to Modern Literary Arabic.* Cambridge: Cambridge University Press, 1958.

Dauzat, Albert. *Dictionnaire des noms de famille et prénoms de France.* Paris: Larousse, 1951.

Davies, Trefor R. *A Book of Welsh Names.* London: Sheppard Press, 1952.

de Felice, Emidio. *Dizionario dei cognomi italiani.* Milan: Mondadori, 1978.

Dictionnaire historique de la langue française. 2nd ed. Alain Rey, ed. Paris: Dictionnaires Le Robert, 1994.

Dorward, David. *Scottish Surnames: A Guide to the Family Names of Scotland.* Glasgow: HarperCollins, 1995.

Eberhard-Wabnitz, Margit, and Horst Leisering. *Knaurs Vornamenbuch.* Munich: Drömersche Verlagsanstalt, 1985.

Ekwall, Eilert. *The Concise Oxford Dictionary of English Place-Names.* 4th ed. Oxford: Oxford University Press, 1960.
———. *English River Names.* Rev. ed. Oxford: Oxford University Press, 1968.

Fucilla, Joseph. *Our Italian Surnames.* New York: Chandler, 1949.

Gage Canadian Dictionary. Rev. ed. Toronto: Gage, 1997.

Gorr, Shmuel. *Jewish Personal Names: Their Origin, Derivation, and Diminutive Forms.* Chaim Freedman, ed. Teaneck, NJ: Avotaynu, 1992.

Graves, Robert. *Food for Centaurs: Stories, Talks, Critical Studies, Poems* (includes "A Toast to Ava Gardner"). New York: Doubleday, 1960.

Grenham, John. *Irish Family Names: The Histories of over 120 Famous Irish Surnames.* Glasgow: HarperCollins, 1997.

Guggenheimer, Heinrich W., and Eva H. Guggenheimer. *Jewish Family Names and Their Origins: An Etymological Dictionary.* Hoboken, NJ: Ktav Publishing House, 1992.

Hanks, Patrick, and Flavia Hodges. *Oxford Dictionary of First Names.* Oxford: Oxford University Press, 1990

ITP Nelson Canadian Dictionary of the English Language. Toronto: Nelson, 1997.

Kaganoff, Benzion C. *Dictionary of Jewish Names and their History.* New York: Shocken Books, 1977.

Kálmán, Béla. *The World of Names: A Study of Hungarian Onomatology.* Budapest: Akadémiai Kiadó, 1978.

Kneen, J.J. *The Personal Names of the Isle of Man.* Oxford: Oxford University Press, 1937.

Le Menn, Gwennole. *1700 Noms de famille bretons.* Saint-Brieuc, France: 1982.

Lévy, Paul. *Les noms des Israélites en France: histoire et dictionnaire.* Paris: 1960.

Lewis, Charlton T., and Charles Short. *A Latin Dictionary: Founded on Andrew's Edition of Freund's Latin Dictionary.* Impression of 1st ed. 1879. Oxford: Oxford University Press, 1958.

Liddell, Henry George, and Robert Scott. *A Greek-English Lexicon.* 9th ed. Oxford: Oxford University Press, 1953.

Mac Mathúna, Séamus, and Ailbhe Ó Corráin, eds. *Collins Gem Irish Dictionary.* Glasgow: HarperCollins, 1995.

MacLysaght, Edward. *The Surnames of Ireland.* Dublin: Irish University Press, 1969.

Mills, A.D. *A Dictionary of English Place Names.* Oxford: Oxford University Press, 1993.

Morlet, Marie-Thérèse. *Dictionnaire étymologique des noms de famille.* Paris: Perrin, 1991.

Mossé, Fernand. *A Handbook of Middle English.* Trans. James A. Walker. Baltimore, MD: Johns Hopkins Press, 1952.

Naumann, Horst. *Familiennamenbuch.* Leipzig: Bibliographisches Institut, 1989.

New Shorter Oxford English Dictionary. Oxford: Oxford University Press, 1993.

Noms et lieux du Québec: Dictionnaire illustré. 2nd ed. Sainte-Foy, QC: Publications du Québec, 1996.

O'Grady, William, and John Archibald. *Contemporary Linguistic Analysis: An Introduction.* 4th ed. Toronto: Addison Wesley Longman, 2000.

Oxford Companion to the English Language. Tom McArthur, ed. Oxford: Oxford University Press, 1992.

Oxford English Dictionary. James A.H. Murray et al., eds. Oxford: Oxford University Press, 1884–1928; corrected reissue, 1933.

Oxford English Dictionary. 2nd ed. R.W. Burchfield et al., eds. Oxford: Oxford University Press, 1989.

Oxford Russian Dictionary. Rev. ed. Colin Howlett et al., eds. Oxford: Oxford University Press, 1995.

Partridge, Eric. *Origins: A Short Etymological Dictionary of Modern English.* 4th ed. London: Routledge & Kegan Paul, 1966.

Pickering, David. *The Penguin Dictionary of First Names.* Harmondsworth, UK: Penguin Books, 1999.

Poirier, Pascal. *Le Glossaire acadien.* Rev. ed. Pierre M. Gérin. ed. Moncton, NB: Éditions d'Acadie, 1995.

Quirk, Randolph, and C.L. Wren. *An Old English Grammar.* 2nd ed. Methuen's Old English Library. London: Methuen, 1957.

Reaney, P.H., and R.M. Wilson. *A Dictionary of English Surnames.* 3rd ed. Oxford: Oxford University Press, 1995.

Robb, H. Amanda, and Andrew Chesler. *Encyclopedia of American Family Names: The Definitive Guide to the 5,000 Most Common Surnames in the United States, with Origins, Variations, Rankings, Prominent Bearers and Published Genealogies.* New York: HarperCollins, 1995.

Schaar, J. van der. *Woordenboek van Voornamen.* Utrecht: Het Spectrum, 1981.

Schimmel, Annemarie. *Islamic Personal Names.* Edinburgh: Edinburgh University Press, 1989.

Shipley, Joseph T. *The Origins of English Words: Discursive Dictionary of Indo-European Roots.* Baltimore, MD: Johns Hopkins University Press, 1984.

Smith, Elsdon C. *American Surnames.* Philadelphia, PA: Chilton Book Co., 1970.
———. *New Dictionary of American Family Names.* New York: Harper & Row, 1973.
_____. *The Story of Our Names.* New York: Harper, 1950.
_____. *Treasury of Name Lore.* New York: Harper & Row, 1967.

Story, G.M., W.J. Kirwin, and J.D.A. Widdowson, eds. *Dictionary of Newfoundland English.* 2nd ed. Toronto: University of Toronto Press, 1990.

Tibón, Gutierre. *Diccionario etimológico comparado de nombres proprios.* Rev. ed. Mexico City: Fondo de Cultura Económica, 1986.

Unbegaun, B.O. *Russian Surnames.* Oxford: Oxford University Press, 1972.

Webster's Third New International Dictionary of the English Language. Springfield, MA: Merriam-Webster, 1993.

Wehr, Hans. *A Dictionary of Modern Written Arabic.* 3rd ed. J. Milton Cowan, ed. Ithaca, NY: Spoken Language Services Inc., 1976.

Withycombe, E.G. *Oxford Dictionary of English Christian Names.* 3rd ed. Oxford: Oxford University Press, 1977.

BILL CASSELMAN BOOKS ABOUT CANADIAN WORDS
FROM MCARTHUR & COMPANY

Casselman's Canadian Words

In this #1 Best-Seller, Bill Casselman delights and startles with word stories from every province and territory of Canada. Did you know that **Scarborough** means "Harelip's Fort?" The names of **Lake Huron & Huronia** stem from a vicious, racist insult. *Huron* in old French meant 'long-haired clod.' French soldiers labelled the Wendat people with this nasty misnomer in the 1600s. **To deke out** is a Canadian verb that began as hockey slang, short for 'to decoy an opponent.' Canada has a fish that ignites. On our Pacific coast, the oolichan or **candle fish** is so full of oil it can be lighted at one end and used as a candle. "**Mush! Mush!** On, you huskies!" cried Sergeant Preston of The Yukon to 1940s radio listeners, thus introducing a whole generation of Canucks to the word once widely used in the Arctic to spur on sled dogs. Although it might sound like a word from Inuktitut, early French trappers first used it, borrowing the term from the Canadian French command to a horse to go: *marche! marche!* Yes, it's Québécois for giddyap!

All these and more fascinating terms from Canadian place names, politics, sports, plants and animals, clothing. Everything from Canadian monsters to mottoes is here.

Casselman's Canadian Words
ISBN 0-7730-5515-0
224 pages, illustrated, $19.95

Casselmania: More Wacky Canadian Words & Sayings

Should you purchase a copy of Casselmania? Below is a quiz to try. If you pass, buy Casselmania. If you fail, buy two copies!

1. "Slackers" is a nickname for what Canadian city?
   (a) Vancouver
   (b) Halifax
   (c) Sackville, New Brunswick

   Answer: (b) Halifax. Why "Slackers"? Because often when Canadian Navy crews put in to Halifax harbour, the sailors had some "slack" time for shore-leave.

2. Eh? is a true marker of Canadian speech. But which of the following authors uses eh? exactly as Canadians now use it.
   (a) Emily Brontë in *Wuthering Heights*.
   (b) Charles Dickens in *Bleak House*.
   (c) Geoffrey Chaucer in *The Canterbury Tales* in AD 1400.

   Answer: All of the above! Eh? is almost 1,000 years old as an interjection in Old English, Middle English, and, of course, in modern Canadian English, too.

3. In central Ontario, a gorby is
   (a) one who follows Russian politics
   (b) one who thinks Mike Harris is good for the province
   (c) a tourist

   Answer (c). A localism in the central Ontario tourist area of Muskoka is "gorby" used by some inhabitants of the area, mostly younger people, to describe loud tourists of the yahoo persuasion. "Oh-oh. Another busload of gorbies!" The origin of gorby is, I believe, in the 1950s camping slang term G.O.R.P., an acronym for Good Old Raisins and Peanuts, a trail mix suitable for canoe nibbling, easily packed, and not subject to immediate spoilage.

Casselmania: More Wacky Canadian Words & Sayings
ISBN 0-316-13314-0
298 pages, illustrated, $19.95

Canadian Garden Words

Trowel in hand, Bill Casselman digs into the loamy lore and fascinating facts about how we have named the plants that share our Dominion. But are there *Canadian* Garden Words? Yes! Try those listed below.

Camas Lily. A bulb grown all over the world for its spiky blue flowers. The name arose in British Columbia where First Peoples cooked and ate the bulbs. Camas means 'sweet' in Nootka, a Pacific Coast language. The original name of Victoria on Vancouver Island was Camosun, in Nootka 'place where we gather camas bulbs.'

A Snotty Var is a certain species of fir tree in Newfoundland. Why? Find out in *Canadian Garden Words*.

Mistletoe! So Christmassy. The word means 'bird shit on a stick.' Oops! Orchid means 'testicle' in Greek. Avocado means testicle too.

While plant names have come into English from dozens of world languages, Bill Casselman has found the Canadian connection to hundreds of plant names and garden lore and packed this book with them. With scholarship and humour, Bill reports on the origin of all the common trees and flowers that decorate our gardens from Fogo Island to Tofino, B.C.

Canadian Garden Words
ISBN 0-316-13343-4
356 pages, illustrated, $19.95

Canadian Food Words

Winner of the 1999 Gold Medal from Cuisine Canada for Best Book of the Year

"A glorious, informative, and funny collection of food-related defini-tions and stories!"
Marion Kane, food editor, Toronto Star, November 18, 1998

"Even readers who are unlikely to fry a doughnut in seal blubber oil will enjoy this latest romp by writer and broadcaster Bill Casselman . . . he mixes in so much entertaining information and curious Canadian lore."
Books, Globe & Mail, October 24, 1998

"There are morsels in Canadian Food Words *to whet any Canadian appetite."*
Howard Richler, Montreal Gazette, May 15, 1999

Do you know that fine Canadian dish, Son-of-a-Bitch-in-a-Sack? It's a real Alberta chuckwagon pudding. In this fully illustrated, 304-page romp, Bill tells the amusing stories behind such hearty Canadian fare as gooeyducks and hurt pie. The juicy lore and tangy tales of foods that founded a nation are all here: from scrunchins to rubbaboo, from bangbelly to poutine, from Winnipeg jambusters to Nanaimo bars, from Malpeque oysters to nun's farts! If you think foods of Canadian origin are limited to pemmican and pea soup, you need to dip your ladle into the bubbling kettle of *Canadian Food Words*.

Canadian Food Words:
The Juicy Lore & Tasty Origins of Foods That Founded a Nation
ISBN 1-55278-018-X
304 pages, illustrated, $19.95

Canadian Sayings

"*Got a big kick out of* Canadian Sayings. *We need more books like this to keep our Canadian spirits up. Most amusing!*"
Albert Wilson Bowron, Library Planner, Toronto, January 2000

"*Eight months on Canadian Best-seller Lists! Eight months in the Top Ten!*"
B.C., humble author, May, 2000

Samples from *Canadian Sayings*:

Thicker than a B.C. pine.
Saskatchewan is so flat, you can watch your dog run away from home for a week.
She's got more tongue than a Mountie's boot.
A grin as wide as the St. Lawrence.
So dumb he thinks Medicine Hat is a cure for head lice.
I've seen more brains in a Manitoba sucked egg.
That smell would gag a maggot on a gut wagon.
Sign in his bathroom: Warning: Objects in mirror are dumber than they appear.
Of childish behaviour in a grown man: That boy never did grow up. One day he just sorta haired over.

Canadian Sayings
1,200 Folk Sayings Used by Canadians
Collected and Annotated by Bill Casselman
ISBN 1-55278-076-7
138 pages, $ 8.99

Canadian Sayings 2001 Calendar

Here are those hilarious and wonderful Canadian Sayings that kept the book on the bestseller lists for 8 months! Plus 100 Brand New Sayings Bill has collected that are not in the book.

You'll find a smile-a-day in this page-a-day calendar for 2001.

Some of the newly collected expressions are:

He couldn't ad lib a fart at a bean supper.

You know you are out in the boonies when you cut your front lawn, and find a car.

She's so stingy, she wouldn't give you last year's calendar.

Rain let up quickly this morning—disappeared faster than a B.C. premier!

I'm so busy cleanin' for the weekend, I just met myself in the hallway.

She's got the crick-cracks in her prayer-bones (arthritis in her kneecaps).

Canadian Sayings 2001 Calendar
ISBN 1-55278-138-0
$ 15.95   4" X 4"   370 pages

All of Bill Casselman's books about Canadian words
from McArthur & Company
are available at bookstores across Canada.

Acknowledgments

For her friendship and advice I thank Daphne Hart, my agent at the Helen Heller Agency. For continuing support and for her ability to machete the tentacles of paranoia that occasionally slither up an author's spine without severing the spine itself (always appreciated) I thank my publisher Kim McArthur. I offer a special salute to efficient and sometimes wonder-working publicity director Sherie Hodds. I thank also the whole team at McArthur & Company. Editor Pamela Erlichman has gazed Medusa-like at six of my manuscripts and seen all my errors. I don't always enjoy watching my pearls turn to stone and be consigned to the crusher, but prose is perkier post *Pamelam.* Finally, my double gratitude goes to this book's designers, Michael Callaghan and Tania Craan, for their rare and appreciated ability to work with an author rather than *above* him.